T0367193

HBCU

HBCU

THE POWER OF HISTORICALLY BLACK COLLEGES AND UNIVERSITIES

MARYBETH GASMAN
and LEVON T. ESTERS

JOHNS HOPKINS UNIVERSITY PRESS | *Baltimore*

© 2024 Johns Hopkins University Press
All rights reserved. Published 2024
Printed in the United States of America on acid-free paper
2 4 6 8 9 7 5 3 1

Johns Hopkins University Press
2715 North Charles Street
Baltimore, Maryland 21218
www.press.jhu.edu

Library of Congress Cataloging-in-Publication Data

Names: Gasman, Marybeth, author. | Esters, Levon T., 1970– author.
Title: HBCU : the power of historically Black colleges and universities /
Marybeth Gasman and Levon T. Esters.
Description: Baltimore : Johns Hopkins University Press, 2024. | Includes
bibliographical references and index.
Identifiers: LCCN 2023022278 | ISBN 9781421448183 (hardcover) |
ISBN 9781421448190 (ebook)
Subjects: LCSH: Historically black colleges and universities—History. |
African Americans—Education, Higher—United States.
Classification: LCC LC2781 .G373 2024 | DDC 378.1/982996073—
dc23/eng/20230718
LC record available at https://lccn.loc.gov/2023022278

A catalog record for this book is available from the British Library.

Special discounts are available for bulk purchases of this book. For more information,
please contact Special Sales at specialsales@jh.edu.

To our daughters,
who bring us joy, inspiration, and love
Chloë Sarah Epstein
Shanna Amel Esters
Laila Amari Esters
Jada Amani Esters

CONTENTS

PREFACE

My Journey at Two HBCUs

LEVON T. ESTERS

When the dark clouds gather on the horizon,
When thunder and lightning fill the sky,
When fate is but a glint in the eye of a fallen Rattler,
And hopes are lost friends,
When the sinew of the chest grows weary,
From those hard charging linebackers,
And the muscles and the legs grow tired,
From those hard charging running backs.
You must always remember that the
RATTLERS WILL STRIKE, AND STRIKE, AND STRIKE AGAIN!
—Florida A&M University Chant

Aggie born, Aggie bred, and when I die, I'll be an Aggie dead!
—North Carolina A&T State University Chant

My decision to attend a Historically Black College and University (HBCU) for my undergraduate degree was not one that I planned from an early age. Though my parents and older siblings all graduated from college, none of them attended an HBCU. Rather, they attended Predominantly White Institutions (PWIs). Many of the kids I grew up with in my neighborhood attended PWIs in my home state of Illinois, such as Illinois State University, Northern Illinois University, Southern Illinois University, or Western Illinois University. I had no desire to attend an in-state school and did not even apply to one when I was thinking about where to attend college. When I reflect on my college choice process, I recall wanting to attend a "big time" institution like

Baylor University or the University of Oklahoma, primarily because I was a college football junkie.

It was not until I went to high school (in 1985) that I slowly started to be exposed to HBCUs and all they had to offer. As context, I attended a predominantly Black high school on the South Side of Chicago, Lindblom Technical High School, which had long been one of the top public high schools in the city. The school had a legacy of graduates who went on to attend college and later became physicians, lawyers, judges, teachers, and entrepreneurs. As an example of the school's rich history of academically talented graduates, five of the six founders of the National Society of Black Engineers (NSBE)* graduated from Lindblom.

During my time at Lindblom, I learned that many of my teachers and guidance counselors were graduates of HBCUs. Schools such as Tennessee State University, Langston University, Alcorn State University, Morehouse College, Spelman College, and Fisk University were just a few of those my teachers talked about during class. As I approached my senior year, I found myself becoming more interested in attending an HBCU. Subsequently, several life experiences confirmed my decision.

The first was seeing *School Daze*, which is my favorite movie of all time. Spike Lee, a graduate of Morehouse College, wrote and directed the film, and it is based, in part, on his experience at Morehouse. The story centers on the experiences of Black students at a fictitious HBCU, Mission College, and their exposure to issues such as colorism, elitism, classism, student activism, and hazing. To say that *School Daze* had an impact on my college choice is an understatement. The movie exposed me to the abundance of Black culture that exists on an HBCU campus. To see this culture portrayed in a way that displayed our unique differences fascinated me.

The second experience that shaped my desire to attend an HBCU was watching the sitcom *A Different World*. In this show, students at

* NSBE was founded in 1975 at Purdue University. Its core activities are centered on improving the recruitment and retention of Black and other minority engineers in both academia and industry.

Hillman College (another fictitious HBCU) explore issues such as relationships, student activism, racism, Greek life, politics, and dating. I saw aspects of myself in many of the characters in *School Daze* and *A Different World*.

Another (more personal) experience that fueled my passion for attending an HBCU involved my then brother-in-law. Soon after my oldest sister was married, I learned that her husband had attended Florida A&M University (FAMU). FAMU was not even on my radar until I met my brother-in-law. I was more familiar with the schools I had heard about during high school: Morehouse College, Tennessee State University, Fisk University, and Hampton University. The more I learned about FAMU, the more I became intrigued by this institution and what it had to offer. I recall my brother-in-law sharing stories about "being a Rattler" and the "Highest of Seven Hills," as well as the Marching 100 band. My interest grew as I read stories in the local newspapers and saw segments on the news about FAMU. It was as if every time I turned around, I heard about FAMU.

I had planned to apply to several HBCUs—including Tennessee State University, Alabama A&M University, Alabama State University, Morehouse College, and the University of Arkansas at Pine Bluff—but after learning about FAMU, it became my first choice. What confirmed my decision to apply to and subsequently attend FAMU was its positive national news coverage.

During the time I was applying to FAMU, it was led by a dynamic individual named Frederick S. Humphries. To this day, I regard President Humphries as one of the all-time best presidents in HBCU history. What impressed me the most about the school, which led to my decision to attend, was how Humphries touted the prestige of FAMU and the academic talents and success of its students. During Humphries's tenure the school's enrollment had significantly increased, and it was now nationally ranked, often in the top five, in terms of enrollment of African American National Merit Scholars, surpassing institutions such as Harvard, Stanford, Duke, Howard, Yale, and MIT (Negron, 1996). Another milestone that could be credited to Humphries was when the Marching 100 band participated as official representatives of the United States in France's Bicentennial year Bastille Day parade. Additionally, about a decade later, *TIME Magazine*/the *Princeton Review* named FAMU as its first College of the Year (E. Jackson, 2021). Humphries led FAMU during a time that I refer to as the Golden Years, which coincided with when I attended (1989–1995).

For many individuals, the institution they attend for their undergraduate degree is most often the school they have the fondest memories of, and for me it is no different. Like my decision to attend FAMU, my choice to attend North Carolina A&T State University (A&T) snuck up on me. After graduating from FAMU, I took a job in the management trainee program with Walgreens. My first role in this program was that of assistant manager at a Walgreens store. I was excited to be working soon after graduating from college, but about six months into the job, I realized that I did not like working in retail. As a 25-year-old, I dreaded working 50–60 hours a week. I had no social life, and the grind of working that many hours in a job that offered no excitement quickly became boring. But once I commit to something, I follow through on my obligation, so I stuck it out for a full year. As I was preparing to resign, I began searching for other job opportunities. One that surfaced was teaching at the top urban agricultural education high school in the United States: the Chicago High School for Agricultural Sciences (CHSAS). My undergraduate degree in agricultural business allowed me to teach and later serve as the coordinator for the agribusiness career pathway at CHSAS, a role I held for three years. During this time, I was also enrolled in an alternative teacher certification program with the City Colleges of Chicago.

Working at CHSAS offered numerous professional development opportunities because it was a premier high school. For example, I was able to participate in college tours. During one tour, we went to see seven or eight HBCUs. One of these was Southern University and A&M College (Southern), where I met Dawn Mellion-Patin. Mellion-Patin was a Black woman who was a well-respected professor of agriculture. I recall her asking about my career goals, and I shared that I wanted to pursue my master's and doctoral degrees. I mentioned that although

I was teaching at a particularly good high school, I did not want to build a career as a high school teacher. I also revealed to her that my goal was to be a college president.

Mellion-Patin asked me if I had narrowed my list of schools; I told her that I had not really explored my options yet. She mentioned that she had obtained her master's degree from North Carolina A&T State University (A&T) and encouraged me to explore this school as an option. Mellion-Patin mentioned a professor at A&T by the name of Carey Ford and suggested I reach out to him for more information about the graduate program in agricultural education. One of the things I appreciated most about Mellion-Patin was her passion for HBCUs and her belief that my choosing to attend one for graduate school would be a good decision. She shared stories about the level of support she received as a student at Southern for both her bachelor's and master's degrees and how important it was in preparing her for the environment of a PWI, which she attended for her doctoral degree.

Soon after I returned from the college tour, I reached out to Ford and expressed interest in his department. I then applied to A&T, got accepted, and embarked on my journey to a master's degree. I soon realized that A&T, like FAMU, was one of the premier HBCUs in the United States. Not only was A&T one of the largest HBCUs, but it was also one of the largest producers of degrees awarded to Black people and was nationally recognized for its excellent academic programs in science, technology, mathematics, and engineering (STEM). As I reflect on my experience at both FAMU and A&T, it is clear that the support I received at these institutions contributed to my academic preparation and readiness for a doctoral program.

Personal Growth and Identity Development

One of the aspects that I enjoyed most about attending college, especially an HBCU, was the journey of personal growth and identity development. For many students, the college years are where you learn about yourself and engage in deep reflection about your purpose in life and what the future will hold. The question "Who am I?" is one that students often wrestle with. Attending FAMU was the first time I lived away from my parents, which brings its own challenges. I quickly started to make friends, however, and to meet people from all over the country. It did not take long before I started to feel comfortable being away from home and living on my own.

While at FAMU, I appreciated being surrounded by students who looked like me. Walking the "yard" at FAMU and seeing nothing but a sea of Black students was powerful and instilled a sense of pride and a can-do attitude in me. Attending an HBCU meant you were part of a family. Many of my friends, who were from different regions of the country, shared common experiences, which contributed to the familial spirit present at FAMU. My professors, most of whom were Black, cultivated a sense of belonging. At a PWI, I would have been lucky to have one Black professor. Taking courses from people who looked like me was powerful and further instilled a sense of confidence that has stayed with me to this day.

Yet another by-product of attending an HBCU is how it contributed to my sense of Black identity. I often hear stories from Black students who attend PWIs about the lack of symbols, images, or other representations of Blackness on campus and what this communicates about the importance of diversity. As you can imagine, the opposite is the reality at an HBCU. Though I attended elementary and high schools where being Black was celebrated, being able to experience the same during college was even more gratifying and empowering. I left FAMU with a greater understanding of and deeper appreciation for what it means to be Black. I would argue that many of my peers, especially those who may not have come from majority Black communities, left FAMU with a deep knowledge of the importance of Black identity development and the positive impact it had on their academic success and personal growth and development.

Like FAMU, A&T was equally fulfilling in terms of how it shaped my personal growth and development. The feeling of being part of a family was present even though I was enrolled as a graduate student. In many ways, the more focused nature of being in graduate school and matriculating as a "cohort" takes the familial nature to an even deeper level. As is the case for all HBCUs, there is a deep history tied to slavery, civil rights, and student activism. A&T has a particularly strong history tied to civil rights, which included protests and sit-ins; it also helped spread these types of movements across the United States. This history is present across campus and in many parts of Greensboro, where A&T is located. As a short history lesson (and one we will discuss later in this book), Greensboro is known as the birthplace of the sit-in movement. Attending an HBCU that was at the epicenter of civil rights activism contributed to the development of my Black identity.

My time at A&T was what contributed most to my becoming a leader and my desire to become a scholar. During my master's program, I was engaged in numerous leadership opportunities. For example, I was elected vice president of the A&T Chapter of Minorities in Agriculture, Natural Resources, and Related Sciences, which is the largest professional agricultural organization for minorities in the United States. I also served as the colead for a student-focused project sponsored by the Southern Food Systems Education Consortium (SOFSEC). SOFSEC was responsible for bringing Historically Black Land Grant Institutions (HBLGIs) into partnership with public schools and community-based institutions to address challenges faced by communities in the southern region. Leading an aspect of the SOFSEC project was my first time engaging with faculty and administrators on a large scale, which provided an invaluable lesson in leadership.

My time at A&T is also when my interest in pursuing a doctoral degree crystallized. I had the benefit of taking classes from outstanding faculty and staff, all of whom encouraged me to pursue my career goals. The faculty at A&T also assisted in the development of my academic self-efficacy, which helped me prepare for the rigors of my doctoral program at Pennsylvania State University. My growth as an emerging scholar and aspirations to become a college professor, and eventually a college president, were cultivated at A&T.

Values Clarification

Attending FAMU and A&T instilled values in me that guide me to this day—namely, public service and social justice. To be fair, valuing service and, in many ways, social justice is a by-product of my having attended and worked at only public institutions. I attended a public K-8 elementary school known for its focus on instilling a keen sense of Black identity and Black history. As mentioned earlier, I attended Lindblom Technical High School, which has a long history of service and social justice. Upon graduation from high school, I attended and worked at only public land-grant institutions: FAMU, A&T, Iowa State University, Pennsylvania State University, and Purdue University. I am a firm believer in the value of a public education and what it can contribute to enhancing the lives of people.

Attending and working at public land-grant institutions offers a unique educational experience in that these institutions focus on public outreach (i.e., extension). Extension was designed to connect the institution's academic and research programs to the needs of society. Simply, public service to communities is a guiding principle of the land-grant mission.

The preparation I was to gain through my classes, research, and leadership experiences at FAMU differed from that of other institutions owing to the "outward facing" nature of the mission. As I reflect on my time at FAMU, where I earned a degree through the College of Agriculture, it is even clearer to me today that this mission is what led faculty and staff to engage with local communities to the extent that they did. In full transparency, learning about the land-grant institutions and their rich history when I was at FAMU was not at the top of my list. It was not until I pursued my master's degree in agricultural education at A&T that I took my first deep dive into learning about these institutions and their educational focus.

My appreciation for social justice as a core value was also influenced by my experiences at FAMU and A&T, institutions whose histories are intertwined with social justice, civil rights, and activism. In a first-year student orientation course at FAMU, one of the assignments was to become well versed in the history of FAMU. I learned that FAMU was founded in 1887 as the State Normal College for Colored Students. In 1909, the school's name was changed to Florida Agricultural and Mechanical College for Negroes (FAMC), then changed again to Florida A&M University in 1953 (Florida A&M University, 2022). I recall my peers and I marveling at the fact that FAMU was once FAMC. We were also impressed to learn that—like many students who attended HBCUs in the south—FAMU students participated in local bus boycotts, which led to the integration of Tallahassee's public transportation system. It was student activism like this that spawned a legacy of social justice and activism at FAMU (Uhl & Evans, 2021).

One of the most important lessons in A&T history is that of the Greensboro Four. In 1960, four Black students from A&T staged a sit-in at a Greensboro, North Carolina, Woolworth, a popular retail store that refused to serve African Americans at its lunch counter. Soon after their protest, sit-ins began occurring across the South. We will touch more on the efforts of these students, who became known as the Greensboro Four, in the Chapter One, when we discuss the role of HBCUs in higher education.

Paying It Forward: A Passion for Mentoring

My passion for and commitment to mentoring Black students were born out of my experiences at both FAMU and A&T. But I must credit my experiences as a student at FAMU for making an impression on me regarding mentoring. The story of my inspiration that I enjoy sharing the most is related to FAMU's motto, "Excellence with Caring," which is ingrained in me and serves as one of the pillars of my approach to mentoring graduate students.

Humphries first popularized the motto in a newspaper interview, when he mentioned that his teacher had instilled in him the concept of "excellence with caring." It is worth mentioning what Humphries said about his teacher's influence on him: "My teacher was a very smart man and he cared about his students. When he realized your abilities, he pushed you to the limit." When Humphries became president of FAMU, the saying became FAMU's motto.

I did not pay much attention to the excellence portion of the motto in my early years as a student. Around my junior year, however, I started to realize that being at FAMU was special and that I was surrounded by some incredibly talented faculty and staff. I vividly recall the advising sessions I had with several of my professors—Zach Olorunnipa, Dave Weatherspoon, and Oghenekome "Kome" Onokpise—and how they challenged and convinced me that I had the ability to do wonderful things, and frankly, that they expected important things from me. The guidance I received from Olorunnipa was the primary reason I chose to pursue a major in agricultural business. What I most appreciated about Weatherspoon and Kome was their expectation of excellence and how they encouraged me to pursue a doctoral degree because they felt I had what it took to do so.

Similarly, regarding the caring part of the motto, I began to realize there were faculty at FAMU who wanted me to be the absolute best I could be, who pushed me, who had exceedingly grand expectations of me, and that to perform below what was expected of me was simply unacceptable. These types of expectations had the potential to scare students away, but that is where the notion of caring came into play. Though faculty had lofty expectations, they made sure to express that they also cared about my growth, development, and well-being. Faculty at FAMU had an influence on me that was similar to Humphries's description of his teacher's influence.

Today, I can say unequivocally that Excellence with Caring guides every aspect of my life. For example, as a leader, I do all that I can to ensure that those that I lead understand that they can trust me as a leader and that I will make sound decisions that reflect the highest of standards. As a faculty member, I am constantly challenging myself to seek out the highest-level opportunities when it comes to grant-writing projects, research projects, and awards. The best evidence I can point to of my commitment to the ideals of Excellence with

Caring, is my mentoring of graduate students—a majority of whom are Black and who attended HBCUs for their undergraduate or master's degrees. One of the three pillars of my mentoring philosophy is the "expectation of excellence." I often tell my graduate students that anything less than excellence is not an option. One of my favorite things to do when ending my meetings with students is to say, "Go forth and pursue excellence."

Even though my excitement for mentoring started at FAMU, my time at A&T was filled with shining examples of excellent mentors. As a master's student the frequency of my faculty interactions was a bit different than it had been during my undergraduate years; it was more in-depth. What I realize today is that my time at A&T was a key influence on my decision to pursue a doctoral degree. For example, my thesis advisor and mentor, Alton Thompson, sparked my love of research and statistics. What is interesting is that I hated this subject in elementary and high school; yet today, I teach research design, statistics, and data analysis to graduate students. Two other professors, Bennie Gray and Donald McDowell, were also excellent mentors and expected nothing less than excellence from me. Collectively, all three professors provided mentoring, guidance, support, and motivation such that I was ready for the rigors of my doctoral program at Pennsylvania State University.

I am a strong advocate for HBCUs and do what I can to help students from these institutions pursue graduate degrees at PWIs. My role as director of the Mentoring@Purdue (M@P) program was further evidence of my HBCU advocacy work; the M@P program has partnerships with over 23 HBCUs, 17 of which are HBLGIs. I also did what I could to encourage students to consider attending HBCUs and help PWIs develop partnerships with Minority Serving Institutions.

Whenever I give a talk and share my educational journey, I like to open by saying that I bleed orange and green, but I am also a die-hard Aggie. To say that I am a proud HBCU graduate is an understatement. To me, there is something special about being a two-time HBCU graduate, which is something that I will forever cherish. Part of the reason this fact is worth mentioning is that it proves wrong those who think that HBCUs are not good enough to prepare students for the real world. I would also like to acknowledge that I am indebted to the faculty, staff, and my peers for what they contributed to my growth and development. Much of who I am personally and professionally can be tied back to my HBCU experiences. Therefore, I will always advocate for HBCUs and encourage students to attend them.

ACKNOWLEDGMENTS

We consider it an honor and privilege to write a book about the power of Historically Black Colleges and Universities. We enjoyed the writing and research process thoroughly and are grateful to everyone who talked with us and shared their HBCU stories. We want to thank all the students, staff, faculty, leaders, and alumni of HBCUs for their passion, hard work, and commitment to the education of African American students.

As all scholarship builds on prior research, we are indebted to those scholars who have conducted research related to HBCUs for decades. We were informed by their work and motivated to dig deeper; we were also warmed by their commitment to telling a compelling and comprehensive story of HBCUs.

We interviewed nearly 60 individuals affiliated with HBCUs for this book, and we are grateful to them for their candidness and their near-constant work for the HBCU community. Without their voices, we would not have been able to illustrate the power of HBCUs. We describe our interview methodology in more detail in the appendix.

We are grateful to Greg Britton, our editor at Johns Hopkins University Press, for his belief in this project and in the importance of HBCUs as well as his feedback on drafts of the manuscript. We are indebted to the anonymous reviewers who gave us important advice about how to strengthen the manuscript. Special thanks to the copyeditor and to the production editor at Hopkins Press as well as the marketing team. We also appreciate Sandy Keller and Ben Keller, who transcribed the interviews that we conducted for the book.

Marybeth Gasman

I am indebted to Levon T. Esters for joining in this project and contributing his passion for HBCUs. We learned a tremendous amount during the writing and research process, and we were lucky enough to have laughed throughout as well.

I am thankful to the staff at the Rutgers Center for Minority Serving Institutions and the Samuel DeWitt Proctor Institute for Leadership, Equity, and Justice. Although they were not involved in this book project, their support overall is a wonderful addition to my life and career and something I cherish. Special thanks to Brandy Jones, Carolyn Nalewajko, Koor Kpogba-Thomas, Alice Ginsberg, Natalie Passov, Andrés Castro Samayoa, and Gisselle Criollo. I also am forever grateful to Rutgers University for its support, especially our dean Wanda Blanchett, our provost and senior vice president of academic affairs Saundra Tomlinson-Clarke, and our chancellor Francine Conway. These three amazing women have supported me so beautifully and model leadership, integrity, and equity.

Although this book was not based on a funded project, I am thankful to the funders who have supported my work over the years as this book would not have been possible without their support of previous projects. These funders include the Kresge Foundation, Educational Testing Service, ECMC Foundation, the Mellon Foundation, AccessLex, Southern Education Foundation, Jobs for the Future, the US Department of Labor, the Spencer Foundation, the Helmsley Trust, Lumina Foundation, USA Funds, the Kellogg Foundation, the Arthur Vining Davis Foundation, the National Institutes of Health, the National Academy of Sciences, the University of Pennsylvania, the Duke Endowment, the Greg and EJ Milken Foundation, the Aspen Institute, the Josiah Macey Foundation, Georgia State University, the Indiana University Center on Philanthropy, and the Rockefeller Foundation.

I want to give a special shout-out to my former students from Georgia State University, the University of Pennsylvania, and Rutgers University, many of whom obtained their undergraduate degrees from HBCUs. I appreciate you and all your support over the years so much.

Thank you for your notes, flowers, Starbucks cards, social media check-ins, and texts. You know how to make a professor feel proud of your contributions. I have also been lucky to have served on dissertation committees across the United States for over 75 students who either graduated from HBCUs or earned their doctoral degrees at HBCUs. Thank you for asking me to serve and allowing me to learn from you.

I am thankful to my good friends Camille Charles, Thai-Huy Nguyen, Leah Hollis, Sanjib Bhuyan, Wayne Bullock, and Brian Melito for their constant and beautiful care and support. As always, I am grateful to my mentors John Thelin, Michael Nettles, Wayne Urban, and the late Asa Hilliard. My mother is my inspiration for justice. Although she could have lived a life focused on only herself given the hardships she encountered, she chose to live a life for others. Finally, but most importantly, I am indebted to my daughter Chloë for her joy, kindness, integrity, justice orientation, love, and humor. You warm my heart with your beautiful soul.

Levon T. Esters

I am thankful to Marybeth Gasman for the opportunity to coauthor my first book. Not only has this been a great learning experience, but it has helped to raise my writing game to another level. The investment of time she put forth to mentor and coach me has been nothing short of spectacular.

I am also grateful to my faculty mentors at Florida A&M University. My love for HBCUs started on the "Highest of Seven Hills." I especially want to acknowledge Zach Olorunnipa, Dave Weatherspoon, and Oghenekome "Kome" Onokpise. Your mentoring and encouragement had a major impact on my growth, development, and confidence as a student and set me on a path of success. Each of you were the epitome of Excellence with Caring.

I offer special thanks to my faculty mentors at North Carolina A&T State University. My love for HBCUs continued in a seamless manner while a student at A&T. There are not enough words to express how grateful I am for the encouragement, advice, preparation, and training that Alton Thompson, Bennie Gray, and Donald McDowell gave me so that I would be prepared for a doctoral program.

I am also grateful to my doctoral advisor, Blannie Bowen, and other faculty mentors at Pennsylvania State University. Professor Bowen, I learned the art and craft of being a faculty member from you, and for that I am honored. I offer many thanks to my colleagues and mentors at Iowa State University. Your support during the initial stages of my faculty career contributed to my success at Purdue University. Likewise, I appreciate my faculty colleagues and mentors at Purdue University. I am thankful for your advice and insights into how the Academy "works." Thank you to my colleagues in the Office of Recruitment, Retention, and Diversity in the Polytechnic Institute. You welcomed me into the college with open arms, which has made a world of difference in helping me to help you.

Special thanks to all my former students and mentees who served as members of the "Esters Lab." You, too, have contributed in significant ways to my success, and I will be forever grateful for the role you played in doing so. In addition, thank you to all the former members of the Mentoring@Purdue (M@P) team. M@P would not be what it is today if it were not for your intellectual contributions and commitment.

Thanks to the entire HBCU community. I am who I am because of having attended two of these great institutions. Your presence will remain in my heart and mind forever. Last but not least, thanks to my daughters (Shanna, Laila, and Jada), mom (Ruby), and siblings (Andrea, Stacey, and Jason). Your encouragement and support over the years have been on time, every time. Each of you is a constant reminder of all the good things in the world.

HBCU

1

On the Higher Education Landscape

We serve as an example of what is possible, because I don't know
what America would have looked like if it hadn't been for
HBCUs, because predominantly White schools were never going
to admit 4 million formerly enslaved people.
—MICHAEL SORRELL, President, Paul Quinn College

The year 2020 was a time of intense racial turmoil in the United States,
resulting from the murder of George Floyd on May 25. A young girl
took a video of the murder, and it played over and over on televisions
across the nation. Citizens saw, with little ability to deny the crime,
police officer Derek Chauvin kneel on Floyd's neck for 9 minutes and
29 seconds until he was dead. They heard Floyd say he could not
breathe and call out for his mother (Levenson, 2021). This murder
came on the heels of many others, including those of Breonna Taylor,
Philando Castile, and Alton Sterling (BBC, 2020). People of all racial
and ethnic backgrounds, across all age groups, took to the streets, coming out of their homes during the COVID-19 pandemic, angered by
the presidency of Donald J. Trump and his indifference to and stoking

of racial injustice. During this turmoil, African American students, craving supportive learning environments that embraced them, began enrolling at Historically Black Colleges and Universities (HBCUs) at higher rates (Lumpkin, 2022; J. Williams & Palmer, 2019). Many African American parents, who in the past may have encouraged their children to attend Predominantly White Institutions (PWIs), began to push their children to consider HBCUs.

At the same time, after a contested and traumatic presidential race, the nation elected Joseph R. Biden as president and Kamala Harris, a proud Howard University graduate, as the vice president of the United States, making her the first Black, South Asian woman and HBCU graduate to hold the position. During her nomination acceptance speech at the 2020 Democratic National Convention, Harris highlighted her attendance at Howard and introduced people with little knowledge of them to HBCUs. Likewise, as the contested presidential election between President Donald Trump and Senator Joe Biden came to a head, one name was on the minds of members of the media, politicians, and even ordinary people: Stacey Abrams, the Spelman College graduate who lost the 2018 Georgia governor's race by 54,723 votes and as a result started the voting rights nonprofit organization Fair Fight (CNN, 2018). In addition to interest in her strategy for engaging voters and working to turn the state of Georgia Democratic—or blue— in terms of majority voters, people took notice of her education and the impact that Spelman College had had on her fight for justice and her intellect. Abrams was not shy about crediting the liberal arts college for Black women in Atlanta, Georgia, for contributing to her success (King, 2020). With Abrams's help, Joe Biden and Kamala Harris won the presidency, and Morehouse College graduate Raphael Warnock along with Jon Ossoff, a protégé of US Representative John Lewis, joined the US Senate (King, 2020).

While these powerful and influential HBCU graduates were capturing the attention of the nation, philanthropists were beginning to take notice in more significant and widespread ways than usual. Corporations and individuals, including Dominion Energy, Michael Bloomberg, Google, Netflix's Reed Hastings, and the social media sensation TikTok, gave abundantly to HBCUs. The individual who garnered the most attention was author and philanthropist MacKenzie Scott, ex-spouse of Jeff Bezos, the founder of Amazon (Gasman et al., 2021). In a noticeably short time, Scott gave nearly $600 million to HBCUs and even more money to two HBCU advocacy organizations, the United Negro College Fund (UNCF) and the Thurgood Marshall College Fund. Her gifts were transformative and a start to leveling the playing field for HBCUs, something that was long overdue.

During this time, the number of Google searches of HBCUs skyrocketed as more people in the United States wondered about these historic institutions. As politicians, activists, philanthropists, and others were highlighting the contributions of HBCUs across a variety of platforms, some Americans were trying to figure out what HBCUs were and why they had never heard of them until now.

The purpose of this book is to look deeply at the true power of HBCUs, including their place in the landscape of American higher education, their unique culture and its impact on the lives and identities of African American students, and their role in moving generations of African Americans into the middle class by expanding their socioeconomic mobility. We examine the role that HBCUs have played in developing and motivating prominent (and not so well-known) scholars and leaders who have changed the lives of those they mentor and advise. Moreover, we examine HBCU engagement in economic development and the impact on the communities where they reside. Given the significant role that philanthropy and alumni giving play in the livelihood of HBCUs, we discuss the history and growing interest of donors and alumni in supporting HBCUs. Finally, we examine challenges faced by HBCUs as well as opportunities, while making recommendations for these institutions and those who care about them to move them to new levels of success and sustainability.

A Brief History of HBCUs

Education has always been a centerpiece for Black people in America. As they arrived in the ports of North American cities in 1619, shackled in slavery, Black people quickly understood that education was the pathway to freedom in a new land (Hannah-Jones, 2021).[1] Although rarely acknowledged in textbooks, enslaved Africans pursued all forms of education despite laws in southern states forbidding them from reading or writing (H. A. Williams, 2005). Enslavers viewed literacy and learning, aside from religious instruction, as a threat to the slavery-based economy, believing it would lead to insurrection and rebellion (Jay, 1835). With a quest for knowledge, and with the support of White abolitionists, a few Black colleges were established in the North even before the end of the Civil War. These institutions included Cheyney and Lincoln Universities in Pennsylvania and Wilberforce University in Ohio.[2] At the foundation of these trailblazing institutions were Black preachers ministering for the African Methodist Episcopal (AME) Church, as well as Quakers who had worked to abolish slavery since before the Revolutionary War (Bly, 2008). Both religious groups worked out of the North and valued education for all (Drewry & Doermann, 2003).

Founded in 1837 as the African Institute, then the Institute for Colored Youth, Cheyney University is the nation's oldest HBCU. Richard Humphreys, a Quaker abolitionist, silversmith, and philanthropist, donated a portion of his estate (roughly $10,000 at the time) to prepare people of African descent as teachers. He was inspired to give in this manner after hearing about a race riot in Cincinnati, Ohio, in which Whites rallied against the equitable treatment of free Black people in the city (Conyers, 1990). The second Black college founded in the North was Lincoln University, established in 1854 as the Ashmun Institute by Presbyterian minister John Dickey and his wife, Sarah Cresson. The couple were Presbyterian and Quaker, respectively. In 1866, one year after the assassination of President Abraham Lincoln, the institution was named Lincoln University to honor the late leader (Murray, 1973). The final Black college established in the North before the Civil War was Wilberforce University in Ohio in 1856. Unlike Cheyney and Lincoln, Wilberforce was the first Black college created and operated by African Americans. Affiliated with the AME Church, the leaders received assistance from the church to provide both classical education and teacher education for Black people. The institution's first president was Daniel Payne, the first African American to lead a college in the country (Du Bois, 1940; McGinnis, 1940).[3]

After the Union won the Civil War, the large task of educating 4 million formerly enslaved African Americans fell on the shoulders of the federal government, through the Freedmen's Bureau. With the help of various northern missionary organizations—both Black and White—the government began creating colleges with the specific purpose of educating African Americans (J. D. Anderson, 1988; Brazzell, 1992). Shaw University in Raleigh, North Carolina, was the first HBCU established in the South. In 1865, Henry Tupper, a soldier in the Union Army during the Civil War and a graduate of Amherst College, founded the institution.

Among Whites, Baptists and Congregationalists were the most involved religious sects in terms of supporting HBCUs. Two of the most widely known White missionary organizations were the American Baptist Home Mission Society and the American Missionary Association (AMA), but there were many others as well (J. D. Anderson, 1988; Brazzell, 1992). These missionary organizations founded several colleges, including Spelman College in Atlanta, Georgia; Benedict College, in Columbia, South Carolina; Talladega College in Talladega, Alabama; LeMoyne-Owen College, in Memphis, Tennessee; and Fisk University in Nashville, Tennessee, among others. According to James Anderson (1988), author of *The Education of Blacks in the South*, the generosity of the White missionary organizations was often marked by racism as well as self-interest. Rather than merely wanting to provide an education to African Americans, the White missionaries were focused on spreading Christianity with the goal of ridding Black people of the "immoralities" of slavery and sparing the nation from the "menace" of uneducated African Americans (J. D. Anderson, 1988; Watkins, 2001).

Although there have always been doubters of African American intellect and ingenuity, from the very beginning HBCUs and their students understood how important it was to foster learning and ensure that access to it continued. One example of this ingenuity surfaced in

1871 when a group of students at Fisk University in Nashville, Tennessee (founded in 1866), organized a singing group called the Fisk Jubilee Singers. The group toured nationally and internationally (and continues to do so) to raise money for and interest in Fisk University. Initially, the group sang spirituals, but over the years it has expanded its repertoire. Despite poor treatment at hotels and on railroads and ridicule from racist White patrons, the Jubilee Singers worked hard to raise much-needed funds to support Fisk (Ward, 2000).

The most active Black missionary groups were affiliated with the AME and the AME Zion churches. Among the colleges established by Black churches were Paul Quinn College in Dallas, Texas; Allen University in Columbia, South Carolina; and Morris Brown College in Atlanta, Georgia. Much like Wilberforce University in the North, these institutions were founded by African Americans for African Americans. They were focused specifically on uplifting Black people. Because African American churches had less access to funding and did not seek funds from White missionaries, these colleges operated on tighter budgets. But unlike Black colleges established by White missionary organizations, they were able to craft their own curricula absent outside influence and control (Watkins, 2001). Many of the earliest leaders and teachers at Black colleges were White and typically had military backgrounds—for example, Union general Otis O. Howard at Howard University—or were missionaries or abolitionists. Of note, at this time, most Black colleges were institutions of higher education in name only as African Americans needed primary and secondary education after being starved of it all their lives.[4]

Amid Jim Crow mentalities, oppression, and lynching[5] across the South, Congress passed the Second Morrill Act in 1890 (Harris, 2021; National Research Council, 1995).[6] This act provided annual federal appropriations to each state to support land-grant colleges. In addition to providing funding, the act banned racial discrimination in admissions for those institutions receiving federal funding. Despite the wording of the act, which was explicit about forbidding racial discrimination and specific in its call for equal distribution of federal monies, the Black colleges resulting from the act received fewer dollars than their White counterparts. Southern states were firm in their stance of treating African Americans as second-class citizens. This inequity cemented a foundation of inferior facilities at the 18 public Black land-grant institutions that these universities continue to work toward improving (S. Adams & Tucker, 2022; Lee & Keys, 2013).[7] Among these institutions were HBCUs such as Kentucky State University in Frankfort, Kentucky; North Carolina A&T State University in Greensboro, North Carolina; and Delaware State University in Dover, Delaware (S. Adams & Tucker, 2022; Harris, 2021; Thelin, 2011)[8]

At the end of the nineteenth century, the small, private, missionary-funded Black colleges had exhausted most of their funding sources, as missionary organizations had little to share. During this same time, the northern part of the nation saw the emergence of wealthy White men focused on industry and capitalizing on its growth. These individuals were also interested in providing philanthropic support to colleges that adhered to their way of thinking and that had the potential to meet their industry needs. Among the industrial giants who offered their philanthropic support to Black colleges were Andrew Carnegie (steel), John D. Rockefeller Sr. (oil), Julius Rosenwald (merchandising), William Baldwin (railroads), and John Slater (textiles) (J. D. Anderson, 1988; Gasman, 2007a; Watkins, 2001).

In addition to a desire for control of industry, these men were motivated by a sense of Christian benevolence. John D. Rockefeller Sr. created a vast organization aimed at supporting (and controlling) education, the General Education Board (GEB). The GEB, a conglomeration of northern White philanthropists, was led by Rockefeller's son, John D. Rockefeller Jr., who dedicated his life to philanthropy and restoring the Rockefeller name after the family was involved in a variety of scandals (J. D. Anderson, 1988; Gasman, 2007a; McGuire, 2004; Watkins, 2001).[9] The GEB donated over $63 million to Black colleges between 1903 and 1964, a considerable amount but only a fraction of what the organization allotted to White colleges and universities (Gasman, 2007a). Of course, the philanthropists had their individual motivations for supporting Black higher education. The funding operation that these industry titans established was evidence of their ardent desire to control all aspects of Black education to enhance their own industries. In the early 1900s, this type of education became known as industrial education (J. D. Anderson, 1988; Watkins, 2001).

The White industrial philanthropists kept the colleges that they supported under their watchful eye. To receive funds, the colleges had to be incredibly careful not to upset the segregationist power structure that prevailed in the South at the time (Watkins, 2001). Black colleges, including Tuskegee and Hampton, were displays of industrial education and were often highlighted by the industrial philanthropists. It was at these institutions that Black students initially learned to shoe horses, sew dresses, cook, and clean "properly" under the leadership and direction of Booker T. Washington and Samuel Chapman Armstrong, respectively. Of course, having Black people learn these skills was absurd given that the same skills were used regularly during slavery (Bieze & Gasman, 2012; Gasman & McMickens, 2010; Krauskopf, 2013; B. Washington, 1901).

The White philanthropists' support of industrial education conflicted with the views of many Black scholars and intellectuals who favored a liberal arts curriculum because it fostered critical thinking skills, which White people disapproved of because it theoretically led to rebellion and independence on the part of Black people (J. D. Anderson, 1988; Gasman, 2007a; Watkins, 2001). Institutions such as Howard University, Fisk University, Morehouse College, Dillard University, and Spelman College operated, for the most part, with a focus on the liberal arts curricula advocated by W. E. B. Du Bois rather than on Booker T. Washington's idea of advancement and independence through labor and self-sufficiency (J. D. Anderson, 1988; Bieze & Gasman, 2012; Du Bois, 2002; Gasman, 2007a; B. Washington, 1901; Watkins, 2001). Regardless of their disagreements of style and approach, the two educational influencers shared a goal of educating African Americans and uplifting their race (Bieze & Gasman, 2012). In essence, Washington favored educating Black people in the industrial arts so they might become self-sufficient as individuals, whereas Du Bois wanted to create an intellectual class among Black people (the "talented tenth") to lead the race toward self-determination and intellectual freedom (Alridge, 2018; Bieze & Gasman, 2012; Brazzell, 1992; Gasman, 2002). Later historians would continue to debate these approaches, while others would agree that both approaches were needed during the early years of Black education (Bieze & Gasman, 2012; Gasman & McMickens, 2010).

Although those interested in HBCUs during the early 1900s focused mostly on the ideas of Washington and Du Bois, Mary McLeod Bethune deserves attention for her steadfast commitment to educating African American women. In 1904, she opened the Daytona Educational and Industrial Training School for Negro Girls. The primary school grew over the years, eventually becoming a high school; then in 1931, it merged with another institution to become Bethune-Cookman College. Bethune was a highly skilled fundraiser; she was even able to persuade James Norris Gamble, the son of James Gamble, the co-founder of the Procter & Gamble Company, to give to the college and serve on the board of trustees. Bethune was one of only six Black women who served as president of an HBCU until the late 1990s, when Black women presidents became more common (A. Washington & Gasman, 2018).[10]

The year 1915 saw a shift in the attitude of the White industrial philanthropists. They began to direct their attention to Black colleges that boasted a liberal arts curriculum (J. D. Anderson, 1988). Realizing that industrial education could coexist with the liberal arts, the philanthropists distributed their money and asserted their power throughout Black higher education in the South. The insidious influence of White industrial philanthropy in the early twentieth century established a conservative and constraining environment on many Black college campuses. Administrators (typically White men) who accommodated segregation were, with few exceptions, the only leaders that the White philanthropists tolerated; and in many cases, they were puppets (J. D. Anderson, 1988; Gasman, 2007a; Watkins, 2001). Attention from the White philanthropists was not always welcomed by institutions such as Fisk University in Nashville, Tennessee, where protests ensued against autocratic president Fayette McKenzie, whom students thought to be a mere lapdog of the White philanthropists

(J. D. Anderson, 1988; Wolters, 1975). Despite these conflicts, industrial philanthropists provided significant financial support for private Black colleges up until the mid-nineteenth century (J. D. Anderson, 1988; Gasman, 2007a).

In the early 1930s, HBCUs became havens for Jewish professors expelled from Germany during Adolph Hitler's regime. Most predominantly White colleges and universities in the Northeast were not welcoming toward Jewish refugees, so the scholars headed south to HBCUs. According to the PBS documentary *From Swastika to Jim Crow* (2000), Black colleges, including Howard University, Talladega College, Tougaloo College, and Hampton University, benefited from having the Jewish refugee professors on their campuses. Ismar Schorsch of the Jewish Theological Seminary explains that the Jewish refugees who taught at HBCUs "found a place where they could make a contribution, and they found a place where they could pursue their intellectual life. They found a place where they could make a difference" (African American Registry, n.d.). The Jewish professors also found the HBCU students to be strong scholars who were eager to learn. Overall, about 50 Jewish professors worked at HBCUs across the South.

In the early 1940s, capitalist philanthropists began to turn their attention away from Black colleges, focusing instead on supporting the expansion of their industries. At the same time, presidents of Black colleges, who were targeting the same people for financial support, were being turned down more and more often. In response, Frederick D. Patterson, the president of Tuskegee Institute (now University) at the time, suggested in an article in the *Pittsburgh Courier* that private Black colleges band together around their fundraising efforts (Gasman, 2007a). Subsequently, in 1944, the leaders of 29 Black colleges created the United Negro College Fund (UNCF) in an act of self-determination (Drezner, 2008a; Gasman, 2004, 2007a; Tucker, 2002; L. E. Williams, 1980). The UNCF began solely as a fundraising organization but has subsequently taken on a large advocacy, developmental, and training role for Black colleges as well (Gasman, 2007a).

The 1940s were also a golden age for some Black colleges, with luminaries from the Harlem Renaissance[11] coming South to instruct

African American students. For example, Charles S. Johnson, the well-connected president of Fisk University, persuaded artists, writers, and poets to come to the campus, making Fisk one of the richest places for art and culture in the South. The campus boasted muralist Aaron Douglass, whose art still adorns the walls of Fisk's Cravath Hall. It also attracted James Weldon Johnson, the composer of "Lift Every Voice," the famed and important "Negro national anthem," and Arna Bontemps, the renowned poet. Johnson also secured painter Georgia O'Keeffe's 101-piece art collection, which had belonged to her late husband Alfred Stieglitz, in 1949. It included work by O'Keeffe, Pablo Picasso, Georges Braque, Arthur Dove, Marsden Hartley, and the famed photographer Alfred Stieglitz himself. With this collection, one that was far more impressive than that of nearby Vanderbilt University, Fisk became a focal point of art in the South (Gasman & Epstein, 2002). In this way, despite the oppressive nature of segregation, Black colleges found ways to inspire their students and local Black communities.

Until the *Brown v. Board of Education* decision in 1954, both public and private Black colleges in the South were segregated by law per *Plessy v. Ferguson* (1896)[12] and were, with a few exceptions, the only educational options for Black people.[13] Although most colleges and universities did not experience the same changes as southern public schools as a result of the *Brown* decision, they were shaped by the verdict (J. D. Anderson, 1988; Siddle-Walker, 1996). The Supreme Court's ruling placed Black colleges in competition with PWIs in their efforts to recruit Black students. With the triumph of integration in terms of the law (although not in practice), many influential White people began to call Black colleges into question and point to them as vestiges of segregation—including prominent philanthropist John D. Rockefeller Jr. (Gasman, 2007a). Private Black colleges, which had always been open to enrollment of students from all racial and ethnic backgrounds if the state laws would allow, were forced to defend issues of quality in a climate that labeled anything all-Black as inferior (Gasman, 2006, 2007a). Many Black colleges also suffered the loss of the top African American students as PWIs in the North and some in the South made efforts to attract the top 10% of students to their institutions once racial diversity was embraced (at least by higher education) (Gasman, 2006, 2007a).

As the 1950s and 1960s rolled in, Black colleges changed greatly and were quite different from those of the 1920s. The leadership moved from White men (and a few White women) to mostly African Americans; Black people had more control over institutional funding, and tolerance for Black dissent against the ills of society and in favor of self-determination grew (Gasman, 2011; Williamson-Lott, 2018). On many Black college campuses, students were active in sit-ins and protesting segregation. The most prominent example among these sit-ins—and noted by historians as the start of the movement—was the case of the four Black college men from North Carolina A&T State University who refused to leave a segregated Woolworth lunch counter in Greensboro, North Carolina, on February 1, 1960 (Favors, 2020; Gasman, 2011; Morgan & Davies, 2002; Williamson-Lott, 2018). Throughout their challenge, these young men were supported by the students at nearby Bennett College for Women, along with its president, Willa Player. Weighing about 100 pounds, Player was a fierce advocate for civil rights, whereas some male HBCU presidents were not as public in their support owing to the general climate in the South and their own fear of losing funding (Gasman, 2007a, 2009a; Sanders, 2019). According to historian Crystal Sanders, Player's

> physical presence as the leader of [Bennett] . . . creates . . . new pathways [for] what was possible for African American women because she is not playing second fiddle to a man. She's not serving in a secretarial role. She's not serving as a dorm matron or as a dean of women, but she is the HNIC.[14] She is the one who's deciding who's hired and fired, who's signing checks, who's determining what course offerings are going to be offered and what course offerings aren't going to be offered.

Sanders added, "Player is a woman before her time, and pushed for civil rights action before the sit in movement happened, even in her inauguration as president at Bennett in 1956." Furthermore, according to Sanders, Player was a significant mentor to students, one who emphasized that "the purpose of education is to help release the chains of racism and that you have a role to play."

Mirroring the Greensboro action, in the 1960s, Fisk University student Diane Nash and her student colleagues began negotiating with local restaurants to desegregate their lunch counters (Plazas, 2020). Nash was a founding member of the Student Nonviolent Coordinating Committee, and she was militant in approach, refusing to acquiesce to the segregated South. She and her colleagues thrust Fisk into the center of civil rights activism and the Black Freedom Movement, making a significant impact on the role that HBCUs played in creating opportunities for African Americans (Barnett, 1993; Favors, 2020). Nash was fiercely brave, coordinating student efforts to participate in the Congress of Racial Equality's Freedom Rides to Mississippi. Though a student, she was arrested for delinquency of minors for encouraging young people to join the fight for desegregation in Mississippi (Holsaert & Noonan, 2013).

At the same time, the federal government began to have a greater interest in Black colleges and higher education overall. To provide clarity, the 1965 Higher Education Act, through Title III, defined a Black college as an institution whose primary mission was the education of African Americans. The recognition of the uniqueness of Black colleges implied in this definition led to increased federal funding for these historic institutions (Gasman, 2007a; Harris, 2021; Thelin, 2011). It also meant that all the HBCUs that could be created had been established; no additional HBCUs could be created from this date on.

Amid these changes, the nation was in turmoil, grappling with protests of both the United States's participation in the Vietnam War and the country's near-constant racial injustices. It was during this time that the Mississippi state police entered the Jackson State University campus on May 15, 1970, and confronted a group of Black students who had been throwing rocks at White motorists driving through campus. That night, the police opened fire, killing 4 students and wounding 12 others. Over the course of the evening, 40 state police officers fired 460 gunshots. The Jackson State incident is relatively unknown because a similar event had taken place on the campus of

Ohio's Kent State University 11 days earlier; the nation was still recovering from the shock of that deadly attack on college students. In addition, Jackson State, being an HBCU, did not receive the kind of empathy that predominantly White Kent State did from citizens, media, and policy makers. As a result of the turmoil on the Jackson State and Kent State campuses, coupled with other issues happening across the nation within higher education, in 1970, President Richard Nixon established the Presidential Commission on Campus Unrest to investigate both incidents (Favors, 2020; M. McGee & Platt, 2015; Spofford, 1988).

The federal government further increased its involvement with Black colleges in 1980 when President Jimmy Carter authorized and signed Executive Order 12232, which established a national program to ease the impact of systemic racism and expanded the capacity of Black colleges in a bid to support their efforts to provide high-quality education. Every subsequent US president has provided funding to Black colleges through this program. President George H. W. Bush followed up on Carter's initiative in 1989, signing Executive Order 12677, which established the President's Board of Advisors on Historically Black Colleges and Universities to counsel the president and the secretary of education on the future of these institutions.

Even with an end to legal segregation by the Supreme Court and increased support from the federal government, desegregation proved to be difficult and slow, with public Black colleges maintaining their racial makeup to this day. In the state of Mississippi, for example, lawyers debated the *Fordice* case for 25 years, with a final decision offered in 2004. *Fordice*, which reached the US Supreme Court, and asked whether the State of Mississippi had met its responsibility, as required by the Fourteenth Amendment's Equal Protection Clause, to dismantle its prior dual and segregated university system. Despite considerable evidence to the contrary, the high court decided that the answer was *yes*. *Fordice* applied only to those public institutions within the 5th District; however, it had a rippling effect within most southern states, resulting in spotty funding for public Black colleges and a lack of sincere access for African Americans (Brady et al., 2000; A. Johnson, 1993; Lee, 2010).

Amid the lawsuits and federal legislation related to HBCUs as well as the tumultuous events taking place across the nation in the late 1960s—including the assassination of Martin Luther King Jr.—a group of presidents and chancellors came together to form the National Association for Equal Opportunity in Higher Education (NAFEO). This membership organization, which was officially launched in 1969, has been instrumental in advocating for HBCUs across the legislative, executive, and judicial branches of the federal government and at the state level (NAFEO, n.d.).

The 1970s and 1980s proved to be a challenging time for HBCUs in terms of financial strain and spending. Because wealthier African American students were beginning to attend PWIs for college, HBCUs were tasked with educating low-income and lower-middle-income students, which took additional funds and led to increased spending. Although HBCUs were able to maintain their enrollments, they did not experience the substantial growth in enrollment that PWIs did during this time. In addition, HBCUs had difficultly retaining Black faculty because they could not compete with PWIs in terms of salary (Griffith, 1996).

In the 1990s, television programs such as *The Cosby Show* and its spin-off, *A Different World*, brought increased attention to HBCUs. *Cosby* regularly featured characters wearing HBCU T-shirts and sweatshirts, and *A Different World* took place at a fictional HBCU, Hillman College, and highlighted the academic and social culture of HBCUs. Both shows were also notable for featuring characters that genuinely wanted to attend HBCUs for college. Research shows (as demonstrated in the preface) that featuring HBCUs on these shows increased interest in and enrollment at these institutions in the late 1990s (Griffith, 1996; Parrott-Sheffer, 2008).

There are currently fewer than 300,000 students attending the nation's 105 HBCUs. This enrollment amounts to 9% of all African American college students (National Center for Educational Statistics [NCES], 2021). On average, the parents of Black students at Black colleges have lower family incomes than those of parents of Black students who attend PWIs. Scholars who study Black colleges, however, have found that African Americans who attend Black colleges have higher levels of self-esteem and find their educational experiences more nurturing (Conrad & Gasman, 2015; Palmer & Gasman, 2008; Strayhorn, 2016). Moreover, graduates of Black colleges are more likely to continue their education and pursue graduate degrees than African American students enrolled at PWIs (Gasman & Nguyen, 2019). Despite only 9% of African American college students attending Black colleges, these institutions produce substantial numbers of professors, politicians, lawyers, doctors, scientists, and teachers— many of whom we talked to for this book (Gasman, Nguyen, Conrad et al., 2017; Gasman & Nguyen, 2019; NCES, 2021; Perna et al., 2009).

Black colleges of today are quite diverse and serve varied populations (Gasman & Nguyen, 2015; Jewell, 2002; Lundy-Wagner, 2015; Maramba et al., 2015; Shorrette & Arroyo, 2015). They garner attention for their academics, athletics, talent, and traditions. They have also been featured by the likes of entertainer Beyoncé (in her 2019 *Homecoming* documentary), have attracted attention for graduating entertainers like Megan Thee Stallion (Texas Southern University) and Anthony Anderson (Howard University), and boasted football coaches like former NFL football player Deion Sanders (Gasman, 2022b). Although most of these institutions maintain their historically Black traditions, on average, 13% of their students are White, 2% are Latinx, and 2% are Asian American (Gasman, 2013; NCES, 2021). Some HBCUs are models for LGBTQ inclusivity, such as Spelman College with its Audre Lorde curriculum project and Bowie State University with its stand-alone LGBTQIA Resource Center, although we should point out that other HBCUs, much like their PWI counterparts, are grappling with how to better serve LGBTQ students (Mobley & Johnson, 2015, 2019; Nguyen et al., 2018; E. Williams, 2013).

Because of their common institutional mission (that of racial uplift), HBCUs are often lumped together and thus treated as a monolithic group, resulting in their being unfairly judged by researchers, the media, and policy makers (Gasman, 2007a; K. L. Williams et al., 2019). Just as PWIs are diverse in their mission and quality, so are HBCUs. Today, the leading Black colleges enroll those students who could excel at any top-tier college or university regardless of racial makeup. Other institutions operate with the needs of African American students in the nearby region in mind. And some offer an open enrollment policy—like a community college, they accept those students who have few other options when it comes to higher education (Gasman et al., 2010). Two-year and community colleges are important and rarely acknowledged segments of HBCUs. Although the majority of HBCUs are four-year institutions, there are 14 two-year and/or community college HBCUs.[15]

Overview

As we move forward in this book, Chapter 2 focuses on the role that HBCUs and their unique culture have played in developing the Black identities of their students. In Chapter 3, we examine the ways that HBCUs have moved African Americans into the middle class and expanded their socioeconomic mobility. Chapter 4 takes a deep look at how HBCUs have shaped the lives of prominent scholars and leaders. In Chapter 5, we explore the contributions of HBCU alumni, leaders, and faculty in mentoring and advising generations of African Americans. Given the vital part that philanthropic and alumni giving plays in the sustainability of HBCUs, in Chapter 6, we examine both the history and the growing engagement of philanthropists in terms of investment in HBCUs as well as the need for alumni support and contributions. Chapter 7 focuses on the contributions of HBCUs to economic and community development in the cities and towns where they are situated. Although in our approach to this book we have kept in mind the power of HBCUs and the overarching positive contributions that they make, we would be remiss in not exploring the challenges that HBCUs face. Chapter 8 looks closely at these challenges from the perspective of those inside the HBCU world and those who work closely with it. Chapter 9 considers the opportunities ahead for HBCUs while making recommendations for these schools and those who care about moving them to new levels of success and sustainability.

2

Culture and Its Impact on Black Identity

From the start, HBCUs have put a different kind of human being into the world, fundamentally different from the graduates of non-HBCUs.
—JOHN S. WILSON, Executive Director, White House Initiative on Advancing Educational Equity, Excellence, and Economic Opportunity through Historically Black Colleges and Universities

When alumni talk about the culture of Historically Black Colleges and Universities, they immediately begin smiling in their recollections of family, community, and a spirit of togetherness that permeates the campus. They are filled with joy when they think of the love they felt, the confidence instilled in them, and the role models around them every day. They hark back to a time when faculty, staff, and even other students believed they would succeed and go on to do great things. As students, they felt wrapped in a protective blanket that cradled them until they were ready to leave campus and pursue their dreams and aspirations. They continue to be grateful for their experiences.

Research demonstrates that HBCUs have a unique and profound culture that has a positive impact on the lives and identities of African American students. Most scholarship related to culture, identity, and HBCUs, however, is focused on students while they are students. Occasionally, scholars have interviewed alumni—mainly about their motivations for giving back to their alma maters—but rarely do they ask alumni about the impact of their HBCU experience on their identity and the impact of HBCU culture (Gasman & Anderson-Thompkins, 2003; Gasman & Bowman, 2012; Winkle-Wagner et al., 2020). The unique and empowering culture of these institutions has an impact on people's lives long after they graduate (Arroyo & Gasman, 2014; Arroyo et al., 2017; Baker et al., 2021; Conrad & Gasman, 2015; Covington & Njoku, 2021; Gasman & Nguyen, 2019; Gasman, Nguyen, et al., 2017; Greenfield et al., 2015; Mobley & Johnson, 2015; Mobley et al., 2021; Nguyen et al., 2020; Palmer et al., 2010; Palmer et al., 2015; Rucker & Gendrin, 2003; Van Camp et al., 2009; Van Camp et al., 2010; L. J. Walker, 2018).

HBCU Culture

When HBCUs are discussed in popular circles, the robust and unique culture is usually the first thing to surface: the family-like environment, the memorable faculty, the diversity of Blackness, the vibrancy of marching bands,[1] step shows sponsored by Black Greek letter organizations, homecoming, football games, and life on the yard. This culture has a long-lasting impact on students and often plays a role in boosting confidence and opening doors for a lifetime. In the words of Makola Abdullah, the president of Virginia State University, "HBCUs, I think along with the Black church, are some of those environments where Black culture exists in its fullness . . . whether it's homecoming or games or different types of activities, . . . it's a place where you're going to get that healthy dose of culture in a manner that's so important."

HBCUs have a culture that permeates families, and exposure to HBCU culture often begins at a young age. This early exposure can be transformative. We found that many of the current and former presidents of HBCUs began their journeys through exposure to HBCU campuses when they were young. Some of these individuals lived across the street from HBCU campuses and were exposed to Black academic excellence and achievement daily. As Rick Gallot, president of Grambling State University, told us, "I was born and reared in Grambling, Louisiana. There is a city that surrounds the university. My childhood home is literally across the street from the campus." Gallot's mother taught at Grambling for 44 years and retired as the head of the history department. As he shared, "HBCUs have been a part of my entire life." Gallot attended lab schools on the Grambling campus—nursery school through his senior year of high school—and then attended college at the institution. Although Gallot applied to and had offers from other institutions, his dream was to be a part of the "world-famed Grambling State University Tiger Marching Band." So, he passed on the other offers to attend Grambling.

Thomas Hudson, the president of Jackson State University, has a similar story. His interaction with Jackson State began when he was in elementary school. As he recalled, "My mom was a single parent who went back to school. She was working in the dining hall—they called it the cafeteria back then—and one of her bosses encouraged her to come back to school. And so, she came back to school, and she took me with her." Hudson added, "I was three, four years old. [My mom] didn't have childcare, right? Jackson State was the first school I knew." At the time, Hudson did not realize that Jackson State was an HBCU. "I didn't know that Jackson State was anything but this place where my mom went to school and class, and I used to go to class with her." As Hudson grew older, he attended a middle school right next to Jackson State. As we were talking with him, Hudson said, "I can look out my [presidential office] window here and see where I went to middle school, so I passed Jackson State every day [when I was young]." This early exposure had a lasting impact.

Michael Sorrell, the president of Paul Quinn College in Dallas, Texas, told us that his "love affair with HBCUs" began when he attended his godfather's graduation from Dillard University. He sat on a white chair on the lawn underneath the oak trees and took in the entire event. According to Sorrell,

> I did not know everything that was going on, obviously, because I was a little kid, but I just remember sitting there and just being awed and inspired, and then listening to my mother's stories about having attended—because our family school was Dillard. My mother went to Dillard. My grandmother went to Dillard. My aunt, who was really her first cousin but they were raised as sisters, went to Dillard. My godfather went to Dillard, and so my first memory in life is being on an HBCU campus as a little kid in dress shorts and sitting on white chairs underneath the oaks.

Sorrell did not attend an HBCU; he attended Oberlin College in Ohio. As he explained to us, "A lot of the ideas that we've implemented here at Paul Quinn College during my presidency were born on listening to my mother talk about what was the Golden Age for HBCUs." He added, "Just the way the professors engaged, the way that the community stood together for years after they graduated. How they all understood that they were doing something larger than themselves. How there was a sense that you were going to succeed, because we had to succeed, and so I was raised with this belief that it could just be the very best of all of us." Despite not attending an HBCU, Sorrell grew up with a fondness for the HBCU community and wanting to be a part of it. He just did not know what his entry point would be.

Others we talked with were drawn to HBCUs because of their marching bands or the spectacle of seeing so many Black people together, learning and socializing. Kevin James, the president of Morris Brown College, is from a family of educators. Both of his parents have PhDs, and he and his siblings all have advanced degrees. When he graduated from high school in 1995, he did not know what he wanted to do. He lived in Columbia, South Carolina, about 45 minutes down the road from South Carolina State University. As James recalled,

> I'm a musician, played the drums, and I was in love with the South Carolina State University marching band, and so I auditioned for a scholarship,

received a scholarship, and I went to school for one reason and one reason only, and that was to be in the band at South Carolina State University, period. I mean, it's just absolutely the truth. I didn't know what I wanted to study, so I just picked a major, music. I love music, so I'm just going to study music, and that's how I started my career at South Carolina State.

Likewise, Damon Williams grew up in a well-educated family that was no stranger to the power of HBCUs. He is the third generation of his family to attend an HBCU. His grandparents attended Southern University, and his parents attended Southern and Shaw Universities. Williams attended Xavier University of Louisiana. As he shared, "I recall when my parents would take us to Southern University. Both of my parents were very, very adamant about education. . . . I mean, we were walking on HBCU campuses. We attended precollegiate programs. My relationship started really early with parents, grandparents, me being on the campuses, me attending Bayou Classic."[2] He added, "I grew up in a small town called Tull, Louisiana, which is between Monroe and Jackson, so I would go to the Jackson State/Alcorn game as well. So, all that academic, socially, just part of my historical nature is how I got involved with HBCUs."

Robert Palmer, a professor at Howard University and a Morgan State University graduate, believes that the opportunity to see Blackness in all its manifestations is a powerful part of the culture of HBCUs and has a profound impact on student identity:

I think that's what HBCUs are about and also providing an environment where Black students for the first time can really meet other Black students who are striving for success and being able to see that not all Black people are the same. There are Black people that come from different walks of life and have different schools of thoughts and diverse ways of thinking. You have Black Republicans, and you have Black people who are more into hip-hop. You have the more studious Black people. You have Black people from the Caribbean and Black people from other parts of the world. So, you have this kind of cultural melting pot, where for the first time in a Black student's life, where they can interact with so many different Black people. They get to really see that "Hey, Black people are so diverse." Culturally, ethnically, in terms of religion, in terms of politics, in terms of sexual orientation.

Palmer added, "That becomes a very powerful learning dynamic, a powerful and transformative learning experience that's really going to help prepare students for the wider world once they graduate."

The culture at HBCUs also boasts opportunities for everyone. According to renowned filmmaker Stanley Nelson,

> One of the things that someone told us as we were working on [*Tell Them We Are Rising: The History and Impact of Historically Black Colleges and Universities*] is that if you're going to Harvard, you know, you can be as smart as a whip and you got into Harvard, but you might not try out as an African American for the role of Hamlet in the play, right?[3] You just might not do that. You might not think that being the editor of, you know, the Harvard newspaper, is a place for you. Now, some people, you know will go out for that and just throw everything aside, right, you know but for so many African Americans they just don't feel comfortable. And that's all the way down the line for all these different endeavors. But you know, at HBCUs, everybody in *Hamlet* is Black. At HBCUs, everybody who's editing, who's working on a newspaper or the college magazine, is Black, and so, yeah, why not go after it?

For Nelson, attending an HBCU meant that Black students were given limitless opportunities that they might not have received at a Predominantly White Institution. With HBCUs, it is not just the issue of access but the opportunity to feel as though you belong.

HBCUs have a long legacy of producing stellar scholar-athletes, including football players Jerry Rice,[4] Walter Payton,[5] and Doug Williams,[6] tennis player Althea Gibson,[7] and sprinter Wilma Rudolph.[8] Sports play a significant role in the college experience for many HBCU students, with many choosing to attend a college based on the success or notoriety of an institution's sports teams and star players (Graham, 2021). Sporting events bring enjoyment to fan bases and contribute to deeper alumni engagement and often increased donations (Gasman &

Bowman, 2010). Within the HBCU community, athletic events serve as culturally liberating activities (Graham, 2021). The most well-known and highly attended HBCU sporting events are football games, which have featured famed coaches such as Grambling's Eddie Robinson.[9] For many students and graduates, sporting events, especially football games, are seen as a cultural phenomenon and part of the fabric of an HBCU. Since the late nineteenth century, football games have been an integral part of HBCUs (Graham, 2021). HBCUs host Classic games, which differ from regular-season games and involve the integration of African American cultural events like step shows, beauty pageants, parades, music concerts, Battle of the Bands performances, and community service outreach (Graham, 2021). Revenue generated from the Classic games supports student scholarships, academic programs, and campus renovations, and these games serve as huge recruitment events for both students and student-athletes.

Harold Martin, chancellor at North Carolina A&T State University, is a leading proponent of positioning his institution for future success by focusing on athletic competitiveness and realizes the importance of sports to the A&T brand. For example, in 2021, he made the decision to leave the Mid-Eastern Athletic Conference and join the Colonial Athletic Association (CAA). When we talked with him for this book, Martin shared: "Everything we've done continues to focus on positioning our university as that aspirational, competitive, doctoral research, land-grant institution. Making the tough decision to accept the invitation by the CAA to become one of its member institutions was ultimately a no-brainer for us. When we began a major conversation about evaluating athletics (seven years ago), we've continued to evaluate the significant role that athletics plays in the visibility, competitiveness, and the brand recognition of our university."

For Martin, the focus is not just on athletic competitiveness but on how athletics can contribute to building the academic brand of A&T and provide better learning opportunities for students through corporate partnerships. Martin emphasized this point, saying, "We have taken an aggressive posture with raising money with corporate partners who are recruiting our graduates in record numbers." He added,

"And they are not only making investments today that support our university from an academic perspective, but they're now in very significant conversations with us around putting a name as a sponsor on facilities. [We are] building out those relationships with corporate partners, much more significantly than we have ever done in the past. And they're responding." Martin elaborated, "We just opened a new engineering research complex. And within that facility are a record number of corporate-sponsored research labs, conference facilities and the like. Those corporate partners want to do more. And that's how it begins with now bringing them to the table to support athletics."

Martin recognizes the importance of investing in the development of successful athletic programs and how it helps contribute to a strong institutional brand as well as increases in corporate and alumni donations. It is also worth mentioning that a by-product of competitive athletics programs is the increased exposure and prominence of an institution, which often results in larger numbers of student applicants and increased enrollment.

Different HBCUs Have Different Cultures

For years we have been telling people with little understanding of HBCUs that these institutions are diverse in nature and are not monolithic. Every HBCU has a different feel and a different culture. We visited 103 of the 105 HBCUs in the United States and can attest to both similarities and vast differences among these institutions—so can HBCU alumni, and they have the intense rivalries to prove it. According to Kent Wallace, a professor and physicist at Fisk University, who attended Grambling for his undergraduate degree, "Coming from Grambling and [now being at] Fisk, these are two diverse types of HBCUs. Their atmospheres are different. Their cultures are different, and after visiting other HBCUs throughout my career, the cultures of the institutions [are different]. People would not know this unless they actually visited HBCUs, and not just one, but many." He added, "People just think, 'Ooh, Black colleges, this monolithic thing, and everybody does the same thing.' It's not [the same]. Different HBCUs have different cultures." From Wallace's perspective, the culture of Fisk University has been instrumental in developing his sense of identity as a scholar. The institution is small yet focused intensely on research. Wallace sees the conflux of the small size and being steeped in research as a unique experience for students. Most HBCUs with a strong research focus are larger, like North Carolina A&T State or Howard Universities.

There are many differences among the various types of HBCUs. For example, there are private HBCUs, such as Hampton University, Stillman College, and Tougaloo College, and 1890 land-grant institutions, such as Florida A&M University, Prairie View A&M University, and Fort Valley State University. In the case of private HBCUs, these are institutions that are independent, set their own policies and goals, are privately funded, and have an academic focus on the humanities, arts, social sciences, and natural sciences. In most cases, these institutions have smaller enrollments than their public university counterparts. On the other hand, the land-grant institutions were created with a focus on agricultural sciences and extension programs. These institutions are publicly funded and have larger student enrollments.

Kevin James emphasized the uniqueness of the culture of the institution that he leads: Morris Brown College in Atlanta, Georgia. Although the college has struggled for over two decades and was written off by nearly everyone, including those in the HBCU community, it is now on its way back, securing support from the federal government and accreditation. Morris Brown College is unique in that it is the only HBCU in the state of Georgia, and one of a few in the nation that was created by African Americans for African Americans. As mentioned in Chapter 1, the vast majority of HBCUs were created by the Freedmen's Bureau and White missionary organizations. In its heyday, the small college was well known for its academics, school spirit, and pride. According to James,

> Morris Brown is world renowned for its band and music program. The Morris Brown College Marching Wolverine Band was featured in the movie *Drum Line* and that's very critical because when I talk to people

and they say, well, where's Morris Brown? And the first thing I always say is, have you ever seen the movie *Drum Line*, and 100% of anyone I have ever asked that question to says, yeah, I've seen that movie. That's one of my favorite movies. And I say that the school in the movie, Morris Brown, is a real school. And 100% of the time, they automatically immediately know who we are because of that movie. They thought the school was a fictional school.

He added, "We are known all around the world and people don't even know they know us. I mean, here we are 21 years later, and that movie is on almost every single day on TBS." The band has been a strong branding component for Morris Brown College and part of the institution's culture even during the difficult years.

James wrote his doctoral dissertation on how music and band programs affect recruitment, retention, and finances at HBCUs. He shared, "I can tell you firsthand that the Morris Brown band was critically important to student enrollment, student retention, and school spirit at Morris Brown College and is even to this day and we don't even have an active program." While we were writing this book, Morris Brown band alumni members were asked to be on *Good Morning America*. According to James, "They called us and said, look, we want to do a story on HBCUs. We know the history of your band. Can you pull together your alumni band and be featured on *Good Morning America*? And we said, absolutely, and we literally did that in two days and put together a 40-piece band in two days with instruments, drums, everything, COVID testing, everything." James added, with great enthusiasm, "Our band is very important to the culture and the history of our school, just like athletics is, just like other programs, like fraternities and sororities and student life here."

Understanding the importance of culture and the uniqueness of Morris Brown College, James shared that as he restores the college,

I have made it a strategy, a strategic chess move, that I am bringing back the band before I even bring back football. I pulled from a strategy that Talladega College used; right now they have a 300-piece marching band, and they don't have a football team. That band, when you look at 300 students, a lot of those students came just to be in the band. And they use their band strategically as literally a marching billboard. They are very strong ambassadors for Talladega College, and so I'm going to use that same approach here at Morris Brown; we are going to be in parades. We are going to be at student orientations. We are going to be out in the community recruiting folks to be in our band and using it as an ambassador of goodwill for our college. Morris Brown College Marching Wolverine Band, keep your eyes open.

Xavier University of Louisiana has a highly unique culture: it is the only Catholic HBCU in the nation. In addition, it has a commitment to producing Black doctors that is hard to match at most HBCUs, and most PWIs for that matter. The institution's track record for producing future Black doctors is awe-inspiring, outpacing every institution (Black or White) in most years (Gasman, Smith, et al., 2017; Hannah-Jones, 2015).[10] When Damon Williams enrolled at Xavier several decades ago, he was taken aback by the students who attended Xavier. Many were second generation, valedictorians, former student body presidents, and homecoming queens. According to Williams, "We were the top talent. We were the talented tenth of Jack and Jill.[11] I saw all this Black excellence and it was like, whoa." He added, "Of course, not everyone had this background. There were low-income students and there were those from all walks of life."

Williams also remembers the deeply Catholic nature of the institution. He joked, "Now, did we like praying? Did we pray every day before class? Of course not. It wasn't like catechism when we were younger, but we were all centered on going out into the community and doing what's best [for the community]." He provided an example:

My favorite professor, Dr. Beverley Mason, would have us go to the other side of the canal [across from the Xavier campus] and say, so what do you see when you see Xavier? What do you think the community looks at when they see Xavier? So, it's your responsibility to give back to the community. It's your responsibility for people to understand that you have a privilege, that you walk around this campus with a book bag, that you look studious, that people might think that you're bougie, but you also have a commitment and a privilege to whatever you aspire to be, and leaders of the community, and you always give back to the community. So, I always think about that when I think about Xavier and its surrounding area.

Mary Schmidt Campbell is the tenth president of Spelman College, which is by all traditional indicators (rankings, graduation and retention rates, and endowment) one of the most impressive HBCUs. Although she did not attend an HBCU, she has surrounded herself with Black culture, literature, and art her entire life. Campbell served as the director of the Studio Museum in Harlem and the cultural affairs commissioner for the city of New York. She understands the unique culture of Spelman and its role in empowering young Black women. To complement and capitalize on this culture—and to stay in touch with students—she created the President's Reading Circle when she arrived on the Atlanta-based campus. Campbell's actions are indicative of the type of leader at HBCUs. As she recalled,

> As president, I know that I would become so tied up in administrative duties and issues that I could find myself in a position where contact with students is just at a very superficial social level. You see them at reception. You go to a meeting with them. They sit on a search committee with you. I thought to myself—I do not have the bandwidth to be able to teach a course for an entire semester or year. I'm going to form this reading circle because I love to read, and I read all the time. And the first book we chose was the biography *Alexander Hamilton* by Ronald Chernow, a pretty substantial biography.

Campbell chose the book because she had recently seen the musical *Hamilton*—when it was off-Broadway—and considered it "the most remarkable musical" she had ever seen. The day the tickets went on sale for the Broadway production, Campbell ordered 40 tickets for the students in her book club. She told them that if they completed the book, they would "get to go to New York and see *Hamilton* on Broadway."

As a bonus, Campbell used her connections to provide a once-in-a-lifetime experience for the students. She called Ron Chernow, and he agreed to come and speak to the students. According to the Spelman College president, "He came to dinner, before we [went] to the play, and he [gave] a brief presentation about why he wrote the book, why he let the book become a Broadway play, how surprised he was when he learned it was going to be a hip-hop musical." Campbell added, "After his presentation, Chernow invited questions. And the students were fantastic. I mean, they were asking him probing questions about the biography. Afterwards, he said 'Wow, that was really something. Do you think they'd like to meet the cast?'" As Campbell recalled, "We [went] to see the play. Afterwards, the theater emptie[d]. We move[d] up to the front. The entire cast from *Hamilton* [came], [sat] on the edge of the stage, and [talked] to my Spelman students for an hour and a half."

Recalling the importance of the President's Reading Circle, Campbell shared,

> What it told me in that first year, first, the students who were in that group still keep in touch. We forged lasting connections. But it revealed something to me about the structure of the President's Reading Circle. I decided that we were going to read the book, but then we're going to have a related experience. And what it did is it really got me underneath that sort of superficial level of contact to understand who the students were, how they were thinking, the kinds of issues they bumped up against as they were going through their Spelman journey.

As we were writing this book, Campbell announced her retirement. She was in her seventh year at Spelman and was starting yet another reading circle. The reading circle and its sense of empowerment and intimacy are representative of the strong culture at Spelman and how leadership engenders culture and cultural traditions. As Campbell shared, "It gave me a real sense of how the college serves our students because they would talk about those experiences whether they were in class or out of class and how meaningful this was or that was. And so, it really gave me an inside glimpse into the students' lives." In addition to the structured activity of a reading circle, Campbell also enjoys those chance encounters: "You go to the cafeteria, and you put your tray down and join students for lunch, or you go to the Student Government Association meeting, or you go to the Miss Spelman Pageant. You show up. You're present. But the reading circle is what has given me the deepest insight into our students and the things at the college that work well on behalf of their success."

Overall Diversity of HBCUs

Often when discussing HBCUs, those unfamiliar with their history and culture assume that these institutions are not diverse—they see them as all Black. This assumption is based on a misunderstanding of the richness and diversity of Blackness as well as a lack of knowledge related to the history of HBCUs as places that have always welcomed people of all racial and ethnic backgrounds. HBCUs boast rich diversity in their student body in terms of race, ethnicity, religion, socioeconomic status, gender, sexuality, and country of origin (Gasman & Nguyen, 2019; Palmer & Williams, 2021). Their faculties are also the most diverse among colleges and universities in the nation (Esmieu, 2019). As Kent Wallace, a professor at Fisk University who loves teaching, explained,

> The student does not have to be Black. One of our former student government presidents, a proud graduate of Fisk University, was Afro-Latino, and one was just straight Latino. Also, the research shows HBCUs tend to have more diversity in their faculty than their majority-serving counterparts. The HBCU name carries an [assumption] with it, that it's a Black school. However, there is so much more diversity here than [we are] given credit for. We welcome and tend to be a very nurturing environment for varying perspectives.

Lynn Wooten, a North Carolina A&T State University graduate and president of Simmons University in Massachusetts, agreed, sharing,

> You know, the one thing is that people think HBCUs don't have diversity, but they do. There's socioeconomic diversity. There's sexual orientation diversity. There's gender diversity. But the one impact that goes back to

what I talked about is when you get to an HBCU, it doesn't matter who you are. You're learning [on] a level playing field. Everybody is given the same treatment and there's equity. You're given what you're needed. And so, the notion of community, the notion of collaboration, the notion of helping is kind of the first thing.

As Wooten explained, diversity in terms of sexual orientation is present on HBCU campuses. Although acceptance of this type of difference has not always been welcome—an issue on most college campuses—HBCUs have, in recent years, been vocal in terms of their support of LGBTQ communities (B. Jones et al., 2020; Lenning, 2017; Mobley & Johnson, 2015, 2019). For example, Bowie State University has one of the most comprehensive LGBTQ centers on an HBCU campus and is forthright in its policies that support LGBTQ faculty, students, and staff. Likewise, Spelman College has been a leader, creating guidebooks pertaining to how to support LGBTQ students and hosting national conferences aimed at helping their HBCU counterparts—and other institutions—to implement best practices to support LGBTQ students, faculty, and staff (Guy-Sheftall, 2012; E. Williams, 2013).

The Curriculum

HBCUs have highly diverse curricula. Some have a more Afro-centric approach, others are more traditional, and still others have woven issues of equity throughout their courses. Overall, a respect for Blackness permeates the curricula across HBCUs. As Alton Thompson, a graduate of North Carolina Central University and now a professor at North Carolina A&T State University, explained, "One thing about HBCUs, when I was at Central, it [was] like having Black History Month every month. I mean, you lived in a Black culture, so you celebrated Black history every month. In the eastern part of North Carolina, Black history wasn't in our curriculum. So, the Black history that I learned started at HBCUs. And I also learned about significant contributions that African Americans have made to American society at HBCUs."

The role that HBCUs play in terms of educating African American students about Black history and culture is not by accident, according to Paul Quinn College President Michael Sorrell: "From a historical perspective, I think it's important to understand that the charge for HBCUs was unlike anything else that we've seen. I mean, higher education itself was created to ensure that the landed gentry had educated clergy, and their sons were educated to perpetuate their wealth. Higher education wasn't created to provide access to better lives for everyone right." He added, "We never intended to do that, except for HBCUs, because when slavery ended 4 million freed people needed to be made a part of the fabric of America, and look, we can talk about how there really wasn't a full intention to do that, but that was the charge. And so, everything that the formerly enslaved people were going to actually be was going to come from this experiment, right?" Sorrell noted that we call American democracy the great American experiment but that HBCUs were really the grand experiment. In his words, "There's been nothing in history like [HBCUs], and I don't think that [fact] gets credit enough. You created a set of schools [for] people who weren't even considered people, right, who were considered chattel, to help them access a life in a land that never wanted them there in this way."

Sorrell believes the reason that HBCUs had to provide a curriculum that bolstered African American history and culture is that they were producing more than doctors and lawyers. HBCUs were (and still are) tasked with "producing a society." In Sorrell's words, "Our job was to produce people who could fight the fights that the formerly enslaved people and their progeny needed to fight." Although African Americans now have more choices, HBCUs continue to provide a curriculum rooted in African American perspectives and knowledge, adding to the overall culture at HBCUs.

Antoine Alston, a professor at North Carolina A&T State University, believes that the curriculum at HBCUs must teach African American students that "they do have a place in this world." He reminded us that most school systems in the United States teach history and social studies from a Eurocentric perspective (Wong, 2015). As he recalled from his own education, "I remember when I was in high school, we had a world history book. It had about 30 chapters and 25 of them were on Europe. [When we got to] Africa, we just breezed over that and kept it moving and [the book] taught Egypt as if it were a part of the Middle East, but Egypt is clearly on the African continent." Alston continued, "It really empowers us to let us know our place in the world, let our folks know that [we] have intellect and [we] have a place in this world and that we can have an impact in this world."

If you spend time in HBCU communities, you often hear that the curriculum at HBCUs meets students where they are intellectually and takes them to where they need to be. As Armando Bengochea, program officer at the Mellon Foundation, shared, "There is a great care taken to meet students where they are and then to add value, as opposed to force fitting all undergraduates into somebody else's vision and somebody else's notion of what their trajectory ought to be when they are undergraduates." He added, "HBCUs set out to train a certain kind of population—historically subjugated and presently excluded. And thus, they do all they can to ensure the conditions under which those students can rise to become leaders and become upwardly mobile."

With such a deep emphasis on curriculum and teaching, faculty at HBCUs often teach very heavy course loads. They also do a great deal of mentoring and advising outside the classroom and often after hours. As Mary Schmidt Campbell shared,

> One of the realities of working at an HBCU is the faculty teaching load, which, over time, must be addressed. But what I've witnessed is faculty who not only are sustaining that teaching load but also taking on the very serious responsibilities of advising, mentoring, coaching, watching out for students, making sure that they are pointed in the right direction for this opportunity or that research project and doing it with a real sense of being there specifically to help that student to find the way that's going to help that student succeed.

As a result, HBCU faculty know their students well. From Bengochea's perspective, "HBCU faculty are often in the forefront of work around teaching and learning." Although being experts at teaching and learning is not always valued in many majority institutions—especially larger universities—HBCUs do the work that prepares their students for success in larger universities when they pursue graduate degrees (Conrad & Gasman, 2015).

The Ability to Make Mistakes

As we talked with those who attended or taught at HBCUs, they shared that one of the luxuries of attending an HBCU is the ability to make mistakes. In a society that rarely allows people to stumble anymore, the HBCU environment of learning and forgiveness is indeed at the forefront of nurturing students. As Kent Wallace explained,

> I feel that being at HBCUs, you have more of a likelihood of being in a nurturing atmosphere. HBCUs offer students the opportunity to make mistakes. For example, what I mean by that is at any university, you'll have to teach students about plagiarism and sometimes they just don't know, or sometimes they just get scared or they're behind, they don't want to fail. When they plagiarize, usually what we try to do, if it's a first offense, is use it as a teachable moment, and explain to them and hold them accountable, but still give them the opportunity to learn from it.

Wallace added, "If a person of color gets into a situation like [this] at a majority institution, they are just going to be kicked out. In an HBCU, although I do believe that they need to be held accountable, I feel like it's more of an environment where [we're] going to give [the students] an opportunity to learn from their mistakes. You don't have to be perfect."

Expounding on his discussion of HBCUs and how they allow students to make mistakes, Wallace shared, "We will bend over backwards, trying to just make sure that you do not fail." He believes this personally and professionally, as he has come close to failing himself. As Wallace told us, "I had to go through [a situation like this] when I was a student at Grambling. If I had gone to Penn State, I would have been gone. So, I do believe that being at HBCUs gives you an opportunity to make mistakes, but also provides an environment where they're going to push you to be successful."

Trina Fletcher, a graduate of the University of Arkansas at Pine Bluff and professor at Florida International University, agrees with Wallace and has firsthand experience with making mistakes. As she shared, "I had behavioral problems most of my K–12 experience because of things that were going on at home. I actually ran away from home and that's part of why I didn't have a 3.0 when I graduated from high school." Fletcher believes that many HBCUs are giving an opportunity to students who, based on how African Americans are treated in this country, might not be recognized as talented. In Fletcher's words,

> Black girls make up a majority of suspensions, a significantly higher amount than their White counterparts.[12] I truly believe that for students like myself, students with behavioral problems or those coming from areas that are very known to be racist and discriminatory against Black people, [HBCUs] are giving us a chance to stay out of the criminal justice system. They are giving us a chance to create a foundation that otherwise we would not have, especially as it relates to education. We all know that education is key to a better life.

She added, "Speaking for myself and some other students who I mentor who have similar backgrounds as I did, if it had not been for the University of Arkansas at Pine Bluff, I honest to God do not know where I would be at. I really do not know and don't want to know." Fletcher explained to us, with a great deal of emotion in her voice,

> I had family members in and out of the jail system. I have family members in jail now. The prison system and the criminal justice system have been very heavy on Black people in the state of Arkansas. So, in my honest opinion, I could be in jail. And some people are like, you're just exaggerating. I'm like, no I am not. I think that HBCUs are not only providing that path to the middle class, but also a way to keep some folks who don't have the best background and [don't] come from the best homes

an opportunity to see that they can have another life. There are better avenues and paths for them to take versus the ones that they have seen people in their families and their communities take.

Mistakes might also include having to drop out of college and then coming back years later to finish. HBCUs educate many students in this situation. Jeffrey Miller, a graduate of Morris Brown College and now a trustee of the institution, recalled,

> I started [college] in '88, but I did not graduate. I came back and finished in 2012. So, as a traditional student, I was on SGA [Student Government Association] as the chief of staff and I began to learn that leadership is great. The title's wonderful. But if you're not really serving your constituents, what good are you? So, when I came back, I came back as an adult and I decided to run for SGA president to help mentor the traditional students who had enrolled in Morris Brown, those who had [taken] a chance on a college that at that time was completely unaccredited.

Miller gave back to those who came after him and believed his younger classmates were part of his legacy.

Family-Like Environment

A common theme of the literature related to HBCUs is the idea of family as representative of the culture of HBCUs (Conrad & Gasman, 2015; Gasman & Nguyen, 2019; L. J. Walker, 2018). Students regularly describe HBCUs as operating like a family and having a support system that is deeply family oriented. Being family oriented means that those on campus look out for each other, hold each other accountable, and ensure the success of others. Most importantly, family at HBCUs means that faculty and staff believe in student success inherently. Roslyn Artis, the president of Benedict College in Columbia, South Carolina, told us what makes for the family-like culture of HBCUs:

> The secret sauce, I think that's really the question [you are asking]. What is the secret sauce that we're mixing up here? Reading, writing,

and arithmetic are not novel concepts. They're taught at every higher education institution across the world. I think [it's] the way that it's taught in an environment that is culturally sensitive, I think that for students who tend to be outsiders in the world they live in, to be able to come into an environment where race is not an issue, where race is not something you wear on your sleeves, where when you get up in the morning, you're getting dressed to be comfortable or to go to class—not necessarily to please a world that may judge your outward appearance. I don't have to worry about straightening my hair if I don't want to at an HBCU.

When you strip away all the pressures that many students face as they work toward their degrees, college is about learning, growth, and the development of human potential that happen on these campuses. According to Artis, "I provide physical safety for kids. No harm will come to you on this campus if I can help it."

Despite a protective nature regarding outsiders and racism, Artis believes students should be challenged:

Intellectually, I'm going to assault you, right? That noodle is a muscle and I want it to hurt, I want you to get outside your comfort zone and be pushed. I think one of the things that we can do here is push students, intellectually, politically, and [in] other ways. We can push them beyond their comfort zone, and it's done with love. I always say loving correction, right? So, when I say to a young lady, I need you to cover this up, right? We're going to class. They can hear me because they know it comes from a place of love. I want you to be better for you. This isn't about my judgment of you. This is about my support for you, and my desire that you do well. I think that it's that loving correction that we provide that is not seen as chastisement, but simply as loving correction that allows them, the young people that matriculate to our campuses, to grow and to mature and to develop into their very best selves.

Much like Artis, David Wilson, the president of Morgan State University in Baltimore, Maryland, also sees HBCUs as a family: "HBCUs are such powerful places and spaces. They are powerful and they are empowering and that should never be trivialized. We throw around certain words in describing HBCUs so much that people don't pay as much attention to those words as they should, but it's a family. It's a nurturing environment. It's a place where you never ever have to guess whether it cares about you and whether you belong on that campus."

Makola Abdullah, the president of Virginia State University, sees a kind of playfulness and realness at HBCUs that not only manifests among the students but also includes him, as the president. As he shared, "It's having an impact on the culture. It has been really personally fun. I mean, there is a playfulness and a not take yourself too serious attitude that has started to prevail at Virginia State." He offered an example:

> When I first got introduced to campus, the students had a big pep rally for me. They gave me some gifts and they taught me a line dance. What they didn't know is I love to line dance. I know all of them, every one of them. So, after they taught me a line dance, I said I'm going to teach you one, and they looked at me like I was crazy, and I taught them a line dance. And while I was teaching, I asked the vice president at the time, I said how come you're not dancing, and she looked at me and said we can do that. Right. Now, fast forward four or five years later, the administrative team did the Carlton[13] [dance] at the pep rally. This is just what we do. And so, to have the kind of playfulness that I have, or my sense of humor start to permeate activities. That's been fun as a leadership thing.

Howard University professor Robert Palmer is demonstrative of faculty perspectives at HBCUs and feels that he benefits from the student body as well:

> Faculty are very nurturing, very supportive, there's a family-like environment, which I really appreciate at Howard. The students are amazing to work with, just to walk into a classroom and have people respect me. I don't feel like I must prove myself, or I must talk about my past work experience to kind of lend credence to my credentials. I feel when I walk into a room that there's this respect and there's this appreciation, so that has been a really beautiful experience to have at Howard, in terms

of the students and knowing that the students are interested in Black or brown issues. A lot of those students are interested in research, and they know that I have published a lot and so they gravitate to me because they want to publish. So, working with the students at Howard, that's been an amazing experience.

Whether it was a student, faculty member, president, or alumnus that we spoke with, there is a deep appreciation for and acknowledgment of the unique culture of HBCUs. This culture plays a profound role in shaping the identities of African American students in addition to nurturing them as they grow.

Black Identity Development

Although there is ample research related to identity development in college, there is less related to Black students and even less related to Black students at HBCUs. Those researchers who explore the HBCU context are most focused on the realization of Blackness that takes place there (Greenfield et al., 2015). Other scholars focus on how students purposely choose to attend HBCUs with the hope that they will deepen their connection to Black people and explore their Blackness (Van Camp et al., 2009; Van Camp et al., 2010). Still others write about the link between identity and student success or intersections of identity development (Covington & Njoku, 2021; Mobley & Johnson, 2015; Palmer et al., 2010; Rucker & Gendrin, 2003).

Students' college choices can be influenced by a variety of factors, including academic, social, economic, and race-related factors (J. M. Johnson, 2019; Van Camp et al., 2010). Regarding race, racial identity has been found to shape college choice decisions (Van Camp et al., 2010). Racial identity refers to the quality or extent of identification a person has with his or her racial group (J. M. Johnson, 2019). Racial identity development is a critical part of psychosocial development and is associated with social adjustment, mental health, and academic performance (Hatter & Ottens, 1998; Miller-Cotto & Byrnes, 2016; D. R. Williams & Williams-Morris, 2000). For Black students attending college, a positive racial identity is critical for academic success and personal development (Bakari, 1997).

Researchers have found that individuals interested in opportunities to develop their racial identity while in college were more likely to consider attending HBCUs (Freeman, 1999; J. M. Johnson, 2019; Van Camp et al., 2010). Black students are also more likely to attend and persist at these universities primarily because the campus culture offers them a sense of community (K. C. Smith et al., 2019). Yet another reason Black students are drawn to HBCUs is that the missions of these institutions often focus on maintaining Black historical and cultural traditions and producing graduates who can address race relations and work for the betterment of Black communities (Brown & Davis, 2001). HBCUs offer something unique to their students, including the opportunity to develop their racial identity in a predominantly Black environment (Van Camp et al., 2010).

The Role of Blackness

As we talked with individuals across the HBCU spectrum, they expressed a sense of self-discovery and immersion in Black culture that changed them fundamentally. Historian and Florida A&M University graduate Ibram X. Kendi shared, "I felt I was able to gain a personal sense of who I was as an African American to be exposed to that diversity of people and even diversity within Black people. And my sense of myself was derived from a larger conception of Blackness as opposed to being derived in some sort of opposition to Whiteness."

Likewise, Jeffrey Miller, who grew up in nearby Columbus, Georgia, expressed,

> I got to Morris Brown, and I had a sister who went to Clark Atlanta. It was Clark College at that time. Then I found out more about Spelman. I took classes at Clark Atlanta and Spelman and then I finally found where Morehouse was. And I didn't know anything about the Atlanta University Center.[14] And I was just blown away by the Blackness of it. Columbus, Georgia, isn't a bad place or anything like that, but the school that I

went to at that time, it was majority White. Columbus is a majority White city. And just being around all these Black people in Atlanta, in my opinion it was really operating as the Black mecca when I got there, pretty much at the height of it. And I just never wanted to go back home ever.

Miller added,

We all walked on the campus, and we were not concerned about some of the things, the racism, we were concerned about excellence, that we were being successful, if that makes sense. So, I think for myself, and other students, particularly since we have seen an increase in the pandemic, the murders and police brutality on Black women and Black men, that people want to go to HBCUs because they just feel like the campus climate is something different. It fosters something that's successful, rather than me having to fight for everything, just to be seen in the classroom.

For Lynn Wooten, a North Carolina A&T State University graduate, attending an HBCU transformed her identity in myriad ways, and she sees these same changes happening in many students who attend HBCUs. In her words, "Three things happen at HBCUs—from adolescence to adulthood. You develop your leadership identity. You develop your academic identity that puts you on your professional calling and you become more salient about your racial identity." Wooten believes the development of these three identities has boosted her confidence throughout her life.

For many we interviewed, attending an HBCU made an impression on their identity as a Black person. Being immersed in a college culture where Blackness was centered in all aspects of their personal lives was instrumental to how they developed as adults. Those we interviewed also spoke of how the development of their Black identity while attending an HBCU was transformational and has had a lasting impact.

Role Models That Look Like You

In addition to experiencing a full spectrum of Blackness within the HBCU context, another benefit that students and alumni regularly share is that of being surrounded by role models of the same race (Conrad & Gasman, 2015; Gasman & Nguyen, 2019). For Black women, having role models of the same race and the same gender can be even more empowering and inspiring. In recent years, researchers have found evidence that same-race role models are particularly important in the sciences in terms of success (Madyun et al., 2013; Main et al., 2020).

Grambling State University graduate Kent Wallace has experienced the benefits of same-race role models both in his own life and in the lives of his students in the sciences at Fisk University, where he teaches. According to Wallace, "One of the strongest factors of unpacking a scientific identity is role models. There is a much greater likelihood that a student is going to see a faculty member and be engaged by a faculty member that represents their ethnic and cultural background, which has a positive impact on their sense of cultural and scientific identity. So, there's something built into the model of an HBCU that other schools cannot replicate [because their faculties do not have enough African Americans on them]." Unfortunately, PWI faculties are not representative of the diversity among their student bodies, especially in the sciences. Overall, the faculty in colleges and universities across the nation is 75% White (NCES, 2018). People of color account for a mere 10% of faculty in science and engineering (Gasman & Nguyen, 2019; P. Stewart, 2020).

Like Wallace, Thomas Hudson, a Jackson State University alumnus, benefited greatly from the role models he encountered while an undergraduate at the institution. As he shared,

HBCUs [are] one of the first places and only places where I was able to see African American leadership at all levels of the administration. I went to a PWI for law school, and you had one or two African Americans who had roles, significant roles, who were really geared towards the minority students, but the chief financial officer (CFO) was not African American. The person who was over facilities was not African American. The president or the chancellor was not African American. Most of your professors were not African American, so when you're looking at what you can strive to and what I can be, did I really see examples of what I could do in that university setting?

He added, "At an HBCU, you can imagine yourself as president. You can imagine yourself as the CFO of a major corporation, director of human resources, [or a] vice president for fundraising. HBCUs are one of the few places where you can see prominent African American leadership at all levels and it's not a strange thing. It's within the fabric of [the institution]."

According to Robert Palmer, a Morgan State University graduate,

> When you think about how this sense of self-efficacy—having students, particularly Black men, . . . who've gone through a system in K–12 where they didn't have . . . Black role models in terms of teachers and role models in other forms—and they get to this college campus and they meet the Black faculty, the Black president, and the executive leadership. The way in which these individuals at HBCUs are able to pour into those students and mentor those students [is incredible]. That mentorship often extends beyond the classroom. It extends beyond academics.

Palmer also reminded us of the ethic of care with which HBCU faculty often operate: "I may have talked about this ethic of care, in terms of having a Black faculty or role models. Black faculty and administrators really work hard to really pour into students and really develop them holistically and meet students where they are. HBCUs provide Black students an environment where they can kind of grow and bring their authentic self to campus."

Those we interviewed recognized the importance of attending an institution where they were able to learn and interact with individuals who looked like them. Additionally, having Black women and men who were professors and who held prominent leadership roles was profound and demonstrated to students that they too could reach similar levels of success. HBCUs provide access to same-race role models that empower and inspire in ways that do not exist at most other institutions.

"It's the Confidence"

An increased sense of identity within an environment filled with role models can lead to a sense of confidence that can have a profound impact on an individual. HBCUs bolster self-confidence. Some of the individuals we talked with claimed to be able to spot an HBCU graduate with immediacy. Antoine Alston, a professor at North Carolina A&T State University, told us, "When I went to Iowa State as a graduate student, I could always tell an HBCU graduate from a Black student who had gone through undergrad at a PWI. It is not because we were smarter, but we just had a certain oomph about us, a certain swag, if that makes sense." He added,

> I could tell because you had that pride that an HBCU instills in you, letting you know this is who I am. I'm proud to be African American, my heritage, the traditions, the history of our people, the struggles, and the achievements of our people. Because more than any other group in society, society is built on the backs of literally, of African Americans, and so HBCUs train you about your heritage, that you have an intellect and that you need to express your intellect, that you need to go back and lead your community. So, we train leaders, we train scientists, we provide that confidence for African American students, but also non-African American students, too.

Stanley Nelson, the Emmy-winning director of the HBCU documentary *Tell Them We Are Rising*, agrees. When we asked him about the power of HBCUs, he responded, "It's the confidence. It's the confidence. White institutions beat you down, you know? They beat [you], they just do, and especially when, when you're like 18 to 21 you know, when you're at a critical part of life, and you're not sure of who you are, they beat you down." He added,

> Many African American students now are choosing to go to HBCUs because, you know, the real smart ones are saying, well, maybe for four years of my life, I don't want to have to deal with race up front on a daily basis, because when you get out, you're going to have to deal with race.

You know, if you have any amount of success in this country, you're going to have to deal with, with race on, daily. So, in those final formative years, HBCUs, you know, offer people a chance to get away from that, at least for a moment.

Belle Wheelan, the president of the Southern Association of Colleges and Schools Commission, believes that one reason HBCUs disproportionately prepare students to be doctors, professors, teachers, and lawyers is that they engender a culture that develops a strong sense of confidence:

> I think one of the things that [HBCUs] contribute, obviously, is the Black intelligentsia to the rest of the universe. They educate the largest number of doctors, lawyers, teachers, and everything else. Interestingly, I think they also contribute a sense of "I can" among the students who come there. There's that support there, that you may not have felt that you were going to have much worth before you got here but I promise you, by the time you leave, you will. That sense of I care and I'm going to help you get through this, because life can be tough and if you don't have someone on whom to fall back, then you'll have great difficulty achieving your goals and that's important.

She added, "I think that's one of the reasons that more Latino and White students are beginning to come to HBCUs, because they understand that sense of support, that sense of caring, that sense of I can do this and they're going to help me."[15]

Wheelan did not attend an HBCU, but her thoughts ring true to the experience that Lynn Wooten, president of Simmons College, had when she was a student at North Carolina A&T State University. According to Wooten, HBCUs are powerful because you are "living in a learning lab every day and learning about social justice, learning about equity, and learning about my history." Affirming that this environment had a significant impact on her and her friends, Wooten added, "We talked about the confidence boost, that you can be a conqueror and that you can do anything. And then the pathway, I believe in the potential and the pathway that HBCUs must really close the wage gap and make economic situations better. The long-term life outcomes. All those things that the Gallup data talks about that HBCUs score higher on well-being are really magical."[16]

HBCUs are vocal about the contributions and the impact that their students can make. According to Louis W. Sullivan, former president of the Morehouse School of Medicine and Morehouse College graduate, HBCUs help students make a powerful contribution by "being affirming institutions, by taking young people and really telling them that there is a positive contribution that they can make, they should make, and that the world is waiting for their contribution to be made." Filmmaker Stanley Nelson agrees that HBCUs instill confidence in their students. He shared,

> Students kind of really must go for themselves and push themselves at HBCUs, you know? And so, the ones who could come out on top and succeed are just amazing. We would play a game, you know, after we made the film, and you know, that we could tell by talking to someone, like they were an intern and they came for an internship, if they went to an HBCU or not. We can tell, we can tell by how they walked in the door.

Leah Hollis, a professor at Morgan State University, understands the way that HBCUs push students to be their best. As she shared, "Howard [University] produced Chadwick Boseman. He came up with people who just pushed him along the way and as I understand, even paid for a scholarship for him to go to London, and hence the *Black Panther*[17] is born." She added, "I mean, those kinds of things that happen at HBCUs not only change the lives of the students but also change the communities in which they operate and serve."

As evidenced by many we talked with, HBCUs instill a level of confidence that radiates among their graduates. This confidence helps graduates reach various levels of success, which also leads them to transform others and their communities. More importantly, this confidence serves as an example for prospective students as to how students are nurtured, valued, and prepared to contribute in meaningful ways to society.

A Sense of Belonging

One of the ways that HBCUs shape identity and instill confidence is by engendering a sense of belonging in their students. According to scholars, a sense of belonging enables students to excel academically and emotionally (Gopalan & Brady, 2020; Strayhorn, 2018, 2019). Feeling that you belong at a college or university means that you are treated well and respected in the environment. According to Rick Gallot, the president and an alumnus of Grambling State University, "There are a few things that I often say to prospective students as I'm recruiting, and the first one is at Grambling, and at other HBCUs, you'll be celebrated, not tolerated, and that certainly resonates loudly in this post–Donald Trump, George Floyd–type moment that we're still in." He added, "You know, I think that is something, that we provide a safe space for students to be able to find themselves and to develop their whole self, without fear of being marginalized, of being made to feel unwelcome." As Gallot talked with us, he recalled a story about a Grambling alumnus that he often shares with students:

> One of our alums, Charles Blow, [is] a *New York Times* columnist and he's written a couple of books.[18] His son attended Yale and was going to the library one Saturday evening and the police saw a young Black male with a backpack going into the library, and he was stopped and had guns pulled on him, because he was a young Black man going into the library. And so that is just one example of how African American students are not always accepted or supported at PWIs. I often say you'll never be profiled and have guns pulled on you by university police at Grambling for going to the library.

Historian and Stillman College graduate James Anderson felt that sense of belonging that Gallot alludes to. As he recalled,

> Because I have the contrast of having gone to an HBCU—Stillman—and then coming to [the University of] Illinois, a large, Predominantly White Institution, there are times when I'm in circles and I'm talking to Illinois graduates and I realized that we were here at the same time, in

the same college, and the campus was large, but the college has always been relatively small, and I have no memory whatsoever of them, of being here, because when I was coming in, coming through, and it hasn't changed profoundly since then, it's still there, we were kind of an enclave of African American students trying to make it through what we viewed as a hostile environment and so we clung together. And so that group you knew, but you didn't know the larger group, where at Stillman, you were always part of that larger group, you knew them, you became lifelong friends or acquaintances, or if there's a conversation, you go, yes, yes. I do remember this. I remember them. And so, one of the experiences that you get from an HBCU, I think, and I wish for everybody, you ought to have memories when you come through college. You ought to have this sense of belonging. I think that's important. I mean, I know people are looking at that now, but when I walked into Stillman as a freshman, it never occurred to me that I didn't belong.

Beaming with pride, Anderson told us, "Stillman was my college, my sophomore class, the president of the student government was my president. The editor of the newspaper was my editor, so that strong sense of belonging." When Anderson went to the University of Illinois, he had the opposite experience: "You had the sense, well, it's their college. I'm here. Let me get my degree and get out, but that was not that sense, over time that changed. When I came back to the faculty and worked with students, that sense of belonging started to change. But you ought to be able to go to a college and you ought to feel that you belong. I think that's one of the things that you get in HBCUs." During our conversation, Anderson shared a quote from Fisk University graduate W. E. B. Du Bois: "If you remember in Du Bois's autobiography, he said, 'I was in Harvard, but not of Harvard,' and that is the crunch.[19] That's the crucible right there. When you go to an HBCU, you're not just in there, you are of FAMU, you're of Stillman, you're of Morehouse, you're of Spelman, and that is an aspect of the HBCU that should be translated to all higher education. Wherever you go, you should be of that institution, not just in the institution."

Walter Kimbrough, the president of Dillard University in New Orleans, notes that to succeed in college and beyond, students need to know that they matter. When we talked with him, he shared a story of one of his students who felt at home on the campus. She talked of mattering and knowing that she mattered. In the words of Kimbrough, "A student said something, it was so powerful. Coming here to Dillard, she said, this is a place where I came, where I mattered, and so this whole idea of mattering, to be highlighted and uplifted, and that kind of reinforcement for folks." He added,

> She's a senior now, who is a captain of our mock trial team. She could have gone anywhere in the country. She's sharp, but sort of quiet and mild mannered, and we've just watched her really grow into this really strong and powerful young woman. That happened because she was able to be in this environment. People talk about nurturing a lot, but in this case, you're seeing it. I think it's a place where a student who comes in with a lot of raw talent and skill can be identified and amplified, I think in a quick amount of time.

Aaron Walton, the president of Cheyney University of Pennsylvania, agrees with Kimbrough and offered his own perspective:

> I'm going to say the impact of HBCUs is transformational. You get a raw product that comes to the university that is an open vessel. You have an opportunity to shape that vessel into something extremely meaningful and purposeful. And I think that the experiences that the students can gain at an HBCU, creating a sense of belonging, a sense of self-worth, encouragement, and motivation, which is not necessarily the case in other settings. There's a comfort level that exists [at HBCUs] that encourages the students to do their best, and to develop associations with other students that they would not have that opportunity to have, depending on prior exposure.

HBCUs engender a sense of belonging that makes a difference in the lives of students and is critical to their academic success. The power of this institutional practice contributed to students feeling as though they mattered and helped motivate them to reach levels of success that they might not have otherwise reached. In many ways, the sense of belonging that exists on an HBCU campus is a major contributing factor to what many describe as the family-like environment present at these institutions.

Through our interviews with HBCU graduates, leaders, and those who work closely with HBCUs, we learned about the uniqueness of the culture and the long-term impact it has on the lives of alumni. Cultural elements such as the family-like environment, caring and inspiring faculty, diversity of Blackness, sporting events, and general life on the yard are just some of the areas that contribute to these institutions being the college choice for thousands of students each year.

Our interviews also enabled us to highlight some of the subtle differences among HBCUs. In addition to cultural nuances, there are also differences in the student bodies and the various identities of individuals as well as the type of curriculum offered. We also gleaned from those we interviewed how HBCUs nurture and foster identity development, especially Black identity development. Simply, HBCU campuses provide students with opportunities to learn about their Blackness in ways that are not often afforded to students at PWIs. For many graduates, opportunities to learn about and explore their role as Black people in society exist at an HBCU. The power of HBCUs also manifests itself in the showcasing of same-race role models. Finally, our interviews revealed the confidence and sense of belonging that are cultivated on an HBCU campus. It is clear that the power of the culture of HBCUs has an impact on students long after they graduate.

3

Onward and Upward

I think that HBCUs are not only providing that path to the middle class, but also a way to keep some folks who don't have the best background and come from the best homes an opportunity to see that they can have another life.

—Trina Fletcher, Graduate, University of Arkansas at Pine Bluff

The impact we have on the lives of students is taking those first-generation students, and really turning them into something great. One of the things we say at JSU is become who you were meant to be, and that's what we really do as HBCUs.

—Thomas Hudson, President, Jackson State University

Historically Black Colleges and Universities have a long and noteworthy history of providing access to a college education and advancing opportunities for millions of Black students. Ample evidence suggests that HBCUs serve as important promoters of Black socioeconomic mobility, especially for those who are among the most disadvantaged members of society. In addition, HBCUs, which operate with a significantly lower level of institutional resources than their Predominantly White Institution counterparts, serve these vulnerable students as they move into the middle class and beyond (Elu et al., 2019; Hardy et al., 2019; Nellum & Valle, 2015; Nelson & Frye, 2016; Palmer & Gasman, 2008; Saunders et al., 2016; K. L. Williams et al., 2018).

The Middle Class and the Value of a Degree

According to the Pew Research Center, the middle class in the United States is defined as households that earn somewhere between two-thirds and double the median household income ($61,372). Thus, the middle class is made up of households making between $42,000 and $126,000 (Casselman, 2015; Frankenfield, 2021; Fry & Kochhar, 2018; Kochhar et al., 2015; US Census Bureau, 2017). At present, the middle class constitutes only a slight majority of the US population, with 52% of households falling into this socioeconomic category (Frankenfield, 2021). As a result of increases in wealth among the upper echelons of the middle class and the expansion of the lowest-income population, the middle class is shrinking. According to Pew Research (Kochhar et al., 2015), 19% of households are upper-income and 29% are lower-income. Of note, only those households in the upper-income class have been able to fully recover from the two previous economic recessions. Pew Research (2018) also reported that the median income for an upper-income household of three people was $187,872, a middle-income household of the same size was $78,442, and a lower-income household was $25,624 (Fry & Kochhar, 2018).

The *American Middle Class Is Losing Ground*, a 2015 report by Pew Research, demonstrates that there is a significant racial wealth gap in the United States. For example, in 2015, a mere 12% of Black households and 10% of Latinx households were in the upper-income quintile, whereas 28% of Asian households and 21% of White households were. On a positive note, African American families saw some advancement in wealth: between 1971 and 2015, they were the only racial group that experienced a decline in the share of low-income households (48% to

43%). Likewise, the share of African American upper-income households rose from 5% to 12% during the same time (Frankenfield, 2021). Despite this progress, according to Aladangady and Forde (2021) of the US Federal Reserve, "the average Black and Hispanic or Latino households earn about half as much as the average White household and only has about 15 to 20 percent as much net wealth." If Black households were to hold their fair share of the wealth in the United States in proportion to the share of the population that they occupy, they would hold $12.68 trillion. Currently, they hold only $2.54 trillion, exemplifying a hefty wealth gap of $10.14 trillion (Williamson, 2021). To understand how the wealth gap plays out even more clearly, consider this: "The 400 richest American billionaires have more total wealth than all 10 million Black American households combined. Black households have about 3% of all household wealth, while the 400 wealthiest billionaires have 3.5% of all household wealth in the United States" (Williamson, 2021).

Access to a college degree is clearly important as postsecondary training remains the most viable route up the economic ladder in American society, and a precise path to upward mobility and wealth accumulation (Committee on Education & Labor, 2019; Espinosa et al., 2018). Research indicates that bachelor's degree holders earn about $32,000 more than those whose highest degree is a high school diploma. Bachelor's degree recipients are also 47% more likely to have health insurance through their employer. Further, over the course of a lifetime, a bachelor's degree holder earns $964,000 more than an individual with only a high school education. A bachelor's degree can significantly improve an individual's quality of life (Association of Public & Land-Grant Universities, 2020; Carnevale et al., 2016; Pew Research Center, 2014; Trostel, 2015). Only 14% of African Americans have earned a bachelor's degree compared with 23.7% of Whites and 11% of the Latinx population (A. H. Nichols & Schak, 2014; Schak & Nichols, 2014). HBCUs are instrumental in ensuring that more African Americans earn bachelor's degrees and as a result achieve further social mobility.

Socioeconomic Mobility by the Numbers

Historically Black Colleges and Universities have received much positive attention in the past couple of years owing to calls for racial justice across the country. But if we step back a few years, federal and state officials were calling into question the value of HBCUs. Some states cut funding, and state and federal lawmakers affiliated with the Trump administration—even Donald Trump himself—questioned the constitutionality of HBCUs (Boland & Gasman, 2014; Stratford, 2017). With this questioning in mind, several organizations—including the American Council on Education (2018), the Rutgers Center for Minority Serving Institutions (2019), and the United Negro College Fund (2021)—examined the role that HBCUs play as a vehicle of social mobility among African Americans. Social mobility is the defined movement between social classes. Each of these investigations relied on data from Opportunity Insights (formerly the Equality of Opportunity Project) (Espinosa et al., 2018; Hammond et al., 2021; Nathenson et al., 2019).[1] Opportunity Insights is the brainchild of professors Raj Chetty, John Friedman, and Nathaniel Hendren of Harvard University. The Chetty-led team is "united in their passion to understand how to improve economic opportunities for all Americans" and are open to sharing their data, and subsequent database, with researchers interested in using it for their own projects (Opportunity Insights, n.d.). The data are robust and offer a fresh opportunity to study income mobility rates by parental income from masked income tax returns and the US Department of Education. The data set is particularly interesting in that it pulls from a wide range of colleges and universities and allows for comparisons that have been difficult to make in the past.

Prior to this social mobility–focused work, only a few quantitative studies had attempted to understand the impact of HBCUs on Black students. Kim and Conrad (2006) found that, despite HBCUs having fewer financial resources, the graduation rates for African Americans at these institutions were comparable to those at PWIs. While this research demonstrates that HBCUs are performing well with limited financial support, graduation rates are only one factor in mobility, and one that is constrained as it does not pertain to long-term labor market outcomes. Fryer and Greenstone (2010) and Price et al. (2011) also compared the labor market earnings of HBCU graduates with those of non-HBCU graduates; however, they found conflicting results, and their data were old, making it difficult to draw a conclusion about students in the past few decades.

To understand the impact of HBCUs on socioeconomic mobility, especially in comparison with PWIs, it is important to consider PWIs within commuting distance of HBCUs (Nathenson et al., 2019). According to Hillman (2016), college choice is often a localized decision, with most students choosing to attend college close to their homes. It is also essential, when examining socioeconomic mobility, to account for students' origins—for instance, "the mobility trajectories of students with low-income parents" (Blau & Duncan, 1967; Nathenson et al., 2019, p. 2). The best way to understand socioeconomic mobility is to compare the impact of similar and nearby colleges and universities. For example, in Atlanta, the higher education landscape includes HBCUs such as Spelman College and Clark Atlanta University, and PWIs like Georgia State University and Clayton State University (Nathenson et al., 2019). A much fairer comparison can be achieved by using this type of approach.[2]

HBCUs are considered institutions that address the systemic racism that is at the foundation of higher education in the nation (Gasman, 2007a, 2011; Nathenson et al., 2019; B. D. Tatum, 1997; Williamson-Lott, 2008). Price et al. (2011) suggested that HBCUs have a positive impact on students' "identity, self-image, and self-esteem," which, they claim, yields a wage increase in the labor market (p. 106). Recent research related to socioeconomic mobility has found that more than 50% of students at HBCUs experience some measure of upward mobility. Moreover, upward mobility is about 50% higher at HBCUs than at PWIs, because PWIs enroll far fewer lower-income students. Close to the same number of students at both types of institutions move into the middle class, and at least 70% end up there (Espinosa et al., 2018; Hammond et al., 2021; Nathenson et al., 2019). If we take a closer look at Dillard University in New Orleans, for example, the median family income for a student is $30,800. As a result, a greater share of the student body has the possibility of moving up the economic ladder once they graduate than at an institution like Louisiana State University, which is 160 miles from Dillard and has a median parental income of $108,800 (Donastorg, 2021). Of course, students only have a true opportunity to move into the middle class or beyond when they are nurtured and supported by faculty and staff at their colleges or universities. Their mere presence on campus does not contribute to their success, and this is where HBCUs excel, as demonstrated by the voices in this book.

Although Morehouse College, Spelman College, and Howard University, the most highly ranked and well-regarded HBCUs, propel a proportion of low-income students into high-income careers that is similar to that of PWIs, these schools enroll lower percentages of low-income students than the majority of the HBCUs. In contrast, Xavier University and Tuskegee University enroll more low-income students than Morehouse, Spelman, and Howard, while at the same time achieving a higher mobility rate than almost any other HBCU (Espinosa et al., 2018; Nathenson et al., 2019). According to Hammond et al. (2021), authors of *HBCUs Transforming Generations*, "On average and across institutional type, when it comes to mobility rates HBCUs outperform all other categories [of colleges and universities] and boast mobility rates more than double the national average" (p. 8). To emphasize the impact that HBCUs have on low-income populations, they note "the evidence suggests that HBCUs support nearly five times more students than Ivy Plus[3] ranked institutions in facilitating students' movement from the bottom 40% in household income to the top 60%" (p. 8). For example, the average mobility rate at HBCUs is 34.4%, whereas at Ivy Plus institutions it is 7.4% because these institutions do not have a commitment to enroll low-income students in significant numbers (Hammond et al., 2021).

Students at Xavier University are the most likely to advance in terms of socioeconomic status of any HBCU, at nearly 80%, while schools such as Florida A&M University achieve levels on par with the higher end of PWIs. HBCUs that can boast about creating middle-class opportunities for more than 70% of their students include Prairie View A&M University, Elizabeth City State University, and Tennessee State University (Espinosa et al., 2018; Hammond et al., 2021; Nathenson et al., 2019). Overall, two-thirds of low-income students at HBCUs move into at least a middle-class income quintile, a proportion similar to PWIs (70%). While the share increases with parental income, the gap is never more than 5 percentage points between PWIs and HBCUs (Espinosa et al., 2018; Hammond et al., 2021; Nathenson et al., 2019).

The most highly ranked HBCUs—for example, Howard University, Spelman College, and Morehouse College—move more than one-third of their low-income students into the top fifth of income earners in the nation. Other HBCUs with far larger percentages of low-income students also boast large gains in terms of their students' upward mobility. For example, nearly 65% of the students at Xavier University are eligible to receive a Pell Grant (compared with 49% at Morehouse), and almost one-third of these students move into the top fifth of income earners. Bennett College, Tuskegee University, Florida A&M University, Clark Atlanta University, and Dillard University also do a particularly good job fostering upward mobility for their large populations of low-income students (Espinosa et al., 2018; Hammond et al., 2021; Nathenson et al., 2019).

Regarding those students at Xavier University who come from affluent backgrounds, at least 70% replicate this status more than a decade later. Approximately two-thirds do the same at the most highly ranked HBCUs, such as Spelman College, Hampton University, Howard University, and Morehouse College. A few other HBCUs, such as Florida A&M University, Clark Atlanta University, Southern University and A&M College, Virginia State University, North Carolina A&T State University, Lincoln University of Pennsylvania, and Dillard University, also achieve intergenerational retention of upper-middle-income status (Espinosa et al., 2018; Hammond et al., 2021; Nathenson et al., 2019).

HBCUs are doing the important work of fostering the upward mobility of their students, especially considering the large share of their students who come from lower-income backgrounds. According to UNCF president Michael Lomax (2021) and research conducted by his organization, "Within a decade of obtaining a degree from an HBCU, the average graduate earns $71,000 annually." Moreover, over the course of an HBCU graduate's lifetime, they will earn an additional $927,000 (56%) more than they would without an HBCU degree (Bridges, 2018). The one area, however, where HBCUs lag is in their ability to move students into the top quintile of earners as an adult. As mentioned, HBCUs are much better at enrolling low-income students, and the leap from the bottom to the top of the socioeconomic ladder is steep (Reeves & Joo, 2017). Still, Hammon et al. (2021) ask us to remember that "even a 10% shift in income can translate into life-altering access to health insurance, educational options, and expendable income that may ultimately drive outcomes that are both useful and necessary" (p. 4).

Personal Stories of Socioeconomic Mobility

Educational access and opportunity enable individuals to achieve socioeconomic mobility (Greenstone et al., 2013; Organisation for Economic Co-Operation and Development, 2018; Smeeding, 2016). Many of those we interviewed for this book shared the ways that HBCUs have served as a pathway to socioeconomic mobility for them. We learned that HBCUs were often the only institutions that provided access and opportunity for Black students to pursue a college degree.

Alton Thompson, executive director for the Association of 1890 Research Directors and a graduate of North Carolina A&T State University, shared his experience of being able to pursue a college degree at A&T and the impact this opportunity had on his future success:

If you think about many HBCUs, particularly 1890s, their mantra is opportunity and access. For example, I attended school in a rural area and my standardized [test] scores were low. I mean, [they] were [so] low [that] I could not have been admitted to North Carolina State University or to other universities around the country. So, even though my standardized [test] scores were low, HBCUs will give a gift [to] students who could not get admitted into the PWIs—an opportunity for success. I think opportunity and access is one of the significant contributions HBCUs make to society overall. Just think, I was an African American student, 18, not able to get accepted to the University of North Carolina or North Carolina State University. So, if I could not get accepted into an HBCU, what would be my options? A high school degree, maybe community college. But think about the value added to society by me going to an HBCU, which gave me the opportunity to go on to The Ohio State University. So, my being at Ohio State was a direct result of me getting accepted into an HBCU.

Thompson's account highlights how HBCUs are especially important for those with low standardized test scores; these institutions offer students the opportunity to succeed. Importantly, research has shown that standardized test scores are not strong predictors of college success or completion (Allenson & Clark, 2020; J. L. Hoffman & Lowitzki, 2005). In Thompson's case, North Carolina A&T provided access to a postsecondary education that was instrumental to future educational attainment and success.

Louis W. Sullivan, president emeritus of Morehouse School of Medicine, believes that HBCUs are spaces that allow for the cultivation of students' talent, which in turn leads to more socioeconomic mobility. He told us, "I think the most significant contribution that HBCUs make is taking young people from poor backgrounds, many who have less than optimal educational experiences in the K through 12 years and really recognizing the talent that these young people have, helping to develop it, also giving them aspirations and hope for the future and encouraging them to develop those talents and contribute to society and their own livelihood." Sullivan highlighted his experience as a student at Morehouse College and the positive influence that former Morehouse College president Benjamin Mays had on students. Sullivan told us, "One of Dr. Mays's sayings to us as students was this. 'Each one of you was born with a purpose to achieve in life. Your goal is to find out what that is, then work like hell to be sure that you make that contribution because if you do not, then that contribution will not be made to our society.'" He continued,

> His saying was really we have something positive to contribute to our lives. So, when you take someone who's grown up in an environment that has been an oppressive environment that has been saying to them that they are not worthy, they are not intelligent, that they are not good but really turns that around and says no, you are intelligent. You do have some things now to contribute. It will make a difference not only for you personally but for society and you should work to do that because your life will have greater significance and greater importance in doing that.

Sullivan believes HBCUs contribute to the social mobility of African Americans, which in turn benefits society overall.

Sharing a personal narrative as well, Thomas Hudson, the president and a graduate of Jackson State University, told us how Jackson State helped his family and later contributed to his realizing greater social mobility. "Jackson State evolved from being the place that helped lift my family out of poverty, to a place that was aspirational, in terms of that's where I'm going to go to as a student. This is where I went, [it] set me on a trajectory to do some cool things in my career. Hey, I'm here. I went to work, starting in a lower position and I've worked my way up to president." Hudson continued, "Jackson State has just been there at all stages of my life, from beginning, aspirational, actual in terms of being a student and then coming back as an employee, to now actually running the institution. That is, I think, a quintessential HBCU story. Just the holistic experience you get from [an HBCU]." Personal stories from HBCU alumni bring to life the numbers associated with the socioeconomic mobility that HBCUs fuel.

Shaping the Socioeconomic Mobility of Students

Many of those we spoke to emphasized the importance of HBCUs in providing educational access and opportunity to students who have been historically disenfranchised. For example, Armando Bengochea, senior program officer at the Mellon Foundation, expressed sentiments similar to those of Alton Thompson (mentioned previously). He stated, "I think by definition, of course, HBCUs set out to train a certain kind of population, a historically subjugated and presently excluded population of students. And thus, they do all they can to ensure the conditions under which those students can rise to become leaders and become upwardly mobile." Filmmaker Stanley Nelson agreed as he reflected on the impact of HBCUs: "The great contribution that HBCUs gave and still give to society is that they say to people, who might not be able to get a college education, that there is a place for you, and that's what they've been doing from the beginning, from Jim Crow and segregation, when Black people just couldn't go to colleges, and I think that's what they're doing [to] a certain extent today." Myriad scholars have also noted the role HBCUs have in providing access to the Black middle class for Black students (Allen et al., 2007; Bracey, 2017; Palmer et al., 2011).

Xavier University president Reynold Verret pointed to the institution's success in producing graduates who achieved increased socioeconomic mobility:

> One of the interesting metrics that we have become aware of, because others have been tracking it, is socioeconomic mobility. To be able to say that students who come from the lowest quintile of the socioeconomic ladder in this country migrate to the upper three-fifths which is not saying that they are in the upper 5%, but the upper three-fifths, that's quite a stride. Xavier is ranked very often in the top 10 for social mobility, transitioning students from the lowest quintiles to the upper three fifths. And that's something that other HBCUs do also. So that social mobility was [and is] producing wealth and equity at a time when there were governmental decisions that precluded access to wealth for the descendants of slaves. HBCUs have been doing that quite well.

Agreeing with Verret, Walter Kimbrough, president of Dillard University, acknowledged the impact HBCUs have on the socioeconomic mobility of students who are eligible for Pell Grants, which is an indicator of low-income status. In his words, "Do people really understand that, to see that you have a sector where two-thirds of the students are eligible for Pell Grants, and any kind of way that you cut that data, the institutions that are doing the best in terms of social mobility are HBCUs?"

Because HBCUs perform well in terms of moving African Americans up the socioeconomic ladder, they have been instrumental in building the Black middle class. With this idea in mind, Kevin James, president of Morris Brown College, discussed with us the role of HBCUs in creating the Black middle class: "Overall, HBCUs have done more with less. HBCUs from a data perspective are primarily responsible for a lot of the Black middle class. The leadership in this country, both on a government level, state level, local level, educational level, every field of endeavor has been impacted by HBCUs and just what we offer from a perspective of access, equity, relationships, resources, and community." For Trina Fletcher, a University of Arkansas at Pine Bluff graduate, what stands out is how HBCUs empower students who grew up in poverty. As she emphasized, "Oprah Winfrey and Spike Lee, these folks who came from the gutter, the depths of poor communities and no connection to money, who are now wealthy, who are doing very well and sharing their knowledge and expertise with other Black people. There are so many examples of Black people who came up with nothing who are now a part of the middle class because of that motivation and strength and this idea of I am somebody. I am great." For Fletcher, HBCUs are carrying on the work and legacy of her ancestors by building the Black middle class.

The Power of STEM

Changes in an individual's socioeconomic mobility are mostly related to increased levels of education and jobs with higher earnings potential. For example, STEM jobs tend to pay higher salaries than non-STEM jobs (Deming & Noray, 2020; Noonan, 2017; Pew Research Center, 2018). According to the US Department of Education, STEM graduates earn an average starting salary of $65,000—$15,500 more than non-STEM majors. This advantage sets them up for higher earnings across their lifetime (Jacobs, 2014). Among the producers of Black STEM graduates, HBCUs have a notable presence and have awarded 25% of all STEM baccalaureate degrees earned by Black students (Gasman & Nguyen, 2016; Lomax, 2021). Additionally, given their ability to effectively produce Black STEM graduates, HBCUs represent meaningful sites of preparation for medical school or other professional health degree programs (Gasman & Nguyen, 2016; Nguyen et al., 2020; Perna et al., 2009; Perna et al., 2010; Washington Lockett et al., 2018).

Leah Hollis, a professor at Morgan State University, highlighted the role of HBCUs in producing Black women STEM graduates. She stated, "As I understand Morgan State is number two in the country for training Black women engineers, second only to North Carolina A&T State University. That is phenomenal because women are so often locked out of STEM." Hollis continued, "To have universities cultivate that kind of professional crop of graduates is just amazing. I mean, those kinds of things that happen at HBCUs not only change the lives of the students but also change the communities in which they operate and serve. I think that is huge." She also told us that she

think[s] that HBCUs have a very rich history that deserves more attention. Regardless of how they were established, during postslavery or the Reconstruction period, no matter how we got here, these institutions have been set up as a model. You can get a medical degree. You can go to Fisk. You can go to Howard, you can go to these places and get an education, even if the dominant culture was locking you out during Jim Crow. There was something to aspire to, that was life changing, even if you are coming from a Black community.

Adding to the discussion of HBCUs and STEM, and also sharing an example related to how HBCUs serve the educational needs of marginalized populations, Damon Williams, a Xavier University graduate, stated, "There was a time where we could not go to school, right, as people of color, we were marginalized [and] HBCUs provided access for us to get education, to [help] eliminate the wealth gap, but they also [continue to create access today for students who might not be able to afford [earning] a [degree] at Penn, Rutgers, or Northwestern." Williams shared with us how HBCUs contribute to Black students being able to pursue STEM degrees as well as graduate and medical professional degrees in STEM (Rodríguez et al., 2017; Sibulkin & Butler, 2011; Toldson, 2019; Upton & Tanenbaum, 2014). He noted, "You all know the data of how many [students earn] MDs, PhDs, master's, or postbaccalaureate [degrees]. The data speaks for itself." As noted above, STEM degree holders from HBCUs have a significant advantage in terms of salary, which leads to greater social mobility over time.

HBCUs have played an important role in providing a path toward increased socioeconomic mobility for African Americans. Those we interviewed shared stories of how earning a college degree, and all that it has to offer, was fortified by an HBCU. HBCUs have done the lion's share of the work in terms of the socioeconomic mobility of African Americans from lower-income backgrounds. Quite simply, without HBCUs, there would not be a Black middle class in America. Finally, due to increased attention and funding on all fronts, HBCUs have an unprecedented opportunity to increase socioeconomic mobility for African American students and, in effect, their future families.

4

Inspiring Leaders and Scholars

It's not just the Kamala Harris effect that everybody talked about, but when you start looking at somebody like Stacey Abrams, and at Raphael Warnock, you start looking at all of mayors of these southern Black cities, here and Atlanta and Birmingham and Montgomery, I guess even St. Paul, Minnesota, the mayor there is a graduate of FAMU. You start adding those up pretty quickly and you see that there's this oversized impact [of HBCUs]. Even during the summer of George Floyd [2020], and everybody's trying to figure out what should we be reading? Everybody's reading Ibram Kendi, who went to FAMU, or Ta-Nehisi Coates, who went to Howard.
—WALTER KIMBROUGH, President, Dillard University

Although Predominantly White Institutions are often lauded as being superior to Historically Black Colleges and Universities, research—including that of some of the most prominent researchers in the field of higher education—demonstrates that HBCUs outperform PWIs in many areas. According to sociologist Walter Allen and his various coauthors (Allen, 1992; Allen & Jewell, 2002; Allen et al., 2007; Allen et al., 2018), HBCUs offer better psychological adjustment, cultivate enhanced cultural understanding and awareness, and foster higher academic achievement among African Americans. Moreover, low-income African American students attending HBCUs do better than their Black counterparts at PWIs. According to Allen and countless other researchers, the campus climate—including the racial composition—along with the faculty-student relations has a positive impact on student academic achievement beyond that of what Black students experience at PWIs (Allen, 1992; Fleming, 1984; Gasman & Arroyo, 2014; Hardy et al., 2019; Hawkins, 2021; K. L. Williams et al., 2022; Wilson, 2007).

The culture and support at HBCUs make an enormous difference in the lives of the students who attend them, producing scholars and leaders who go on to change the nation and the world. Some of these individuals are well known, while others are lesser known but are having a profound impact on the lives of many. Roslyn Artis, president of Benedict College, says it best: "The fact that an entire two generations, the last two or three generations of some of the finest, greatest leaders in the United States of America have been born of Historically Black Colleges and Universities. The depth and breadth of the experience, the self-efficacy that really develops on this campus, on these campuses, I think has made a tremendous contribution." As we saw in Chapter 2, one's identity can transform because of experiencing the culture and diversity of Blackness at HBCUs. As the nation talks about diversity and the increased need for it, HBCUs have long been promoting and benefiting from diversity (Palmer & Williams, 2021). HBCUs have also played a key role in diversifying many professions across the spectrum—from teaching to medicine to research to law (Simen & Meyer, 2021; Yancy & Bauchner, 2021).

For over a century, HBCUs have taken the students who come to their doors and helped to shape them intellectually and professionally—from sociologist W. E. B. Du Bois (Fisk University) and educational leader Booker T. Washington (Hampton University), to singers Roberta Flack (Howard University) and Lionel Richie (Tuskegee

University), to director Spike Lee (Morehouse College), to civil rights activists Martin Luther King Jr. (Morehouse College) and Jesse Jackson (North Carolina A&T University), to Reverends William Barber II (North Carolina Central University) and Louis Farrakhan Sr. (Winston-Salem State University), to television icon Oprah Winfrey (Tennessee State University). Over the years, HBCUs have transformed individuals and, in effect, communities. As Walter Kimbrough, president of Dillard University, explained, "With the advent of HBCUs, you saw the rapid increase in literacy in African American communities. So, I think from a historical point of view, that was one of the key contributions, that the illiteracy rate dropped precipitously once you started to have HBCUs." In her important book *Self Taught: African American Education in Slavery and Freedom*, Heather Williams details how literacy was kept from Black people so that they would not be able to communicate. Regardless, Black people found ways to learn to read and taught each other even in the small ways available to them. HBCUs changed the landscape for African Americans in terms of advancing literacy, and thus advancing the lives of generations of African Americans.

In the words of Makola Abdullah, president of Virginia State University, "We have graduated and sent off into the workforce, into the entrepreneurship space some incredible individuals who have done some incredible things and their work has really, in my mind, defined the reputation of our institutions. I tell my alums all the time 'Our reputation is based on the accomplishments that you make when you graduate.' So, by far our biggest contribution to society has been incredible graduates who do incredible work." Antoine Alston, a professor at North Carolina A&T State University and an HBCU graduate, agrees. He sees HBCUs as having a special ability to change lives: "The Black college has a history of taking that raw product, giv[ing] them a chance. Somebody will take them under their wing and they [are] going to make it and they [are] going to be successful."

As someone who did not attend an HBCU but who works closely with many of their leaders, Bill Moses of the Kresge Foundation shared, "HBCUs have contributed to society overall by serving students who otherwise wouldn't have had an opportunity or a voice, which is different from being the intellectual leader of the Black community and different from disproportionately educating African Americans. These contributions overlap with each other obviously, but I think supporting students with few choices for an education has been a critical part of HBCUs' contribution."

Scholars and Leaders of the Past

Although increased interest in HBCUs is a somewhat recent development, these institutions have long been producing leaders and scholars who have changed the nation and the world. As historian James D. Anderson articulated,

> I think what has happened in more recent years is . . . people [are] now talking about Ta-Nehisi Coates and Nikole Hannah-Jones going to Howard University [as faculty], they're pretty excited about it and they act like it's something new. Well, that's not anything new [for] Howard. I mean when [influential attorney] Charles Hamilton Houston[1] was there, or when [scientist] Percy Julian[2] was there, when [biologist] Ernest E. Just[3] was there, they had intellectuals for a long time, very powerful people, but now we are in an era where the University of North Carolina-Chapel Hill will compete for them. Back then they couldn't get a job there.

As Anderson demonstrated in an article written in 1993, even with the most impeccable qualifications—those on par with White scholars at the time—African American scholars were not hired by PWIs in the South or the North. The first African American hired into a full-time position at a PWI was William Boyd Allison Davis, an anthropologist at the University of Chicago. Aside from him, it was nearly impossible for African Americans to be hired at PWIs. Anderson cited a study done by the Julius Rosenwald Fund, which demonstrated the ways that institutional racism and color-blind policies perpetuate inequity. More specifically, in 1945, Fred Wale, the director of education for the Rosenwald Fund, sent letters to nearly 600 college and university presidents asking if their institutions would be willing to hire "high quality" African American scholars. Wale mailed a list of roughly 150 Black scholars with impeccable qualifications to the same group of presidents. Over the course of a month about a third of the presidents replied to Wale; the other two-thirds never replied (J. D. Anderson, 1993). Among the 200 or so presidents that Wale corresponded with, "virtually none" saw the "complete absence of African American scholars" from their faculties as an indication of "racially discriminatory hiring practices" (J. D. Anderson, 1993, p. 158; Gasman, 2022a). As a result of large-scale institutional racism, the most prominent African American scholars were housed at HBCUs throughout the late 1970s, and HBCU students benefited immensely from the rich diversity of their presence. They continue to benefit from this richness; however, there is considerable and recent competition for African American faculty and scholars (Griffith, 1996).

Portraits of Leaders and Scholars

It is important to get a flavor for the deep and meaningful contributions of HBCU graduates, and so in this section we look more closely at graduates across a variety of areas, including literature, leadership, politics, civil rights, medicine, science, research, art, and business. We highlight some of the contributions of these individuals and the ways that HBCUs shaped their individual thinking and lives, while also alluding to the countless others who have been shaped by HBCUs. These profiles capture various stages of individuals' lives and careers.

A Profound Impact on Literature

Toni Morrison
Toni Morrison, author of *The Bluest Eye*, *Song of Solomon*, and *Beloved*, among many other works, graduated from Howard University in 1953 with a degree in English. Morrison was the recipient of the Pulitzer

Prize in Literature, among other awards. In 2012, President Barack Obama awarded her the Presidential Medal of Freedom for her life's work.

Morrison grew up in a working-class family in Lorain, Ohio. She enrolled at Howard University in 1949 and earned a master's degree from Cornell University in 1955; however, it was her experience at Howard that was life changing. As she shared with host Terry Gross on the National Public Radio show *Fresh Air*, at Howard University, "the criteria for excellence had nothing to do with color. It had only to do with talent" (Lefrak, 2019). While at Howard, Morrison was the homecoming queen, acted in plays sponsored by the theater department, and served as the dean of pledges for Alpha Kappa Alpha Sorority, Inc.[4] She took advantage of all the opportunities available to her and found her assertive and activist voice, pushing back against segregation in the local Washington, DC, area. Hailing from Ohio, according to Morrison, she did not encounter segregated restaurants and public transportation until she attended Howard University, as Washington, DC, adhered to the segregation of the South.

Morrison often talked about the influence of Howard University on her career and lauded the university's "history of opposition, debate, and argument, starting with the school's explicit rejection of the 19th century notion that blacks didn't deserve a chance at higher education" (Streitfeld, 1995). She returned to Howard in 1958 to teach and focus on her writing. While there, she joined a writing group. The group—made up of faculty and local writers—met "to read to each other and critique each other. Some of them were professional writers, and some were not." Morrison added, "And so I brought to these meetings little things I had written for classes as an undergraduate— some fiction, some not and so on. And they had really, really good lunches, really good food during these meetings. But they wouldn't let you continue to come if you were just reading old stuff. So, I had to think up something new if I was going to continue to have this really good food and really good company. . . . So I started writing" (Fresh Air, 2015). Morrison eventually worked as a book editor for Random

House and cultivated talent such as Angela Davis. She published her first book—*The Bluest Eye*—in 1970. The influence of the Blackness of Howard shaped Morrison's centering of Blackness and Black narratives in her work. For example, in *The Bluest Eye*, she places Black girls at the center of her story, changing American literature forever (Als, 2020).

Morrison was a faculty member at Princeton University from 1989 to 2006, when she retired. While at Princeton, she developed the Princeton Atelier, which is a program that brings together students, artists, and writers from across the nation. Together, they produce creative art that is presented to the public. Morrison died in 2019 at age 88, contributing political and literary commentary up until the end of her life (Fox, 2019).

Ta-Nehisi Coates

Writer and journalist Ta-Nehisi Coates—author of *Between the World and Me*, which won the 2015 National Book Award for Nonfiction—attended Howard University. Coates has written extensively for many of the nation's media and literary outlets, serving as a national voice on racial issues and politics.

Coates grew up in Baltimore and was interested in writing from an early age, perhaps because his mother required him to write essays when he misbehaved and his father was active with Black Classic Press.[5] He enrolled at Howard University in 1993, stayed for five years, but did not graduate (Howard University, 2019). Instead, he left to pursue a career in journalism. He wrote for a variety of small media outlets and the occasional national outlet and broke through to a larger audience in 2008 with the article "This Is How We Lost to the White Man" (Coates, 2008) for *The Atlantic*. The essay focused on comedian and actor Bill Cosby and conservatism, as Cosby was regularly offering strong critique of low-income African Americans at the time. With this essay, Coates became a senior editor at *The Atlantic*; he also became highly influential and was a regularly sought-after commentator.

In his book *Between the World and Me*, Coates (2015) refers to Howard University as Mecca (a place of sanctuary and refuge), stating, "My only Mecca was, is, and shall always be Howard University" (p. 39). Coates elaborates, proclaiming, "I was admitted to Howard University, but formed and shaped by The Mecca. These institutions are related but not the same. Howard University is an institution of higher education, concerned with the LSAT, magna cum laude, and Phi Beta Kappa. The Mecca is a machine, crafted to capture and concentrate the dark energy of all African peoples and inject it directly into the student body" (p. 40). As he further explains, "The Mecca derives its power from the heritage of Howard University, which in Jim Crow days enjoyed a near-monopoly on black talent" (p. 40). Coates adds that part of the power of Howard University as a Mecca for African American students is its location in Washington, DC—"Chocolate City" as he and so many affectionally call it. Howard is at the center of Black power and federal power. From Coates's perspective, "The result was an alumni and professoriate that spanned genre and generation— Charles Drew,[6] Amiri Baraka,[7] Thurgood Marshall, Ossie Davis,[8] Doug Wilder,[9] David Dinkins,[10] Lucille Clifton,[11] Toni Morrison, Kwame Ture.[12] The history, the location, the alumni combined to create The Mecca—the crossroads of the black diaspora" (p. 41).

While at Howard, Coates discovered his identity and cultivated it. As he writes,

> I first witnessed this power out on the Yard, that communal green space in the center of the campus where the students gathered, and I saw everything I knew of my black self multiplied out into seemingly endless variations. There were the scions of Nigerian aristocrats in their business suits giving dap to bald-headed Qs[13] in purple windbreakers and tan Timbs. There were the high-yellow progeny of AME preachers debating the clerics of Ausar-Set.[14] There were California girls turned Muslim, born anew, in hijab and long skirt. There were Ponzi schemers and Christian cultists, Tabernacle fanatics and mathematical geniuses. (pp. 40–41)

In providing a picture for the reader, Coates states, "It was like listening to a hundred different renditions of 'Redemption Song,' each in a different color and key. And overlaying all of this was the history of Howard itself. I knew that I was literally walking in the footsteps of all the Toni Morrisons and Zora Neale Hurstons,[15] of all the Sterling Browns[16] and Kenneth Clarks,[17] who'd come before" (p. 41).

Coates could experience all this Blackness—"the vastness of black people"—in the matter of a "twenty-minute walk across campus" (p. 41). In just a short time, he recalls, "I saw the vastness in the students chopping it up in front of the Frederick Douglas Memorial Hall, where Muhammad Ali had addressed their fathers and mothers in defiance of the Vietnam War. I saw it in the students next to Ira Aldridge Theater, where Donny Hathaway[18] had once sung, where Donald Byrd[19] had once assembled his flock" (p. 41). Coates elaborates, "Some of the other students were out on the grass in front of Alain Locke[20] Hall, in pink and green, chanting, singing, stomping, clapping, stepping. Some of them came up from Tubman Quadrangle with their roommates and rope for Double Dutch.[21] Some of them came down from [Charles] Drew Hall, with their caps cocked and their backpacks slung through one arm, then fell into gorgeous ciphers of beatbox and rhyme" (pp. 41–42). As we read Coates's work, we were struck by how he captured the essence of Howard (and in many ways HBCUs overall): the buildings named after prominent African American intellectuals, the descriptions of deeply common cultural memories, and the depiction of Black fraternity and sorority culture.

In *Between the World and Me*, Coates offers a sense not only of the uniquely beautiful and empowering environment of Howard University but also of an HBCU campus more generally. He ties the students to the history and culture and makes the imagery come alive for the reader. As he recalls, "Some of the girls sat by the flagpole with bell hooks[22] and Sonia Sanchez[23] in their straw totes. Some of the boys with their new Yoruba names beseeched these girls by citing Frantz Fanon.[24] Some of them studied Russian. Some of them worked in bone labs. They were Panamanian. They were Bajan. And some of them were from places I had never heard of. But all of them were Hot and incredible, exotic even, though we hailed from the same tribe." Here Coates makes sure that the reader understands the influence of the vast, contrary, and diverse African diaspora on Howard University students, and how all these perspectives of and about Blackness can exist at an HBCU. As Coates puts it, "The result is a people, a black people, who embody all physical varieties and whose life stories mirror this physical range. Through The Mecca I saw that we were, in our own segregated body politic cosmopolitans. The black diaspora was not just our own world but, in so many ways, the Western world itself" (p. 43). In essence, both Howard and HBCUs center Blackness, and that centering is immensely powerful for African Americans as they develop and contribute to society (Coates, 2013).

In 2021, Coates joined the faculty at Howard University as a writer in residence in the English department, where he holds the Sterling Brown chair.[25] In the words of Armando Bengochea, program officer at the Mellon Foundation,

> It's no surprise that Hannah-Jones and Coates are now at Howard. I mean, it's an exemplary institution. It is research driven and has capacities that other HBCUs don't have, not in a rural environment but in a major metropolitan area. I hope it isn't just the exceptionalism of Howard within the HBCU community. I think it doesn't hurt other well-positioned HBCUs to attempt to create those possibilities. I don't know how much they have reached out and tried to create those kinds of arrangements with the best well-known Black academics or figures. I hope it happens, but [Hannah-Jones and Coates] wound up at Howard, and Howard is Howard. That's why we call it Mecca.

Bengochea also shared that, with Coates taking on a faculty position at Howard, "there is a sense that this is where the smartest people come from. This is where the smartest people go. I hope that HBCUs, like any other college that has highly accomplished alumni, that those folks continue to create and that the institutions continue to place media stories around the success of HBCUs. There are just so many in so many realms of life, but you only hear about them and know about them in private circles, in academic circles."

HBCU Contributions to the Arts

HBCUs are widely known for graduating entertainers, politicians, and even professional athletes. Often lost amid accomplished alumni are those who have become successful artists. HBCUs became the major sites for the education of Black artists and, until the 1970s, presented the best opportunity for the exhibition and preservation of their work (Moffitt & Schmidt-Campbell, 2021). Black artists have also had unique roles in American culture, not only highlighting talent but also telling the stories of a people in a nation where they are often overlooked and undervalued (The Hundred Seven, 2021). Aside from the fact that many prominent artists have graduated from HBCUs, these institutions have also amassed a rich collection of African American art, preserving this heritage to offer students, faculty, and art enthusiasts a better understanding of these artists' contributions to the history of this country (Tom Joyner Foundation, n.d.). During the nineteenth and twentieth centuries, many of the great African American artists worked at HBCUs because they could not display their work in mainstream American institutions (Tom Joyner Foundation, n.d.).

Artist and art historian David C. Driskell, an acclaimed authority on African American art, shared the following in the 2021 HBO documentary *Black Art: In the Absence of Light*: "When nobody else was out there championing these [Black] artists, HBCUs were there, claiming them, showcasing them, putting them up on walls, teaching about them" (Bynoe, 2021). Sarah Elizabeth Lewis, a Harvard University professor who was also featured in the HBO film, underscored the importance of HBCUs to art history, stating, "Without the work of Historically Black Colleges and Universities we wouldn't have a repository of African-American art that we can draw on" (Bynoe, 2021). Important in the discussion of HBCUs and their role in the arts is that these institutions used their limited resources to train Black artists, acquire work created by artists of African descent, and provide Black artists with professional guidance and support. HBCUs were the first patrons of African American art (Bynoe, 2021).

The contributions of HBCUs to art span a number of institutions. For example, Talladega College houses historic public murals painted by Black artists, and Fisk University and Spelman College, among others, house major repositories of work by Black artists. Had these institutions not had the foresight to train artists and preserve their work, a great deal of the legacy of Black artists would be lost. Three HBCUs have made an indelible mark on the history of the art world: Hampton University, Howard University, and Clark Atlanta University (CAU). Hampton University Museum was the first HBCU to collect African American art with its acquisition in 1894 of the oil paintings *The Banjo Lesson* and *Lion's Head* by Henry Ossawa Tanner (1859–1937) (Bynoe, 2021). The museum also has the oldest collection of Kuba-related[26] material in the world. Howard University was the first HBCU with an art department led African Americans. Howard University's art department has influenced generations of Black artists through its approach to classroom instruction, pedagogical art practices, scholarship, and mentorship of students. Howard University's art collection consists of over 4,500 works. CAU established its art program in 1931. Renowned artist and printmaker Hale A. Woodruff started the program and hired celebrated artist Nancy Elizabeth Prophet to teach sculpture. By the mid-1930s, Atlanta University (which later became Clark Atlanta University) was regarded by many as the leading institution in the American South for Black people to study art (Bynoe, 2021).

HBCUs have a long history of providing an environment in which Black artists and art professionals thrive. As Kinshasha Holman Conwill, former director at the Studio Museum in Harlem, New York, shared in an interview, "In addition to their collecting activities, these institutions also provided primary training for African American artists, art historians, professors, and curators" (Lynne, 2021).

Bisa Butler

Bisa Butler, a contemporary artist and HBCU graduate, is known for her vibrant quilted portraits celebrating Black life; her representations range from everyday people to notable historical figures. Butler graduated from Howard University with a bachelor's in fine arts. She cultivated her talents under the mentorship of faculty such as Lois Mailou Jones,[27] Elizabeth Catlett,[28] Jeff Donaldson,[29] and Ernie Barnes.[30] She later earned a master's in art from Montclair State University, where she took a fiber art class. Butler began to experiment with fabric as a medium and became interested in collage techniques. Early in her career, Butler was a high school art teacher.

Butler uses her unique artistic style, which combines portraiture and quilting, to accord dignity and respect to her Black subjects—those she discovers in historical photographs, as well as members of her own family (Logan, 2020). In a recent interview, Butler recalled exhibiting her work wherever she could, which included churches, community centers, and the like (Logan, 2020). Butler shared, "Back then, my quilts weren't life sized, because I didn't have enough time for that. I knew I could tell more of a story with the full body, and multiple people. I always wanted to do more."

The fact that HBCUs are places where Black identity is valued and developed is reflected in the work of Butler, who shared in an interview, "My subjects stand in defiance against racist stereotypes. My work proclaims that Black people should be seen, regarded, and treated as equals." The role of Black identity is further supported by Michele Wije, curator of exhibitions at American Federation of Arts, who mentioned during an interview that Butler's work "is, and has always been, about Black identity." Wije continued, "So, [Butler's] work is very relevant to this moment in history, when we are seeing a societal reckoning over racial inequity" (Logan, 2020, n.p.).

Shaping Visionary Leaders

Ruth Simmons

> Ruth Simmons is the one who flapped her wings as a butterfly and it caused a storm, or a tornado to whip through higher education.
> —John Wilson, Former Executive Director, White House Initiative on HBCUs

Ruth Simmons is the president of Prairie View A&M University in Prairie View, Texas, just outside of Houston. Before coming out of retirement to assume the presidency of the Texas-based HBCU in 2017, Simmons served as the president of Brown University in Providence, Rhode Island (2001-2012), and Smith College (1995-2001) in Northampton, Massachusetts. She was the first African American president of both institutions and the first Black president of an Ivy League institution.

Simmons grew up in Houston, Texas, in a "segregated, poor community" called Fifth Ward. She did not know anyone who had gone to college, and she did not set her sights on acquiring a college degree. While in high school, she encountered teachers who insisted that she go to college. Still, according to Simmons, "I was not familiar with the college world, and as Texas universities were just beginning to integrate, [my teachers] didn't think that it was safe for me to go to a newly integrated university in Texas given the racial issues in Texas at the time." One of her teachers had graduated from Dillard University and thought the small college in New Orleans would be an "ideal place" for Simmons. The teacher helped her apply to Dillard and to get a scholarship to attend the HBCU in 1963.

Simmons describes Dillard as "very much a mixed experience" initially. She shared, "I was, of course, a very poor student. I don't mean that in the sense of academics, but my family was very, I won't say destitute, but certainly did not have the means to support me when I was in college. And so, I felt rather like a fish out of water going into college directly from my family situation here in Houston." She added, "I'm the youngest of 12 children, and the one thing that you feel when you are the youngest of 12 is you can't be away from your family. And so, to be sent off to New Orleans away from my family was kind of devastating for me." At Dillard, Simmons entered a culture that was foreign to her. "I mean there were all these young people, African American people, many of whom were from New Orleans, who felt pretty self-confident, and they were able to move about the world in a certain way. And I didn't feel that comfortable at all. And so, my first year was a little difficult, and if I had been able to drop out at that point, I certainly would have." Simmons did not have enough money to go home, however, and when she thought about all her teachers who had helped get her to Dillard, she decided to "try it as long as [she] could."

Like many other students at Dillard and colleges across the nation, Simmons was able to settle in after the first year (Farmer et al., 2019). She "began to understand the worth" of what she was doing and "the value of the environment" that she was in. Specifically, Simmons understood "that just as in this segregated high school in Houston, people had taken me in their care, wished the best for me, and pushed me to achieve the most that I could achieve. I finally began to understand that I was in the same kind of environment at Dillard, that the people there were engaged in trying to help me become the best possible scholar, the best possible person, the best possible individual to weather the tumultuous times that we were in." Simmons's experience of being shaped and mentored by individuals at Dillard is similar to the experiences of other HBCU graduates (Conrad & Gasman, 2015; Gasman & Nguyen, 2019).

In 1963, during Simmons's first year of college, John F. Kennedy was assassinated, and, according to her, "that was a time of terror in this country. Nobody really knew how we were going to get out of it." In addition to the "deep segregation" that she had experienced growing up in Houston, there was uncertainty in national leadership and the activity of the civil rights movement. Fortunately, Simmons felt safe in the Dillard environment. As she shared, "I felt empowered to be there. Strangely, I felt empowered to be there as who I was, and that was as a very difficult person, to be perfectly honest with you."

As a child, Simmons was not shy about asserting herself, stating, "The only way I survived being the youngest of 12 was to be very obstreperous, certainly always vocal." She added, "My mouth got me into a lot of trouble in my family. When I went off to college, I used the same garrulousness to assert myself, through my essays, my challenges to the administration, my work on the newspaper—everything that I did must have been offensive to somebody." Simmons was confident and fierce in her convictions. She noted, "If there was a rule in college, I violated it." As an example, Simmons shared that she found required chapel to be unnecessary and "oppressive." She stated,

> I reasoned, as a 17-year-old, that [it] didn't seem quite fair because it was a Protestant chapel. We were affiliated with the Methodist church, but surely everybody didn't have the same faith tradition. How would you force someone to go to a service of another faith by making it a requirement? And so, I said what about Catholics? What about Jews? What would you force them to do as a student at Dillard? Of course, there were no Jews at Dillard. It was all pyrrhic, but that's what I was all about as a 17-year-old. I was about justice, and I was about the ideal. And so, I would refuse to go to chapel.

Simmons's refusal got her into quite a bit of trouble at Dillard. In fact, during her senior year, the university administration wrote to her family, "telling them they regretted to inform them that I would not be able to graduate because I did not complete the chapel requirement." Looking back, Simmons realizes that it was safe to be a rebel at Dillard. As she explains, it "wouldn't have been safe for me at the University of Texas or at any other institution [in Houston] because I wouldn't have stopped using my mouth the way I did at the time."

Unlike many who graduate from HBCUs and share memories of halcyon days, Simmons is nuanced in her memories of Dillard. For her, the New Orleans HBCU "never became the kind of ideal academic experience that I treasured." She added, "I castigated professors who were not rigorous enough. You get the picture. I really thought that I deserved a different kind of environment, a more intellectual environment than Dillard was at the time." Simmons recalled an incident when she was called to the president's house as a sophomore and was terrified. She thought, "Everything had caught up with me and I was being kicked out of school." But it turned out that the president decided to send her to Wellesley College for her junior year. Simmons never found out if she was sent away for being a nuisance or because the Dillard administration thought it might be a good experience for her. After a year, she came back to Dillard for her senior year and graduated, understanding that there are "certain things that I garnered because I went to an HBCU."

Simmons won both Fulbright and Danforth fellowships while at Dillard, enabling her to study abroad in France and to have her graduate education completely paid for, wherever she decided to attend. She eventually attended Harvard University. According to Simmons, "Harvard was pretty uncomfortable with me. They didn't know what to do with me, they said, because surely there would be no career for somebody like me in academic life. Why? Because I was studying French, and 'what was an African American doing studying French?' It didn't make sense to them." Nevertheless, she was paying her own way, and she finished in four years.

Much like other HBCU students who attend graduate school at PWIs, Simmons credits her Dillard education for her success at Harvard (Wagner et al., 2013). She noted, "I always say that I was able to [finish my PhD in four years] because my HBCU prepared me well for what I was going to endure at Harvard. If people thought I did not belong, that was of little consequence to me. If people thought that I was not worthy to be there, I knew that was a lie. If people thought I could never go anywhere in the profession that I had chosen, I knew that I could disprove that." Simmons fully understands the power of her HBCU experience. Attending an HBCU gave her a deep knowledge of self and a sense of confidence. As she shared with us, "HBCUs are still doing for students what I had needed an HBCU to do for me."

Simmons explained that with

> the racial situation in the country being what it was, how is a child to understand how to navigate [it]? It doesn't come naturally to us as human beings to face up to hatred and discrimination. Our question is always why. Why do you see me as being different? Why do you see me as being less than? So, we're questioning the oddity of that, the rationality of that. But nobody really can tell us how to deal with it. HBCUs help students deal with that.

She added that HBCUs

disprove[e] common presumptions and notions about who they are. You are poor, and therefore you won't fit in. You wear your hair differently, and thus there's something wrong with you. You don't speak the same as I, therefore you must not be intelligent. To be in a kind of proving ground where all of those things that you learn that people think or say about you are not only flawed but downright pernicious lies [is powerful]. You emerge from that environment armed better to deal with the world that you actually live in.

Simmons is convinced that HBCUs are powerful and that the world we live in right now needs them. With passion, she shared that "we have not rid ourselves of all of the things that people try to do to weaken many of our young people, to try to dismiss them, to try to disenfranchise them. And HBCUs are a bullwork against that." As president of Prairie View A&M University, Simmons understands the importance of her role and of her institution in the lives of the students. She recognizes the profound impact that the institution can have on students. "I love my students at Smith and at Brown just as I love my students at Prairie View. What is the difference, and what have I enjoyed? The profound need that I am meeting at Prairie View. My students at Brown were wonderful, but they were well off, and without me they were going to succeed anyway. The same was true for students at Smith." She added, "I know there are students at Prairie View who, but for what I do to help them, would have enormous difficulties and would not be able to perhaps succeed in the same way that for me as a young person, if certain individuals had not stepped onto my path, I know I would not have been able to have the life that I have, unquestionably."

Moving back to Houston and leading Prairie View has been special to Simmons. As she describes it,

One of the things that I've always held to be important is that I not lose touch with the people who are my true peers, the people I grew up with in this ward [Third Ward, Texas], the people who live the life that I lived as a child. And so, I'm thankful that I'm still in the midst of people like that, and therefore I know what my life would have been if I had not had those people step onto my path. So, I understand the importance of that kind of educational intervention, and to me, when I walk across the Prairie View campus, I can see daily evidence of the impact that we are having on these young people. And that's different from a well-endowed institution that has enormous means and that principally selects its students from the most economically viable families in the country.

Simmons's stature has moved Prairie View A&M University to new levels in terms of its academic achievement and its ability to garner philanthropic support.

Lynn Wooten

Lynn Wooten is the president of Simmons University in Boston, Massachusetts. Before coming to Simmons, Wooten held a named deanship and was a professor of management at Cornell University. She earned a PhD at the University of Michigan in Ann Arbor and an MBA from Duke University in Durham, North Carolina. Wooten earned her bachelor's degree at North Carolina A&T State University, an HBCU in Greensboro. According to Wooten, "My parents were strong believers [in] HBCUs. They are both natives of Virginia and I would say especially more my mother than my father, but everybody in my family, cousins, aunts, and uncles who are older than me who went to college went to Virginia State in Petersburg, Virginia." Her mother was one of 10 children, 5 of whom went to either Virginia State. Her father, who grew up on the Virginia–North Carolina state line, went to college at age 14 at Virginia State as well. In Wooten's words, because of the impact that HBCUs had on her family, she "always knew about the power of HBCUs."

Despite her family's devotion to HBCUs and her personal knowledge of them, Wooten really did not want to attend one. Recalling her college admission story, she shared, "Every day I think it's an amazing story." The dean of the North Carolina A&T Business School wrote to Wooten "out of the blue." Her mother saw the letter and said, "A&T's

a good school. You should follow up and you should apply." Wooten did just that and received a prestigious scholarship. According to Wooten, "The ironic thing is that A&T was really starting to grow and a couple of people who I was loosely tied to, who I grew up with, were also recruited by A&T. One of my classmates from high school, they were recruited for an ROTC scholarship. Another girlfriend because her boyfriend went because A&T was known for engineering. One of my other good friends was recruited through this SAT search." Between the friends she knew, the friends she made, and the culture of North Carolina A&T, she felt empowered. As she recalled, "My mother always felt that an HBCU was going to love you, take care of you and make sure you were successful."

During our conversation with Wooten, she quoted Nelson Mandela's wise words: "I am because they are." She shared, "A&T definitely shaped my leadership and who I am now. I'm a person who probably always liked to lead. I was active in my high school. I was a Girl Scout. I was active in my church. But my four years at A&T elevated my leadership practices to another level." How? As Wooten explained, "It's having a group of faculty and the support staff who believe you could accomplish. So, the level of mentorship and investment that I received in my future is priceless. The opportunity just to lead in a variety of situations, whether it be leadership in my dorm, honor society, or my sorority life, or just on-campus leadership." She added, "What I learned at A&T is the power of collaborative and collective leadership and that everybody can be equal and that you can build consensus, that you can do teamwork, that you lift as you climb. That's truly what I learned at A&T, and I saw it through a variety of ways." Wooten witnessed this power through the faculty that mentored her, the friendships that she had, and "the ability of everybody to pool their strength to accomplish something."

As she was talking with us, Wooten offered an example of the strength of community at North Carolina A&T: "I was valedictorian of my class at A&T, and I had a straight-A average all through [college]. My line sisters and my big sisters [in my sorority Delta Sigma

Theta, Inc.][31] would let me go study because they were so proud of my accomplishments and wanted me to succeed. So, this is an example of everybody cheering you on and even to this day, still being proud of my accomplishments."

After North Carolina A&T, Wooten headed to Duke University to earn an MBA. She noted that Duke was much different from North Carolina A&T, and despite its less than accepting culture (as it was the 1990s), Wooten had the confidence to succeed. She felt much like Ruth Simmons when she went to Harvard. Wooten was only 21 years old, lacked experience, and, unlike most of her peers at Duke, went straight from her undergrad to an MBA program. When we asked Wooten about the level of confidence instilled in her while at North Carolina A&T, she said that "there are two institutions that I believe give you confidence, the Black church and HBCUs. You may not be able to sing in the Black church, but they'll clap their hands and make you think you can sing. It was the same thing at A&T. You've got this. You can do this. We're going to make sure you're successful." She added, "When I got to Duke, I felt like, yes, the curriculum was harder because I was an MBA student, but A&T had prepared me well. My [A&T] professors expected the best out of me, and they gave me the confidence to show up and speak out. And a part of it was you had a community of people who cared about you, your classmates and in particular your professors."

Although Wooten has always thought of herself as a leader and even potentially as a college president, the people at North Carolina A&T knew she would be a president. As she shared, "If you let the A&T people tell it—those who I went to school with—they always said I knew I was going to be a college president." Wooten was inspired by Black women such as Johnnetta Cole, the famed anthropologist and president of Spelman and Bennett Colleges, and Mary McLeod Bethune, the Black women's rights icon and founder and president of Bethune-Cookman University. The first time Wooten saw Cole speak, she said to herself, "One day I might want to be a college president of an all-women's college." Wooten credits her drive, commitment, and care toward her students to her experiences at North Carolina A&T State University.

David Wilson

David Wilson, president of Morgan State University in Baltimore, Maryland, attended Tuskegee Institute (now University) for his undergraduate education. He grew up the son of an Alabama sharecropper. When he left for college, his father gave him five dollars toward his tuition—all the money that he had. His father's small donation and belief in his ability are what fueled his success in life and leadership.

Wilson enjoyed his experience at Tuskegee immensely. From his perspective, Tuskegee was the "best college in America." He shared, "I started there in 1973, long before the acronym HBCU existed and so Tuskegee and others were known as 'Black colleges.' In the view of all of the students at Tuskegee, there was no other college in America, with all due respect to the Ivy League, the Big 10, University of Chicago, that was better than Tuskegee. And so that was my first encounter with institutions that would later take on the acronym, HBCU." Wilson's experience at Tuskegee was "absolutely hands down the best college experience that I think anyone on the face of the earth could ever have. I felt like a kid in a candy store every single day on that campus. I grew astronomically. I encountered students from practically all 50 states, from 30 countries, professors who were extraordinarily diverse and some of my best professors at Tuskegee were White professors, Indian professors, they were so committed to your success. That was my first experience."

Of course, when Wilson entered Tuskegee, it was his first experience with college, and he experienced what many students encounter when they leave rural communities and move to a college campus. But there was something special about Tuskegee being a Black college. Wilson also experienced some of the frustrations that HBCU students and alumni often express. As he explained, "I also encountered, much as all students who went to places like Tuskegee did during that time, long lines at financial aid. We encountered rats in the cafeteria. There were pigeons that were, you know basically in the roof area of the residence hall. But you know what? As students, we just kind of whatever, kind of chucked it up and went along and did not let that get in the way of the great experience there." For Wilson and his peers, the quality of the academic experience and the overall culture of Tuskegee made up for the lack of resources and poor infrastructure.

After earning both a bachelor's degree and a master's degree at Tuskegee, Wilson left the institution in 1979. He moved to Philadelphia to begin work at the Research and Development Institute of Philadelphia, eventually deciding to attend graduate school at Harvard University. While at the Cambridge, Massachusetts–based university, he won a Woodrow Wilson Fellowship that took him to Kentucky State University (an HBCU) as an executive assistant to the vice president for business affairs and finance. As Wilson explained, "I worked for the youngest college president in America at the time, Raymond Burse, who was a Rhode[s] scholar, Harvard Law. He was about 31, 32 years old and that was an experience, because he was a perfectionist and basically would not accept anything but perfection." Wilson added, "I became fascinated by the process that Kentucky State was embracing to become a desegregated campus. When I was there, I think about 25 to 30% of the students were White." For his doctoral thesis at Harvard, Wilson decided to write a case study of the desegregation at Kentucky State University that was based on his experience there (Wilson, 1987).

Although he was enjoying his time at Kentucky State, the Woodrow Wilson Foundation asked if Wilson would vacate his fellowship, move to Princeton, and direct the fellowship program that he was a part of. He became an officer of the Woodrow Wilson Foundation in Princeton and considers this one of the "best moves of my life." Wilson shared with us, "I arrived in Princeton and my office at the Woodrow Wilson Foundation was next to Robert Goheen, who was the former president of Princeton University and who led Princeton during the turbulent 1960s. The president of the Woodrow Wilson Foundation was Richard Cooper, who was the former president of Hamilton College in upstate

New York, as well as the New York Public Library and it had all of these just incredibly bright, transformational, forward thinking historical leaders there at the Woodrow Wilson Foundation." Among these brilliant minds, Wilson was the only African American, and he benefited from the "special interest" that they took in him. He shared, "I just grew astronomically." After Wilson finished his doctorate at Harvard, his newfound connections led to an introduction to the president of Rutgers University, Edward Bloustein, and securing the position of assistant provost. He stayed for 9 years before moving to Auburn University to become vice president for 11 years. Wilson was the first Black person in the history of the state of Alabama to be appointed a senior administrator at a PWI.

It was not long before the University of Wisconsin came knocking on Wilson's door to be chancellor over two statewide institutions, a UW extension that housed Wisconsin Public Radio, Wisconsin Public Television, all the online degree programs in the UW system, and all the economic development activity, in addition to overseeing the 13 freshmen/sophomore liberal arts campuses. He took the job and "was in hog heaven." He loved Madison, Wisconsin, and thought of the small city as "the best place, beyond Cambridge, Massachusetts, that he had ever lived. A very, very progressive city."

As Wilson was enjoying his time with the University of Wisconsin System, he often received offers to become presidents of various HBCUs. But he did not have the desire. He had even been offered the presidency of his beloved alma mater Tuskegee a few times and said no. It was not until Shirley Malcolm, a senior advisor at the American Association for the Advancement of Science and a board member of Morgan State University, called him that he began to rethink his decision to stay at Wisconsin. She said, "We have had a president for 25 years. We've done a search. We're not satisfied with the pool, and I was told to reach out to you." Wilson replied, "Thank you very much, but I'm happy where I am." He thought that was the end of the conversation, but Malcolm did not take no for an answer. She was persistent, saying, "Look, all I'm asking you is, are you open to my flying out to Wisconsin to have dinner with you?" Wilson agreed to have dinner and insisted that he was happy where he was. That fact was precisely the reason she wanted him to come to Morgan State. Malcolm thought Wilson was "ideal for where the institution is now and where it could go."

Wilson eventually agreed to visit the campus informally. As he explained,

> I flew out there one Friday afternoon, rented a car and came upon the campus. I had a baseball cap on, turned it back. Jeans, sunglasses, walked through campus. The first time I'd ever been on the campus, even though my wife at the time was a Morgan alum, she had come here but we never came. She did her undergraduate degree here in biology and chemistry and then went on to Howard dental school, but she never spoke about Morgan in the way that I spoke about Tuskegee. And therefore she, myself, and our son, never came. When I came here, that was the first time that I had stepped foot on this campus. And that was the first time since Tuskegee that I've seen that many Black people in one place on a college campus.

The sight of so many Black people together was "powerful" to Wilson. As he shared, "Oomph. That was powerful because I didn't know. I just didn't know what I had lost. I'm walking the campus now and I'm seeing all these young people who look like me."

At the point when he was walking across the Baltimore-based HBCU campus, Wilson said that his father, who had passed away, "kind of whispered in [his] ear." Wilson shared that he heard his father say, "'Son, you need to leave Wisconsin and you need to be here.' And I was trying to fight that." Wilson met with the board and answered some questions. Congressman Elijah Cummings, who was a member of the Morgan State Board of Trustees until he passed away, asked the last question: "Let me see if I'm hearing you correctly. You have this grand vision, but I'm not sure if Morgan is ready for a grand vision. So, help me understand how you would think about implementing a grand vision at an institution that might not be ready to think about a transformation of itself in the way in which you have presented yourself here." Wilson responded while drawing on his legal pad,

Congressman, if I'm hearing you correctly, you're saying that Morgan State University is this matchbox, and it may have 12 matchsticks in it, and you are looking for a president to come in and not do anything with this matchbox but change the position of the matchsticks? I said "If that is what I'm hearing from you, I think the flight out of Baltimore back to Madison leaves soon and I need to be on it." I said "But if the board is ready for a president who is seeing perhaps a box like this turned upside down, or indeed, no box and you want to grow the institution in ways that the institution has not experienced, understanding that there will be numerous bumps along the way, then we can talk."

The board asked Wilson to step out. When he came back in, they placed an eight-page contract in front of him.

Although Wilson is enjoying an extraordinarily successful presidency now, the first few years were full of considerable growing pains and bumps. Several members of the board were not ready for the type of transformation that he brought to campus. The previous president, Earl Richardson, had also been transformational, and in many ways the institution was looking for a president to just steady the ship, not set sail on a new course. But once Wilson and the board of trustees were on the same page, Morgan State began to grow and excel (Dance, 2012; Gasman, 2012). Wilson shared, "I have enjoyed almost everything imaginable about leading Morgan. The students here are terrific. They are so amazing, and they are brilliant in their own way, without being arrogant. And so many of them don't understand how brilliant, how talented, how innovative in thought they are. I have enjoyed having them in conversation, in dialogue and listening for the most creative thoughts that they utter in that conversation." He enjoys "opening doors of opportunities for [students] to see the world and to understand the world and to grow and to develop as leaders."

Wilson also appreciates working with the faculty at Morgan State and sees them as "the most committed and dedicated and well-prepared faculty that [he has] been around in higher education." He elaborated, "They teach [four courses a semester] at a research institution. They publish books by some of the best publishing houses. We had faculty members just last year have books published by Oxford University Press, Princeton University Press, and Harvard University Press. They are so committed to the institution, to the mission of the institution, so I enjoy that."

Wilson is dedicated to leading Morgan State University. As he shared, "When I left Tuskegee, I didn't think that I could ever, ever fall in love with another university, in the vernacular, that ain't happening, but I've fallen in love with this one and that's why I have stayed here." Despite being asked to lead major, majority research institutions, Wilson has opted to stay on at Morgan State and continues to transform the institution into what his "good friend John Wilson [former president of Morehouse College] has called a cathedral." Wilson ended our discussion by saying, "I enjoy every aspect of the body of work that we are about here at Morgan, because I don't see what I do as a job. It's a calling and I'm rarely unhappy in this calling." Much like other presidents of HBCUs, Wilson sees his work and role at Morgan State as a contribution to the greater good and the larger African American community.

Roslyn Artis

Roslyn Artis is the president of Benedict College in Columbia, South Carolina. Before this, she was the president of Florida Memorial University in Miami Gardens, Florida. At both HBCUs, Artis was the first woman president; she has been a trailblazer most of her life. She grew up in southern West Virginia, which has very few African Americans (just over 3%). As a result, there was little discussion of HBCUs around her dinner table. As Artis explained, "I'll be honest and say I didn't know what the acronym stood for. I didn't know there was such a thing as a Historically Black College or University when I was growing up."

Artis was the first in her family to attend college. "When I got prepared to go to college, that was my idea, not my parents. Neither of my parents is college educated. My father was a coal miner. My mom was a nurse's aide, and both really encouraged me to get a job with a utility company, where there were good benefits and a great shot at just having a normal life." Instead, Artis "kind of quietly applied to colleges" by herself. Because she was a strong student, she was admitted to every college to which she applied. Her family, however, did not have any money for college. She grew up in the "Reagan eighties" (Ehrman, 2006), when Pell Grants were limited and there were few other options for paying for college. As Artis conveyed, "We were considered working poor, and because my dad worked, the penalty is I got no Pell Grant, so there was no opportunity for me to go to school, so I signed up for the military." She added, "I was on my way to the Air Force and was preparing to be sworn in, because I understood they had tuition assistance and that was going to be my ticket [to college]. Then I got a letter from West Virginia State, then College, now University, offering me a full academic scholarship, which incidentally had laid on the kitchen table for a couple of days." Artis's mother "thought it was another acceptance letter, so didn't bother to open it." Eventually her mom went through the mail and "opened up a full scholarship letter and almost had a cow."

When Artis left for West Virginia State, she still did not know what an HBCU was. She arrived on campus and thought it was odd that there were lots of Black people. "Huh? Well, this is interesting," she thought to herself. Then she started noticing that not just administrators and teachers but everybody was a person of color. Artis saw the president and the first lady and the first daughter, all of whom were people of color, and was still baffled by this. As Artis explained, "I accidentally got there and learned very quickly how special of an environment [it] was. And so, while most people say that HBCUs are places where you can be yourself, for me an HBCU was a place I learned who 'myself' was." She added, "I didn't choose it. I didn't understand how much I needed that exposure. I was listening to Bon Jovi. I had no idea."

Artis was able to experience life freely at West Virginia State, unlike her world prior to attending. As she described,

I had a whole intricate set of workarounds for how to get along with White people. Never sit with your legs extended, always sit crisscross applesauce and nobody wondered why [my] knees were darker, never jump in the pool. Always be the chick that watches the towels and the radio, cause your hair will go crazy. I had all kinds of elaborate work-arounds to help me to sort of go along and get along in the environment I found myself in, and then I get to this environment where a lot of people, most people, all people look like me, and that was pretty amazing. So, I got there accidentally, and I will never be ungrateful for that accident, that changed my whole life.

Much like David Wilson, Artis loves being the president of an HBCU and enjoys being with the students. When we asked her what she enjoyed the most about leading Benedict College, she shared the following example:

Like today I was walking into the office and a little girl was walking into the door ahead of me, and she stopped and said, smile for Chat, and held up her phone. She's like, that's the president, y'all, that's the president. While that may seem like a little thing, on a Friday after a super long week, navigating COVID, the fact that she cared to say, oh my God, that's the president. Like will you smile for my Snapchat? It is very familial, and I'm the mom, and that's awesome. My kids will be seen publicly with me, right? Isn't that what all parents want? They want their kids to be seen publicly with them, and still like them when they're adults, and so it's the familial environment and the way that I get to love these kids, as though they were my own.

Despite her love of leadership and particularly leading an HBCU, Artis did not see herself as a college president. Her plan was to be a lawyer. Growing up, she watched LA Law on TV and was inspired by the glamorous lives of the lawyers. As she tells it, "I wanted to be a sharp, smart attorney, and so once I graduated from West Virginia State, I went on to West Virginia College of Law and got a law degree, exactly on the plan. Took the bar exam, got a job with a law firm and I was living the dream. I practiced almost nine years in southern West Virginia." At that point, a friend asked her to teach a course as an adjunct instructor. Artis did not know anything about teaching. After instructing a 16-week course, however, she realized that "students are like a jury in a box, except they're not there from a subpoena. They chose to be there. They want to hear what you have to say." At the conclusion of the course, one of the students left Artis a note that said, "You changed my life." The student was studying to be a paralegal. She did not know that Black women could be lawyers. She had never met one. According to Artis,

> I was the only Black lawyer in the city, so it really shaped and shifted her trajectory, and she is now a lawyer. I remember thinking, if an hour and 15 minutes, twice a week can change somebody's life, that's pretty heavy stuff, and so I wanted more. I caught the bug. I started teaching more and more and more, and then ultimately resigned my law practice and took a full-time job at the local university and realized pretty quickly that I would need a terminal degree, so I literally stopped practicing law and went back to school at Vanderbilt to earn my doctorate in higher education, leadership, and policy.

It did not take long for Artis to realize that she wanted to be a president: "I was really, really purposeful. Once I settled into a career in higher education, I was crystal clear that I wanted to be the president." She added,

> Not because I'm a type A, bossy, got to be in charge of everything person, although those things are probably true about me. I realized that my ability to impact the trajectory of an institution, the strategic direction of an institution, was always going to be limited, no matter the role that I occupied. When I was a chair, I could only impact my department. When I was a dean, I could only impact my school. As a vice president, I could only impact my division, but the ability to globally shape the trajectory of an institution, its strategic direction, its DNA, if you will, to sort of alter the DNA of the system rests with the president and the board of trustees, and so I was clear from the first moment of full-time appointment at a higher education institution, I was going to be the president.

Artis was purposeful about seeking out opportunities to develop her skills, "to accumulate a diversity of experiences that would make [her] a competitive candidate for a presidency." She "stumbled into a career in higher education, but the second the higher education bug bit [her], [she] was dead set on being the president" at an HBCU. Artis's experience at West Virginia State as a student propelled her to pursue leadership roles and to serve her larger community, and HBCUs have benefited from this leadership.

Justice-Focused Politicians and Civil Rights Activists

Kamala Harris

Kamala Harris is the first African American, the first South Asian American, and the first woman to serve as vice president of the United States. She is also the first HBCU graduate in this role. Before becoming vice president, Harris was a US senator and the attorney general for the State of California. She was born in Oakland, California, in 1964 to college-educated parents; both her mom and dad were researchers. Influenced by their yearning for knowledge, she pursued a bachelor's in economics at Howard University.

Harris was a student at Howard in the 1980s and a child of the civil rights generation. While at the DC-based university, she encountered global movements to end apartheid in South Africa and was part of the backlash against the Reagan administration's policies (Ehrman, 2006). She was not only groomed to be an African American leader but also exposed to social activism, began to use her voice to make a difference for the larger community and nation, and learned that strength comes from community. These foci are part of the fabric of HBCUs. As Harris stated, "Howard taught me that while you will often find that you're the only one in the room who looks like you, or who has had the experiences you've had, you must remember: you are never alone. Your entire Bison family will be in that room with you, cheering you on, as you speak up and out. We're with you every step of the way" (McClay, 2021). Harris and her classmates "came to Howard with a sense of commitment to not only improve the lives of ourselves, but others as well" (McClay, 2021). They understood that they were change agents who had a seat at the table because of those who had come before them (McClay, 2021).

Attending Howard was a conscious choice for Harris. She wanted to immerse herself in Black culture and Black life. Although her mother was South Asian, she raised Harris and her sister Maya to be "strong Black women" (James, 2021). Howard was the place to embrace and cultivate her Blackness. Much like Ta-Nehisi Coates, and so many other Howard students, an appreciation of the diversity of Blackness came alive for Harris at the Yard at Howard. She hung out there regularly with her friends and loved seeing all the hair, fashion, political activity, and diversity of Blackness on the Yard.

While at Howard, Harris was active in student leadership, running for and being elected class president. According to her friend Melanie Wilcox, "She was always a leader. She used to say [being at] Howard [in] D.C. was like having your finger on the pulse of the world" (James, 2021). Much like others who attended HBCUs, Harris was nurtured and supported in her development and given the opportunity to grow as a leader—one who eventually would have a national and international impact. In her nomination acceptance speech at the Democratic National Convention in 2020, Harris thanked her "HBCU brothers and sisters" for their support and the influence they had on her life—raising HBCUs to a platform and exposure that they had not benefited from in the past (CNN, 2020).

Harris's attending an HBCU and serving as the vice president are both a testament to the power of HBCUs and a spotlight on the talent that HBCUs produce. She has raised the profile of these important institutions with her mere presence in the leadership role.

Stacey Abrams

The name Stacey Abrams invokes images of strength and justice. She has used her intellect and power to ensure that everyone in the state of Georgia and beyond has the ability and opportunity to vote and have a voice in democracy. The daughter of a librarian and a shipyard worker, Abrams attended Spelman College in Atlanta. Both of her parents were active in the civil rights movement integrating public transportation and pushing back against the disproportionate imprisonment of African Americans. The Abrams family emphasized education, and she credits the public schools for "saving" her and her siblings (Rothberg, 2021). An excellent student, she was valedictorian of her high school in Atlanta, where her parents moved to attend theological seminary at Emory University.

At Spelman College, Abrams learned to be an activist. In 1992, during her first year, she led a protest in response to the Rodney King verdict. She also cocreated a student group called Students for African American Empowerment. As part of this group, Abrams participated in a protest at the Georgia State Capitol in which the state flag, adorned with the "stars and bars" from the Confederate flag, was burned.[32]

According to Jeffrey Miller, who was a student at Morris Brown College in Atlanta while Abrams was at Spelman,

> Unfortunately the Rodney King verdict happened while we were both in school and we were both on some leadership committees at the same time. She was more fiery then. I mean, you don't understand. She was a part of this group. They went down and they burned the Confederate Georgia flag; she did not play. When I tell you she was fiery, there were some people who started a fire in the grocery store that was near Clark Atlanta [University]. And I'll never forget this. She got on the microphone. She said, "You people burned your own grocery store. That fire should have been burning down the institutions that are keeping us oppressed." I mean when I tell you people jumped up to their feet.

Miller continued, "Listen, the polished Stacey Abrams now who is still passionate and very articulate, I saw the raw form of it, and it was inspiring even then."

Abrams was quoted in the *Atlanta-Journal Constitution* talking about being an activist while a student at Spelman: "Being an activist is like having two full-time jobs." Abrams and other students received considerable backlash as a result of their activism, including threatening phone calls and police harassment. She described activism as an exhilarating but exhausting enterprise (Georgia State University Library, 1992). According to Miller, "The media were saying the radical students are burning the state flag. [But], they got permits. They had a fire extinguisher off camera. They were smart about it. They weren't some crazy students. They were very well planned, organized students who were protesting." Abrams's "fierce advocacy" also led her to serve as president of Spelman's Student Government Association.

Abrams graduated from Spelman in 1995 with an interdisciplinary bachelor's degree in political science, economics, and sociology. Upon graduation, she was named a Truman Scholar, a prestigious annual award given to public-service-oriented students. Abrams eventually earned a master's degree from the University of Texas and a law degree from Yale University. After serving as a tax attorney in Atlanta for several years, Abrams was elected to the Georgia House of Representatives and became known for her bipartisan nature—a reputation that continues today. According to Miller, now a board of trustee member at Morris Brown College, "I can't speak any higher of [Stacey] because in Georgia as a politician, she gets respect on both sides of the aisle. She helped a Republican colleague craft his bill because he couldn't get the language right. She helped him write the language and still voted against it. He said, 'Wait a minute, you helped me craft this. You're not going to vote for it?' She said, 'Oh no. I just wanted you to be able to present it, but I'm not voting for that.'" Committed to a bipartisan right to vote, in 2013, Abrams created a nonprofit called the New Georgia Project, which focuses on increasing voter registrations, especially for but not limited to people of color (McCaskill, 2020; Rothberg, 2021).

Abrams ran for governor of Georgia in 2018 and lost by just over 50,000 votes; a second bid in 2022 was also unsuccessful. She became a nationally known figure as a result of her 2018 run for office because she was the first African American woman to win the Democratic primary for governor in her state. It was during this time that her participation in the burning of the Georgia flag resurfaced, with the Republican opposition using her activism against her (D. Cole, 2018). In response to Republican criticism, Abrams issued a statement noting that her actions were part of a "permitted peaceful protest against the Confederate emblem in the flag" (D. Cole, 2018). During the race, there were ample instances of widespread voter suppression, and these activities fueled Abrams's desire to ensure that voting was available to all citizens (Rothberg, 2021). In 2018, she founded Fair Fight Action, a nonprofit that addresses voter suppression, and her work with the organization was highly influential in helping the Democratic Party win the 2020 US presidential election as well as the Georgia Senate races (Rothberg, 2021). Under Abrams's leadership, the organization registered over 800,000 voters (McCaskill, 2020). In 2020, understanding the impact of Spelman on Abrams's success and mind-set, Spelman president Mary Schmidt Campbell stated, "Whatever party we champion, we all have to agree that [Abrams] rose up 'undaunted' to fulfill the Spelman mandate to make a choice that changed the world. She changed the voting patterns of an entire state and in so doing, inspired others and helped change the country. We salute our history-making shero, Stacey Abrams, for her fearless leadership" (McCaskill, 2020). In using the word "undaunted," Campbell was alluding to the influence of Spelman College, whose school hymn states, "Beacons of heavenly light. Undaunted by the fight" (McCaskill, 2020).

Recently, HBCUs have received attention particularly for their role in producing profoundly successful and influential leaders such as Kamala Harris and Stacey Abrams. According to John Wilson, former president of Morehouse College and former director of the White House Initiative on HBCUs, "I insist that the strength that differentiates HBCUs is the way we prepare graduates for the world. Kamala Harris and Stacey Abrams have very clearly identified themselves with the corrective, transformational agenda. They cannot be mistaken for people who are passionate about conforming to the world they entered after college. They came out to reform and transform. That is an HBCU virtue. That is why Kamala is there. That is why Stacey is there. It is unmistakable."

From historian James Anderson's perspective, HBCUs have long had influence over politics and have produced leaders set on making change. "It's been that way at HBCUs for a very long time, so what would [we] be like as a nation, if they had not led this fight for democracy and social justice, equity for a long time?" He continued,

> When I went on my first civil rights demonstration, in Tuscaloosa, Alabama, I think I was a sophomore or junior and we demonstrated against a new federal courthouse that had put up Colored and White water signs. We went there to protest that and to see people who were beaten with cattle prods and so forth, when I got back to campus, one of the things that really hit me was that, so why did the students at the University of Alabama, literally a stone's throw from here, get to have a college education where they don't have to be cattle prodded. They don't have to be hit over the head with nightsticks. They can just have a wonderful time, join the organizations, go to class, go to football, whatever they like, but why now at Stillman, we've got to take on this extra burden of trying to make this nation democratic? Why does it fall disproportionately on our shoulders to be the ones?

Anderson stressed that he

> still feel[s] this way. I still feel that on the one hand, the graduates of HBCUs have taken up this mantle, taken up this burden for a long time and have fought and continue to fight for it. But that's also chewed up a lot of time and resources, fighting this battle, when we might've done things in other ways, or contributed our talents, our resources, our energies, to other sorts of things. But when you think about it, that old question, if not now, when? If not us, who? It falls, it falls in our lap continuously and I'm not saying that it's only HBCU graduates who are involved in this, but when you look back over time, they have been at the center of these fights, and they continue to be at the center of these fights. If the nation believes in democracy and thinks we must be a democratic society, they should really appreciate the HBCUs and their graduates.

Louis W. Sullivan, who served as the president of the Morehouse School of Medicine and has been on the national landscape of race relations and politics for decades (he is 90 as we are writing this book), sees Harris and Abrams as having a vast impact not only on the reputation of HBCUs but also on society and on the way that Black women are viewed by society:

> I'd say Stacey Abrams and Kamala Harris are good examples of the fact that we really historically have not utilized the full capabilities of our young people in our society by the fact that women have not historically had the kinds of opportunities that men have had. That has changed over the last few decades and continues to change, but these two people show that we have a lot of talent, a lot of wisdom that can be used to help us through difficult times, whether it's dealing with natural phenomena such as the pandemic we have now, or political issues such as the voter suppression activities that are underway in so many areas.

Likewise, Lynn Wooten, a North Carolina A&T graduate, shared with us that she thinks Harris and Abrams have made a vast impact:

> It's the intersectionality of African Americans and women [leading]. And people are starting to pay more attention to what type of institutions produce those leaders. How do we unpack those experiences? What gave them that confidence? What were the academics like? And I believe that you're going to see more women wanting to go, more people wanting to understand what HBCUs are. I've gotten more questions about what my life was like at an HBCU in the last two years than the 35+ years that I've been in leadership.

Bill Moses of the Kresge Foundation believes that HBCUs produce leaders like Harris and Abrams because of the education that they provide to their students: "I think that what HBCU leadership has shown is that you can get the very finest education available at an HBCU, and you can get an education that has a particular angle of social justice and that you can fight to change the world. I think that it's inspirational, in a wonderful way, and that they're accomplishing so much because of the experiences they had at Howard and Spelman." He added that the combination of the supportive atmosphere and the positive feedback loop that helps HBCU graduates to flourish makes a difference in the lives of HBCU students.

Making Advances in Medicine

Louis W. Sullivan

Louis W. Sullivan, a medical doctor, attended Morehouse College in Atlanta and graduated in 1954, when the stalwart leader Benjamin Elijah Mays[33] was president of the small all-Black-men's college. Sullivan is a proud alumnus of Morehouse College; he beams when he talks about the institution and its impact on his life. "I have a strong affinity for Black colleges because Morehouse graduates have really done some outstanding things, whether it's in medicine, the ministry, business, or other fields." For Sullivan, his years at Morehouse were a time of great intellectual challenge and development but also a time of personal development. He stated, "[I was] learning who I was, what I wanted to do with my life, aspiring to do something to make a difference in my life and the lives of my friends, my family, and my community. So, my experience at Morehouse College as a student really helped shape things I have done subsequently throughout my career."

Sullivan's undergraduate years were deeply influential and played a part in his willingness to lead the Morehouse School of Medicine. When he graduated from Morehouse College in 1954 (the same year as *Brown v. Board of Education*), he went to Boston University's School of Medicine. He was the only Black student in his class of 76 students. His classmates were graduates of Princeton, Columbia, Harvard, Amherst, and similarly well-resourced and well-known institutions. Most of them had not heard of Morehouse College. As Sullivan recalled, "During our orientation week, the typical exchange with one of my classmates would be, 'Well, Hi. I'm Bob Abrams. I finished Amherst and I'm pleased to be here and nice to meet you. Where did you go?' I'd say, 'I went to Morehouse.' And the response would be, 'Oh, yes, Morehead. I've heard great things about Morehead.' I'd say, 'No, not Morehead. Morehouse.'"

Sullivan was concerned about how he would do in medical school compared with all the Ivy League graduates. He wondered, "Is my preparation really going to be adequate?" He was nervous. In addition, Sullivan's parents were deeply dedicated to higher education, and so he was really carrying the expectations of his parents, his college, and his friends. He elaborated, "Because I was the only Black, I felt that I was carrying the weight of the Black community." Sullivan had his first examination three weeks after classes began, and he did very well. He then relaxed, knowing that he was well prepared. He was president of his class during his second and third years and graduated near the top of his class.

In Boston, Sullivan found himself living in a nonsegregated environment for the first time in his life. He had a wonderful experience, in contrast to the experiences that many students had in the late 1950s when Louise Hicks, a member of the Boston City Council, became famous for leading the antibusing efforts there against school integration (Formisano, 2004). In 1958, when he finished at Boston University, he went on to New York Hospital–Cornell Medical Center, where he was the hospital's first Black intern. He found himself "going through the same kind of experience" as he did at Boston University's medical school. Sullivan enjoyed his experience at New York Hospital as well and ended up going back to Boston for training in hematology at Harvard University, later becoming professor of medicine at Boston University. He developed a career in hematology research and was "very much committed to becoming chairman of the Department of Medicine by age 45." But he never fulfilled his goal.

Sullivan explained that between 1955 and 1981 there were 47 new medical schools developed in the United States. In Atlanta, Black physicians were extremely interested in this expansion. With only two Black medical schools (Howard University and Meharry Medical College) out of a total of 80 medical schools in the country, one way to increase the number of Black physicians was to develop a third Black medical school (Gasman & Sullivan, 2012). Atlanta was identified as a good place for such a school with the existing HBCUs in the Atlanta University Center.[34]

In 1974, Hugh Glouster, the then president of Morehouse College, decided that the college was interested in a Black medical school and would explore the idea. Glouster recruited Sullivan to serve on a committee made up of alumni who were in academic medical positions; they would advise Glouster on his decision. After a year of meeting and reviewing the idea, the committee felt that Morehouse College had the academic strength, the fiscal resources, and the kind of leadership needed to develop the medical school.

When Morehouse College sought to recruit a dean to create the medical school, the institution's leadership chose Sullivan. He moved back to Atlanta in July 1975 to be the founding dean of Morehouse School of Medicine. The medical program was part of Morehouse College from 1975 until 1981. And, according to Sullivan,

> the plan we developed was for the medical school to become independent from Morehouse College over time and that's what happened. So, in 1981, the Morehouse School of Medicine separated from Morehouse College. Our first class matriculated in 1978 and we started as a two-year school, but it became a four-year school in 1981. So, that is the experience I've had with Morehouse School of Medicine because I served as president until '89 when I was recruited by George H. W. Bush to be the US Secretary of Health and Human Services. I did that for four years. Then when Bush was not reelected, I was recruited back to Morehouse School of Medicine, again, to serve as president and dean and served there until 2002 when I retired.

Sullivan focused on increasing the number of Black physicians as well as women physicians in the country during his professional career. As US secretary of health and human services, he worked to put programs in place to support the training activities for more Black, Hispanic, Native American, and other minorities. He shared, "My career has been intertwined with the issue of diversity all along." As we talked with Sullivan, he was passionate about the importance of Black colleges, noting that these institutions are "a great resource for the nation that really should be strengthened, expanded and enhanced." He stressed that "it'll be good not only for the Black community, but for America at large to see that all segments of our society are well trained so we can contribute to the greater good of the broader community, whether it's in the sciences, in the arts, literature, or other aspects of our society."

Attending a Black college was profound for Sullivan, as was the leadership of Benjamin Mays. As we talked with Sullivan, he recalled the wisdom and mentoring that Mays gave to the young men at Morehouse: "Mays said, those people who find themselves behind in a race must run faster because if you do not, then you'll never catch up. But it is your responsibility to not simply stay in second place and lament that place, but to run so that you'll be in first place. He encouraged us to say we have the capability to be just as good as anyone else and therefore he challenged us to do that." Sullivan saw the Morehouse president as a charismatic figure and said that all the young men wanted to "be like Dr. Mays," which "shows you the [impact] that one person can make in the lives of many people." From Sullivan's viewpoint, "That name is no accident—Morehouse School of Medicine. I wanted the culture of the college to be carried into the culture of the medical school with all those kinds of aspirations that we would lay on our students." Much like his role model Mays, Sullivan, in his role as a president of an HBCU and beyond that role, aimed to transform the lives of those who, in turn, would transform society.

Norman C. Francis

Norman C. Francis is the former president of Xavier University of Louisiana. At the time of his retirement, he was the longest-serving university president in the country. One of five children, Francis was born in Lafayette, Louisiana, in 1931. His early education took place in Catholic schools run by Spiritan priests and Sisters of the Blessed Sacrament, at a time when American Catholic churches were segregated (Skofstad, 2019). In 1948, he received a scholarship to attend Xavier University, and in 1952, Francis became the first African American admitted to Loyola University Law School in New Orleans. After earning his law degree, Francis served in the US Army. He later decided to forgo a legal practice for a career in higher education and became dean of men at Xavier in 1957. In this role, he was instrumental in the university's decision to house the Freedom Riders on campus. The Freedom Riders were an integrated group of activists who were traveling through the South to test the Supreme Court's decision banning segregation in interstate railway and bus travel. The federal government flew the activists to New Orleans after they were threatened and attacked in Alabama (Arsenault, 2007; Mangan, 2013).

The Sisters of the Blessed Sacrament, the religious order associated with Xavier, appreciated Francis's leadership and trusted him. He quickly moved up the leadership ranks. In 1963 he became director of Student Personnel Services and one year later was promoted to assistant to the president. In 1967 Francis became executive vice president, and in 1968, at the age of 37, he was promoted to president of Xavier University. He became the first African American and the first layperson to serve in the position.[35] During Francis's 47-year tenure as president, Xavier's enrollment tripled, the endowment grew eightfold, and the university became the leading producer of African American undergraduates who complete medical school (Skofstad, 2019).

Xavier has long enjoyed a national reputation for placing the most African American students in medical schools and graduating the most African American biologists, chemists, physicists, and pharmacists, in addition to a remarkable number of African Americans completing PhDs in science and engineering (Hannah-Jones, 2015; "Xavier Is Still," 2012). Also impressive is that Xavier enrolls only about 3,500 students and produces higher numbers of Black students who apply to and then graduate from medical school than any other institution in the country, including schools such as the University of Michigan and the University of Florida and Ivy League institutions such as Harvard and Yale Universities (Hannah-Jones, 2015). What makes Xavier's accomplishments even more impressive is that most of its students are the first in their families to attend college, and more than half come from lower-income families (Gasman & Nguyen, 2019).

Considered a leader in the STEM community, Xavier has two programs that have had a significant impact on premedical education and that were developed under Francis's tenure at the institution: its peer- and instructor-led drill system and its peer-led student tutoring centers (Gasman et al., 2017). Both programs were developed for students enrolled in General Chemistry and Organic Chemistry, courses that see high attrition among Black students. The drill system monitors student progress and provides constant reinforcement of concepts and skills with two-hour drill classes once per week (Gasman et al., 2017; Gasman & Nguyen, 2019). Peer-led tutoring is an institutionalized practice at Xavier. Selected by faculty, peer tutors are available throughout the day at centers on campus, ensuring students have ample access to support.

Xavier alumni make up an amazing group of physicians, physician scientists, and other health professionals. Regina Benjamin,[36] former US surgeon general; Claude Organ Jr.,[37] surgeon, medical educator, and first African American editor of the *Archives of Surgery*; and Keith Amos,[38] acclaimed surgical oncologist, are among the ranks of Xavier physician alumni and serve as examples of the countless others who represent Francis's legacy in health sciences (M. Taylor & Thompson, 2015).

Research That Changes Lives and Perspectives

James D. Anderson

James D. Anderson is a professor and historian at the University of Illinois, Urbana-Champaign. His book *The Education of Blacks in the South, 1865–1930* transformed our understanding of HBCUs and their history, ensuring that we grappled with the role that White philanthropists, Black missionaries, and Black people played in the creation and development of Black colleges.

Anderson, who was born and raised in Utah, Alabama (about 30 miles south of Tuscaloosa), attended Stillman College as an undergraduate and has vivid memories of his time at the institution. In high school, he did not think he could attend college. In his words, "It was my senior year. . . . I was thinking about either joining the military to have some success following high school or going North and finding a job. Now, I should point out I was a valedictorian and still didn't know that I was going to college because my family couldn't afford it." Anderson's mother was a cook for a wealthy family in the town where he lived. The family gave the Andersons a place to live and paid his mother eight dollars a week. As he shared, "You can't go to college [on that money], plus I had two younger brothers that [my mother] had to take care of as well and get them to school and so there was just no money to go to college." He did not know he was going to college until the day of his high school graduation, and it came as quite a shock. Anderson was in line and was getting ready to march in the graduation ceremony. He recalled being nervous because he had to give the valedictorian address.

In those days you couldn't read it, you had to have it from memory and my homeroom teacher, Mr. Hughes, who later became Dr. Herman Hughes[39] and ended his career as a math professor at Michigan State, he came and he asked me if I would come to our homeroom, pulled me out of line. That made me very nervous, because I thought something had come up to say I couldn't graduate. So, I went to homeroom, and he says, "I want you to know that before you give your valedictorian address, they're going to announce that you have a scholarship to Stillman College, and I want you to know this, so you won't get nervous and forget the valedictorian speech." That's when I knew I was going to college, and it changed my whole life.

Anderson continued,

[Mr. Hughes] was a graduate of Stillman College and talked to the dean there about admitting me, in part, the challenge was that my high school was unaccredited by Alabama standards and so it was difficult to get into college from an unaccredited high school. We got accreditation in my senior year, so he went there, and he simply made my case to the dean, and it was a handwritten letter, me having a scholarship to go to Stillman College. It was quite a shock.

Anderson spent the summer working, and that fall he went to Stillman College, which he described as a "life-changing experience."

One of the first lessons he learned was that even though he entered Stillman College as a valedictorian, and thus assumed he was OK academically, not all valedictorians are equal. According to Anderson,

Those students who were coming out of Parker High and Allman and Birmingham, where Freeman Hrabowski [former president of the University of Maryland, Baltimore County, who attended Hampton Institute] or Condoleezza Rice [former US secretary of state who attended Miles College] attended, those students had such a high quality education and they were so advanced and it just hit me that, okay, you may be the valedictorian, but you are in the company of a lot of brilliant students and that's one of the lessons that I learned then and I've kept with me my whole career, is that some people look at HBCUs and are thinking, well, a person like me, that gets admitted to [the University of] Illinois, a person that gets admitted to an Ivy League school, that somehow we are the exceptions. They don't generalize about the quality of HBCUs. Well, I know from being in the company, in those cohorts, that there were a lot of students that were a lot smarter, brilliant and you had to work hard to keep up and so it wasn't a case that somehow, I was the exception. I was much more the rule than the exception.

He added, "When I think about the students who won all kinds of awards and whether magna cum laude or summa cum laude, these were a lot of brilliant students and late in life, when people raise questions about the pool, they will say things like can't we find qualified people? And I would just look at them and think, oh yeah, that's not going to be a problem, finding brilliant people, because I was [amid] so many brilliant students that could do anything academically." Profoundly, Anderson stated, "Sometimes people think about the friendships you make, or the nurturing or the character building, or the leadership building that happened at HBCUs, I think first and foremost about the academic brilliance that I experienced."

Anderson spent four years at Stillman and was elected president of his class during his sophomore, junior, and senior years. He had great relationships with other students and recalled that at

senior year commencement, [we had] been together for four years and all the guys were trying to say goodbye without crying, trying to say a manly goodbye, but it wasn't working. I mean, it just hit us that, oh, wow. We're about to leave and who knows when we'll see each other again. . . . It was almost like it was magical. There was me, not going to college and not even thinking I'd have a chance and within a very short time I'm at Stillman and having a wonderful freshman year and then on to sophomore, junior and senior year.

After Stillman, Anderson earned a master's degree from the University of Illinois and began his practice teaching at Marshall High School in Chicago. While pursuing his master's, he took a class with famed educational historian David Tyack. As part of the course, he had to write a term paper. During a meeting with Tyack, the historian asked him what he was going to write about. Anderson replied, "I was thinking about my own education and my high school education and inequalities and the whole Jim Crow system." He also noted how the educational system had failed Black people. Tyack responded, "Well maybe it didn't fail. Maybe it succeeded. Maybe it did what it was designed to do." At first, Anderson was puzzled, but he soon understood what Tyack meant. He thought, "What? It flipped my thinking—like someone would design a system to do what happened to us?" Tyack picked up on Anderson's shock and stated, "You need to look into that and see the extent to which it was an accident or the extent to which it was unintended, or what was actually the purpose of it?" At that point, Anderson's term paper "became an unquenchable thirst" for knowledge. He wanted to know how he ended up in a system like the one he endured. According to Anderson, "I knew growing up that my school—everything was different than across town for the White students in the same town and so I started to really delve into, it's like looking at subordination and oppression as a system by design, as opposed to an unfortunate circumstance that happened to me and kids around me and our parents." He eventually wrote his dissertation on the topic but did not follow up with a book right away.

Anderson received his PhD and went to Indiana University as a professor. There he began doing work on slave literacy. In his words,

Indiana had just gotten all the WPA [Works Progress Administration] slave narratives and that just struck my interest. So, I was going to the library, just reading the WPA slave narratives, something that I was excited about. But as I started to read those WPA slave narratives, suddenly, I started to focus on literacy within those slave narratives and was struck by the former slaves, because they took those narratives in the 1930s, talking about literacy and education and the regret and reading some of them saying that they could forgive almost everything that happened to them in slavery, but they couldn't forgive the denial of literacy.

Anderson continued,

I started to see that [education was] a very strong value within this community and I wanted to see how widespread it was and so I just got wrapped up in that. I think it's because of what I learned from the former slaves and then the narratives about literacy, about education, it brought me back to the study of education and I think about that time, I realized that I really did need to write more, to study more, to learn more and so step-by-step it led to the book.

Because of the publication of *The Education of Blacks in the South*, Anderson was asked to be an expert witness in the *Knight v. Alabama* case, regarding HBCUs and discriminatory funding and practices.[40] In this role, according to Anderson, "I really got to focus in on the history of HBCUs and the history of higher education in the southern states and the way in which it had affected the inequalities for African Americans." Despite the inequities that HBCUs have faced, Anderson is convinced that one of their greatest contributions is their production of scholars who "have made contributions in every field, science, arts, music, you name it and that's been important to the quality of the society that we live in." He added that so many of these scholars support one another and that HBCU contributions to leadership have been profound. He shared, "It is hard for me to imagine where the nation would be without the leadership that came out of HBCUs. They literally changed this nation in that long freedom struggle. People probably resonate or know about the civil rights movement, the modern civil rights movement with people like Martin Luther King coming out of Morehouse College, or Stokely Carmichael (later Kwame Ture), coming out of Howard University or Cleveland Sellers[41] out of

[Howard University]." But even before those graduates, he added, "there were leaders out of HBCUs, like Thurgood Marshall or poet Langston Hughes,[42] who were fighting for civil rights through the National Association for the Advancement of Colored People [NAACP] and other organizations and what that has meant for our nation is that there has been waves of leadership, fighting for a democratic society, in the face of authoritarianism and totalitarianism against it."

As he spoke, Anderson reminded us of the environment in which HBCUs were born and have existed for decades:

> I mean growing up in Jim Crow South, it's like this was a totalitarian society. It was not a society, either in terms of its values, or in terms of the structure of its institutions, that believed in and practiced democratic government, democratic principles. Growing up in the Black Belt of Alabama, where hardly anyone was registered to vote, the nation was very comfortable with that inequity. People were disenfranchised profoundly, and not only were the southern states comfortable with it, but the nation was also comfortable with it, because they didn't pass the Voting Rights Act [until] 1964. So, from the end of Reconstruction until that time, the nation accepted these undemocratic institutions, these undemocratic states.[43]

Anderson elaborated passionately, stating,

> They can pretend to say that they believed in democracy, or they believed in the Constitution, or they were hugging the flag, but the record shows [otherwise]. I mean there were counties in the Black Belt where no African American was registered to vote in 1960, absolutely zero and there were counties in which the percent of Whites registered to vote was above a hundred percent and no one raised a question of fraud or lack of integrity and so forth and so here comes the HBCU graduates, fighting against that.

Anderson, through his own work as a historian and through his experiences at an HBCU, demonstrates the profound impact of HBCUs on society. His intellect and contributions to our understanding of the history of African American education are unmatched.

Ibram X. Kendi

Ibram X. Kendi, a historian and an antiracist scholar, is a professor at Boston University and the director of the Boston University Center for Antiracist Research. Kendi has won numerous prestigious awards, including the National Book Award for *Stamped from the Beginning: The Definitive History of Racist Ideas in America* and a MacArthur Fellowship, or "Genius Grant" as they are commonly called. Although he is still rather young, his contributions and accolades are immense.

Born in Queens, New York, to middle-class parents, Kendi began his career as a student at Florida A&M University (FAMU) in Tallahassee, Florida. He majored in African American studies and later earned a master's degree and PhD in African American studies from Temple University. Kendi's time at FAMU was instrumental in shaping his thinking and life overall. As he recalled,

> I think that in three major ways going to an HBCU shaped my intellectual approach. I think first in going to an HBCU, you're really able, especially one like Florida A&M University, you're really able to be exposed to just the vast diversity of Black people. And so, not just diversity in terms of where people come from, skin color diversity, ethnic and national sort of diversity, but even ideological diversity. So, you're really exposed to, and I was certainly exposed to the gambit of Black thoughts, some of which I've chronicled in my work [about] fierce disagreements between Black thinkers about race and racism and even White supremacy.

He added,

> I think secondarily, I think going to an HBCU and really coming of age in Black spaces, I think you're more able to see just even the depths of anti-Blackness in Black communities that maybe some, let's say, even Black folks who come up in predominantly White spaces where sort of anti-Blackness typically always has a White face. And at HBCU you're able to see levels of anti-Blackness, just as you're able to see those Black folks who have deep and abiding pride in Black people or fighting anti-Blackness.

Kendi then shared the third way that attending an HBCU shaped his thinking (one that we mentioned in Chapter 2): "At least for me, I felt

I was able to gain a personal sense of who I was as an African American, to be exposed to that diversity of people and even diversity within Black people. And my sense of myself was derived from a larger conception of Blackness as opposed to being derived in some sort of opposition to Whiteness."

While Kendi was in graduate school at a PWI, he (much like Ruth Simmons or Lynn Wooten) benefited from the support and confidence in his ability that was nurtured at FAMU (Wagner et al., 2013). As he recalled,

> I think by my attending an HBCU, I felt that not only was I very well trained academically, but even trained sort of socially. I felt that FAMU was under attack and FAMU students were under attack. Our parties would get broken up, as an example. The institution itself became almost like a haven in which I knew that certain things were not necessarily happening to me because I was Black because everyone was pretty much Black. And so, I didn't have to almost be on guard, and I was also able to develop a very strong sense of who I was and myself. And I think because of that, when I went to graduate school, I think that prepared me for being able to better manage this sort of overwhelmingly White space.

He added, "I wasn't as concerned about what people thought about me because I knew I had a very strong sense of what I thought about myself and I hadn't been under attack during my undergraduate years, which gave me the ability to develop that. And I think that sort of helped me navigate graduate school, in my case, that much better." Kendi illustrates the Black brilliance of mind that Anderson talked of and that exists at HBCUs and that outsiders often think is an aberration rather than the norm.

In a period where Black people are faced with an onslaught of issues tied to racism and racial inequality, not to mention what seems like a constant barrage of killings of Black people at the hands of police, Kendi's work is timely. He aims to identify inequalities, including the policies that create and maintain those inequalities, and proposes correctives in six areas: criminal justice, education, economics, health, environment, and politics (O'Neal, 2017). In a recent interview, Peter Starr, dean of the College of Arts and Sciences at American University, shared why Kendi's work resonates with students of color: "For students of color and all students, being able to look to someone like Ibram Kendi, who is a model of intelligent scholarship and activism informed by deep contextual and historical understanding, is powerful. He's got a fire to make a difference in the world that I'm not sure I've ever seen in another scholar, frankly" (O'Neal, 2017). The foundation that Kendi gained at his HBCU alma mater has also given him an armor of sorts against the extreme hate and attacks he has received during political fights against antiracism, critical race theory,[44] and attempts to unearth the racist past of the United States and force citizens to confront it (Kendi, 2021).

Scientists Making a Difference

Kent Wallace

Kent Wallace is a physics professor at Fisk University in Nashville, Tennessee, and leads the Fisk Rocket Program at the historic institution. He attended Grambling State University in Grambling, Louisiana. Although he originally wanted to go to Penn State and play football, his mother said, "No, you need to go to an HBCU." So, Wallace applied to a variety of HBCUs; however, as he shared, "I wasn't academically the hottest student in the world. In fact, I was poor in math and not a whole lot of people knew it, because they just felt based on my demeanor—oh, he's just smart. It was really something that I hid from people."

His mother had a contact at Grambling, and as a result, he was accepted at the Louisiana-based college. Being from Chicago and a northerner, he was apprehensive about Louisiana. "I was kind of scared. I was like, am I going to get hung by the Ku Klux Klan?" When Wallace told his high school football coach that he was going to go to Grambling, he said, "You shouldn't go to an HBCU." According to Wallace,

> He was a White guy, Irish guy, Mr. Miller. I was like "why shouldn't I go?" He flat out said HBCUs make you racist. And never being at an HBCU, these are the things that are kind of going through my head. My

dad wasn't too crazy about it, because he went to University of Illinois, and he was like well, those are party schools. So, I kind of went in not knowing what to expect, but I wasn't hearing a ton of good things.

His mom, however, pushed him to attend Grambling, regardless of the opposition from others.

When Wallace arrived at Grambling, he was not happy. In his words,

I think I wasn't happy, not so much because it was an HBCU, but it was really the first time I was that far immersed in a Black culture, and so I wasn't sure how to socialize because the school, the high school that I went to was kind of a mixed high school, so it was just a different environment. Plus, it was rural, instead of being in a city you're just in the middle of the woods, so what's there is all you got.

As time went on, Wallace became more comfortable. "I started to get a little bit more comfortable in my skin and to be perfectly honest, as I developed my identity as an African American, which really was shaped by being at an HBCU, I started to become more comfortable with who I was."

Much like Kendi and Coates, Wallace was shaped by the diversity at an HBCU. As he relayed, "As I tell many people, HBCUs have a diversity that I think people don't understand, in terms of their staff and faculty." As an example, he noted that the way he became acclimated to math and science was through a White woman named Ms. Gamble. "She was the stereotypical southern Belle, like strong southern aristocratic accent, wore the big, what [are] those skirts that would be kind of fluffy, with the poodle on it from the 1950s." Because Wallace earned a low score on the ACT, he had to take remedial math at Grambling. He was feeling frustrated, and Ms. Gamble asked him what was wrong. Wallace replied, "These inequalities. I never get them, and I just don't think I can get them." Ms. Gamble paused for a moment and replied, "Mr. Wallace, it's really simple. All you must do is remember that the alligator takes the biggest bite." As Wallace recalled, "When she said that, for the first time in my whole life, inequalities made sense, and I couldn't understand the inequalities since fourth grade.

And it was that adulation that I experienced that made me think, well, maybe I can do this."

Eventually Wallace tested out of the remedial math classes and worked his way through physics. Although he had to retake some classes, he credits his professors with encouraging him. According to Wallace, "They weren't always the faces that you would've thought. Dr. Nadu, who is an Indian professor, took me into his research group and he was a research mentor, and then another guy that taught my upper-level physics classes, Dr. Murty." Wallace shared an exchange between himself and Dr. Murty:

> One day I was standing there, and he asked, "Why are you so sad?" I told him "I'm just struggling in these classes, and I don't know if I can make it." Dr. Murty doesn't give out sympathy compliments, and he said, "Kent, you're going to be a physics man. You're going to graduate with a physics degree." And I asked, "How can you say that?" And he said "Kent, no matter how many times I failed you, you always took the class the next semester. You never quit. And because you never quit, you're going to make this program." The fact that Dr. Murty told me I was going to graduate, he didn't give out sympathy compliments, so if he thought that, then he must be right. That was another event that kind of gave me my self-efficacy to get through.

After graduating in physics from Grambling, Wallace attended Fisk University for graduate school, eventually securing an instructor position at the institution. Twenty-three years later, and after earning a PhD, Wallace is still teaching at the Nashville-based HBCU, inspiring African American students to pursue physics degrees.

Attending HBCUs had a profound effect on Wallace. In his words, "My experience with HBCUs is that they are the reason I even exist today, because as challenged as I was in math and science, I look back and know that there's no way I would've survived at Penn State, and I'm glad my mom had that foresight to understand that." He added,

> I'm also grateful for the nurturing atmosphere of an HBCU, because their confidence [in me] affected my sense of self-efficacy, which clearly I had very little of, and it turned into the fact that not only was I

a graduate, not only a proponent, but I chose to make my career here, so that I could positively impact not only students that are really good at math and science, but also those that tend to fall through the cracks because they had poor experiences prior to even getting to college.

As a professor, Wallace thoroughly enjoys engaging students and motivating them to do their best. As he told us, "I have loved the interaction with students. It's really, really rewarding when a student might email you, or you hear through the grapevine from someone who interacted with them and said they say I would not have gotten physics if it wasn't for your class, or I just love the way that you had taught me physics." Regarding his teaching style, Wallace says that he doesn't "just teach physics." Instead, he teaches his students how to solve physics problems—which is "the issue" for the students he teaches. He shared, "The research says that when undergraduates look at physics problems, they try to find a physical representation that they've seen before and replicate that process. So, I got to find this problem. Let me find out an exact problem like it, and I'll do what I did for that problem. Whereas a professor looks at it and they find, try to identify the concept, and then they apply the appropriate, proper concept to the problem."

With his strong knowledge of both physics and education, Wallace feels that he can make a difference with students who might normally be overlooked in physics. As he explained to us, "I [feel] that one of my advantages [is] looking at physics from the education and instruction [point of view], and really using best practices and strategies to identify where students [have] issues with misconception. In many cases, it [isn't] even math. It [isn't] physics, it was their sense of self-efficacy and their scientific identity." Wallace expanded on his idea, noting, "I developed a model in my head that it doesn't matter if I throw a billion dollar curriculum at you, if you don't feel you're smart enough to solve a physics problem, you're not going to, so I really started to develop a strategy of trying to approach a student and get them to look at their scientific identity, and have the self-efficacy to do these problems." Wallace is approaching the teaching of physics exactly the way that experts recommend science be taught; unfortunately, few physics professors use this approach at PWIs (Gasman & Nguyen, 2019).

Wallace is proud to teach at Fisk University in particular. As he shared, "Remember now, the second Black [person] to get his PhD in physics, Dr. Elmer Imes,[45] founded the physics department at Fisk University. So, there's kind of a historic context of being a professor here, because I feel like it's not just the teaching at an HBCU, but I'm continuing a lineage of one of the very first people to be in the field, and that really actually means something to me."

As part of his role as a faculty member and scientist at Fisk, Wallace also leads the Fisk Rocket Team and has since 2006. That year, NASA put out a solicitation for a Student Launch Initiative, which involved the designing, building, and launching of a rocket that could travel a mile. Fisk is one of a few HBCU that competes and is up against universities that have engineering and aerospace engineering programs. Wallace lit up when talking about his work with the Rocket Team, saying,

> We've got physics, and I'm not an aerospace engineer, so there's a lot of learning on my part that I must do to impart to my students, so it's humbling, it really is. When you want to reach out and say, hey, this just isn't my area. Can you help me with this? Because you always feel like a professor at an HBCU, you also have this feeling, you have this obligation to not look weak, because you already feel like they look at you as a second-class citizen anyway. So, it takes some vulnerability to say, to reach out for help, but I've had the fortune of working with some people who've been very supportive of the Rocket Team.

Over the years, the Fisk Rocket Team has developed a powerful reputation, which has been a boon to the physics department in its recruiting of students. Wallace knows how to get students excited about science. In his words,

> The Rocket Team is an opportunity for students from any major to participate in this NASA competition, but it gives them a sense of self-efficacy, because they engage and when they show up to this competition, they're in a competition with the University of Michigan, with Georgia Tech, with Vanderbilt, with MIT, with Johns Hopkins. And so, the students really, I can tell them all day about how great they are, but it isn't until

they show up to the rocket launch that they realize that they're hanging with the big dogs. It's really been exciting to be a part of this.

He added, "The Fisk Rocket Team—it is my baby, I guess, but I'm just really proud that we've been able to exist this long." Faculty like Wallace inspire HBCU students with their presence and their enthusiasm for science. They are one of the reasons HBCUs like Fisk have a considerable track record for sending students to graduate school, especially in the sciences (Gasman & Nguyen, 2019; Wagner et al., 2013).

Trina Fletcher

Trina Fletcher is an assistant professor of engineering education at Florida International University (FIU), a Hispanic Serving Institution in Miami. She is a graduate of the University of Arkansas at Pine Bluff (UAPB), a public HBCU. Fletcher is a twin and one of three daughters of a single mother who raised them in rural Arkansas. According to Fletcher, "We came from a small town. It was predominantly White. I would say 75/25, [in the] formerly segregated South. So, you can imagine kind of culturally how it was even when we were in high school in the early 2000s." She elaborated, "People didn't talk about race a lot in school. Our families would make little comments here and there at family gatherings, but you knew that you were different."

When Fletcher was considering colleges, her counselor suggested UAPB but did not mention that it was an HBCU. They merely said, "You might like this institution." Fletcher was familiar with the HBCU because her biological father's family was from Pine Bluff. She checked out UAPB and looked at a few other HBCUs as well, and in the end she knew that she wanted to attend an HBCU. According to Fletcher, "I felt like there was a culture of community I had missed out on because of where I was raised and I wanted to take advantage of that in college."

While at UAPB, Fletcher took advantage of the various programs focused on fostering success for African American students. She was part of the inaugural class of HBCU-Undergraduate Program [UP], which is a National Science Foundation (NSF) program focused on attracting more African Americans to the sciences. Although she was not interested in the sciences at all when she arrived at UAPB, things changed quickly. As Fletcher told us, "I was at UAPB majoring in physical education because I wanted to be a coach. I had coached middle school girls while I was in high school but found out that STEM could pay a lot of money and then we had this NSF HBCU-UP program. So, I went into it, interned every summer, really enjoyed it." While she was in the HBCU-UP program, she learned a lot about graduate school. The program leaders repeatedly told the participants that the nation needed more African Americans to get PhDs in the STEM fields and in academia. Fletcher was not interested in academia—coming from a low-income family, she wanted to make money. In her words, "When you're like 19, 20, 21, you're like whatever. I'm doing this. I'm majoring in this engineering thing because I'm going to get paid some money. That was my case."

Fletcher went on to work in industry and had some experiences related to diversity and equity that persuaded her to pursue a PhD at Purdue University in West Lafayette, Indiana. Because she was an HBCU graduate, she received a five-year, fully funded fellowship called the George Washington Carver Fellowship. She chose to pursue work related to the role of HBCUs in the production of STEM graduates, noting

I'm passionate about better understanding what's happening with STEM at HBCUs. So, it's kind of full circle. My dissertation wasn't directly focused on HBCUs because of another situation. But as soon as I got this tenure-track position at FIU, I went right back to HBCUs. So, I did some work at the National Society of Black Engineers (NSBE) while I was working full-time and finishing my PhD helping and connecting with HBCUs within NSBE, but at FIU, my first big NSF grant. So, yes, it has carried on and that all started with my undergrad experience at an HBCU in a STEM program.

The NSF awarded Fletcher an early career award for her work pertaining to Black women in engineering in 2022. She is a trailblazer in terms of research related to Black women in science and Black women students at HBCUs. Fletcher is also a staunch advocate for an HBCU education and regularly talks about the life-changing impact her HBCU experience had on her. Fletcher's commitment to Black women in STEM is reflected in the focus of her early career award, which is a five-year, nearly $550,000 grant aimed at developing an asset-based longitudinal and intersectional database focused on Black women's experiences within informal and formal engineering education. Fletcher's project will be in collaboration with NSBE and will highlight the nonmonolithic state of Black women in engineering and contribute toward advancing the literature and broadening participation within STEM education and the STEM workforce.

Producing Bold Business Leaders

Rosalind Brewer

Rosalind Brewer is the CEO of Walgreens Boots Alliance. She is one of only two Black women CEOs of Fortune 500 companies in the United States currently, and one of four throughout history. She was also the chief operating officer of Starbucks and the CEO of Sam's Club before assuming the CEO role at Walgreens Boot Alliance. Brewer is regularly referred to as one of the most powerful women in the United States.

Born in Detroit, Michigan, into a family of five, Brewer is the first in her family to attend college. She attended Spelman College in Atlanta and majored in chemistry, intending to become a doctor. But she changed her mind and took a research technician position at Kimberly-Clark, eventually moving up to become president of manufacturing and operations as well as global president of the corporation. Brewer is also a graduate of both the University of Chicago and Stanford Law School. She serves or has served on the board of trustees of Amazon, Lockheed Martin, Molson Coors Brewing Company, the Westminster School, and the Carter Presidential Center, and she is chair of the board at Spelman College. She is a formidable force in business and leadership, an advocate for diversity and inclusion, and a proponent of expanding racial bias training across corporations. On being a Black woman in corporate America, Brewer has said, "You get mistaken as someone who could actually not have that top job. Sometimes you're mistaken for kitchen help. Sometimes people assume you're in the wrong place, and all I can think in the back of my head is, 'No you're in the wrong place'" (Connley, 2021).

Spelman College has had a profound and long-lasting influence on Brewer. She was a freshman in 1980 and graduated in 1984. Of her experience at the school, Brewer said, "It's a private, all-women's college based in Christianity, and you had to get to know yourself to survive in that competitive environment" (Bloomberg, 2016). Spelman College taught her how to "put her head down and get the work done." As she has noted, when she faced incredible challenges, she reflected on what she learned at Spelman. According to Brewer, as she moved up the corporate ladder, she was often given difficult tasks—ones that higher-ups hoped would be insurmountable—but she was able to overcome them because of her Spelman training and the confidence and strength she developed while at the small college (Brewer, 2018).

Trina Fletcher, mentioned earlier, noted how an HBCU contributed to Brewer's success: "I would say HBCUs create a culture, a safe space where Black people can thrive professionally. Rosalind Brewer [is an example of this thriving]. This woman went to Spelman and is now the CEO of Walgreens, was the COO of Starbucks. I think she was on the board of Amazon. You talk about a woman who had she gone to some other PWI, [may have ended up another person]. I have heard Brewer say, 'Spelman is single-handedly the biggest contributor towards my success behind the love of my parents.'" As Fletcher conveyed, Spelman has had a powerful influence on Brewer.

Brewer recognizes that Spelman challenges students to speak out, to act, and to take on major national and international issues. She also noted that Spelman women are taught to fight, not to sit back and accept what is happening to them and other Black women. Brewer also acknowledges the role that the college plays in politics and changing policy, noting its influence nationwide on the way we think and act.

Recently, Brewer founded a scholarship at Spelman that focuses on purposeful students. She wants to support students who are "on a mission." She knows that first-generation students face many challenges. As she has stated, "When they think the odds are against them, I think they're in their favor because they are fighters. Nine times out of ten these students are breaking the mold when they come to Spelman College" (Edelman, 2021). Not only is Brewer serving as an example for young Black women, but she is also doing her part to empower them and shape their future.

The Power of Shaping and Inspiring HBCU Students

Historically Black Colleges and Universities prepare students for the future, whether the next step is the workforce or graduate or professional school. The faculty and staff at HBCUs are focused on preparing students to be successful. According to Abdalla Darwish, a physics professor at Dillard University in New Orleans, "The first thing I always tell my students is here you are protected. Because you are here, we try to take care of you everywhere possible. But, once you leave Dillard University or your HBCU, you'll not be protected. You will be on your own. So, either you live these four years at a boot camp and know your basics and get your hands on training, do a great job for a great life to live, or [merely] have fun and regret it later." Darwish is responsible for nurturing and mentoring more Black women earning physics degrees than anyone in the nation (Gasman & Nguyen, 2019). In his words, at an HBCU, faculty "cannot just be a professor. You need to be a professor. You need to be a counselor. You need to be a father. You need to be a mother. You need to be everything. It's a one shop stop, as they say. You must, if you cannot be like this, you will not be able actually to advance and to make a difference in their lives." He is "100 percent committed" and this commitment shows in the graduates of Dillard's physics majors (Whack, 2017).

When working with students at Dillard, Darwish tells them that they must be the future leaders in the nation and in the sciences. As he shared, we "open the doors for our students and the rest is up to them. [We] support not just the current student, but the students who will leave and continue. [We] support them as well to go for a PhD program." He added, "I tell them, you will be the leaders of the future. If you cannot take it seriously, then you are not the leader for the future. You cannot make it. If you think you can, then you can. But if you think you can't, you are right, you can't." From Darwish's perspective, HBCUs are a different kind of safe space for students. They do not shield them; they allow them to explore and become without exposure to discrimination. As he shared, "HBCUs are kind of like a haven where you can grow [in] our community. I'm not talking about a safe place, like, okay, it's like a greenhouse, so they will not be affected by the environment. No, it's a place [that gives] them a chance, away from discrimination. A place where you remove elements of discrimination, and you try to teach them equity and inclusion."

From Aaron Walton's perspective in his role as president of Cheyney University of Pennsylvania, if not for HBCUs, a great deal of Black talent would go undiscovered and untapped, and the nation would not benefit from their contributions. When we asked him how HBCUs contribute to society, he said, "I think the exposure to talent and potential that would in many instances go untapped if students had chosen somewhere else to matriculate is one of the most important contributions that HBCUs make." He added, "HBCUs help create a pool of diverse candidates for occupations that have [been lacking] brown and Black people. So, the mere fact that HBCUs has an inventory of diverse candidates that are available for employment for engagement is a plus. If you want that level of diversity, it must be extremely intentional. Well, if you have an HBCU in your environment, it doesn't have to be as intentional because they already exist."

As reflected by those we interviewed, HBCUs are institutions where Black students become inspired to do wonderful things. Once students become alumni, they go on to make significant contributions across all sectors of society. Some of those we interviewed shared how the nurturing environments and mentoring they provided led to students earning their degrees and becoming leaders in STEM fields. They also shared that in many ways, without HBCUs, the contributions and impact of Black talent would be undiscovered. Finally, some of our interviews revealed that the faculty and staff at HBCUs have a vested interest in the success of Black students. The collective efforts of these individuals and their commitment to student success allow for the cultivation of the next generation of leaders.

5

Legacies of Mentoring

For me, the mentorship piece has been one of the most impactful aspects of my HBCU experience.
—ISAAC ADDAE, Assistant Professor, Tennessee State University

The way I was brought up with my mentors and in retrospect, I found that many of my mentors, even though they were at PWIs were products of HBCUs. They said you know; you don't pay me back. You pay it forward.
—LEAH HOLLIS, Associate Professor, Morgan State University

You know, it comes from HBCUs. The kind of mentoring that I got, I don't think people understand this about HBCUs, but when you live through it you know it.
—JAMES D. ANDERSON, Stillman College Alumnus

Notable within the Historically Black College and University community is the way these institutions cultivate a spirit of mentoring among faculty, staff, and students. More noteworthy is how students remain committed to mentoring others long after they graduate. Alumni are quick to share how their HBCU experience inspired them to give back to future generations of students. For many, this inspiration was the result of knowing that prominent alumni such as Spike Lee, Oprah Winfrey, and Thurgood Marshall attended an HBCU. More recently, a new cadre of HBCU graduates, including Stacey Abrams, Kamala Harris, Will Packer,[1] and Keisha Lance-Bottoms,[2] have created an even greater appreciation for how HBCUs produce excellence.

At HBCUs, where teaching is the focus, mentoring is expected and essential to helping students thrive personally and succeed academically. Further, because of the teaching-intensive nature of HBCUs, students often have more opportunities to engage with faculty than their peers who attend Predominantly White Institutions, thus contributing to a greater likelihood for mentoring (Gallup & USA Funds, 2015). Mentoring is important because it benefits students academically and personally while they are in college and beyond (Febus, 2021; Kendricks et al., 2013; Palmer et al., 2010; Palmer & Gasman, 2008). Mentoring equips students, regardless of their backgrounds, with the tools needed for success in the workforce and for advanced educational pursuits (Golden et al., 2017). The value of faculty mentoring is that it can help the mentees convert their talent and potential into tangible outcomes that allow for self-sufficiency and/or the preparation required to move to the next level of accomplishment (Golden et al., 2017).

Exemplary Mentoring Role Models

Understanding the culture of an HBCU means understanding that mentoring is a part of the culture (Golden et al., 2017). Those we interviewed shared how professors at their HBCUs served as influential role models who shaped the educational, professional, and personal trajectories of students. Research suggests that HBCUs provide students with faculty and staff role models, student peer role models, and alumni role models for excelling during and after college (K. C. Smith et al., 2021; G. Stewart et al., 2008). Anthony Driggers, a graduate of Howard University, shared, "I think that the faculty at HBCUs organically engage in mentoring to help students. I cannot even begin to tell you who mentored me because it just feels like that was just the norm. The expectation is high. There's a tremendous amount of love. There's a cultural understanding." He explained how mentoring is ingrained within the HBCU culture, and that in many ways it becomes natural for faculty to engage in this form of student support (Gasman, 2016; Washington Lockett et al., 2018; Shorette & Palmer, 2015).

Sierra Nance, a graduate of Winston Salem State University, was surprised by how many of the mentors she had as an undergraduate attended HBCUs. She explained how their experiences influenced her understanding of what it means to give back to HBCUs. "Some of my professors that were my greatest mentors in undergraduate, they were one of the first Black people to attend and obtain a PhD at a PWI during their time. My mentor, Dr. Morris Clarke, he was one of the few Black people to get a pharmacology degree from the University of North Carolina at the time. He also went to an HBCU for undergraduate." She added, "Most of the mentors that I had at my HBCU also are HBCU alumni, and that's part of the giveback cycle, I think, that helps keep HBCUs going and sustainable." For Nance, having mentors who themselves attended HBCUs had an impact on her educational and career choices, not to mention many of these individuals helped her develop a deep appreciation for and commitment to mentoring students.

James D. Anderson, a historian and Stillman College graduate, shared an experience regarding the care and concern faculty showed toward him as a student:

My favorite mentor out of Stillman was Haywood Strickland, who ended up being president of Wiley College. Well, Strickland had just come back from Wisconsin, out of the history department, he was not that much older than us. I mean, he was, I did not know, we were freshmen. He may have been about 26 years old, or 25 years old or something like that. And you know, what I learned from him is that you could be very smart academically and yet you did not have to give up your culture. You did not have to give up your way of life. He related to us in a very, very personal regular way and he planted the seeds for my becoming a historian.

Anderson continued,

I did not know at the time, because he taught a course on civil war and Reconstruction and gave us W. E. B. Du Bois's *Black Reconstruction* [Du Bois, 1935] to read and my thought was there is no way he expects me to read this book. This is going to be the first chapter, last chapter reading and then pretending [I read] the rest of the book. But he would not let us get away with that. He put in assignments where we had to read the whole book and give a presentation in the classroom, because he knew that we were trying to cut it short. And I did not know at the time, he gave me a Pulitzer Prize winning book to read on the destruction of the American democracy and I had to present in class.

Anderson added, "He would tell me and my classmates, 'Do not sell yourself short.' 'Don't think that because you're at Stillman, you're not the same kind of student who can do the same kind of work as students in Wisconsin, because what I'm giving you is the same thing that was given to me at Wisconsin and when you finish this course, you do this work, you can be confident that you're on a level with anybody, anywhere else in the nation.'"

Anderson recalled,

Strickland [mentored me] and wrote a recommendation letter [for me] to come to Illinois. I developed that taste [for mentoring] even before I left Stillman and I have been doing that the rest of my life and my whole career, realizing that it all begins with mentoring. There are a lot of people with talent, but some do not even know they have it and some do not even know exactly what to do with it, how to guide themselves, but Strickland was there all along, giving us advice, helping us, writing letters of recommendation.

Anderson continues to mentor students and colleagues today. As he explained to us, "It is one of the reasons I am pretty sure I am the only dean on campus that teaches [a class], but I have never stopped teaching, because it is in the classroom that you get to mentor, that you get to know students, that you get a sense of what their needs are and so I will be teaching right till the end."

Paying It Forward

Much like Anderson above, those we interviewed shared how attending an HBCU cultivated an appreciation for mentoring as well as how their mentoring experiences contributed to a commitment to mentoring others. This commitment to paying it forward was expressed by Amber Johnson, a graduate of Tougaloo College: "I don't even think of it in terms of mentoring. It's just like somebody is here, they need me, I'm here. It's a lot of what people have poured into me, it's not even a thought for me. Everything that's poured into me, if I can pour it out into somebody else, I'm doing it." A number of our interviewees mentioned the notion of "pouring into others." For example, Brittini Brown, a graduate of the University of Arkansas at Pine Bluff, is like Johnson in her view of mentoring. She stated with considerable passion,

> Not to get preachy, but you know, to whom much is given, much is required, right? I think that so much about who I am and who I am becoming, so much of the advice that I've gotten, whether it has been tough love sort of advice, or whether it's been advice that lifts you up in an inspirational sort of way, right, so much of that has been because people have taken the time to do that for me, and I think time is a thing that you can't get back once you give it away.

Brown added,

> And many people have done that to me. So many people have poured into me that it is only right that I give it back. Not only is it only right that I give it back, but it's also because I want to, because I know that without those relationships, without people looking out for me and giving me the advice that I needed, the molding, the shaping, the coaching, the yelling, I guess at some point, whatever the case may be, without all

of that, I wouldn't be able to sit in a space where I can now give people opportunities and where I can now share some of the advice that has been shared with me.

In our conversations with HBCU alumni, they discussed their desire to mentor youth and how HBCUs shaped this desire. Danielle Pleas, a graduate of Virginia State University, relayed her experience of mentoring: "We had great teachers. We had people that encouraged us to go above and beyond and to do great things, and so we wanted to provide that opportunity to come back and do the same for a new crop of kids." For HBCU graduates, mentoring youth is often their first opportunity to pay it forward. It is also commonplace for HBCU graduates to share their experiences of attending a Black college. HBCU alumni recognize that mentoring high school students provides opportunities to share their love for Black colleges and helps to recruit future generations to an HBCU (Freeman, 1999; L. Williams, 2018).

HBCU alumni we talked with highlighted how the mentoring they received inspired them to create mentoring programs for students currently attending HBCUs. For example, Sierra Nance cocreated HBCU-DAP with another HBCU alumnus. The mission of HBCU-DAP is to provide resources, mentoring, and support for HBCU students on their journey to a doctorate. Nance explained how the mentoring she received throughout her educational career shaped her mentoring efforts with HBCU-DAP: "Mentoring in general has gotten me to where I am. I could not have created HBCU-DAP without the support of one of my mentors, Edmund Graham. He is the Minority Serving Institutions coordinator at the University of Michigan, but he also went to an HBCU, and he is also in higher education, so he helped us structure HBCU-DAP and what is the appropriate way to mentor."

Nance shared with enthusiasm,

With HBCU-DAP, at this point, we primarily provide a virtual workshop for students interested in pursuing a graduate degree in STEM. As far as mentorship, our first year, we had a cohort of about 8 to 10 undergraduate students who we mentored through the virtual workshop series. So, they would attend the sessions live with us, we were doing them live at first before we switched to prerecording. We also reviewed application materials for those who were applying to that [admissions] cycle. We talked to them about the transition from an HBCU to a PWI. We do that as part of mentorship. I also do a lot of one-on-one mentorships outside of HBCU-DAP. They end up connecting because usually the students who are mentored end up joining HBCU-DAP. We also provide resources for mental health.

Nance continued, "There's a mental component to being a graduate student in these spaces that I did not actually know existed until I came to Michigan. There is a culture shock that people might not realize that you endure when you make that transition, so we try to mentally prepare them for what it looks like and how different it may be from an HBCU."

Nance's commitment to mentoring, which was fostered during her time as a student at Winston Salem State University, carried over to her work with HBCU-DAP. Her efforts are especially important in that they are helping to prepare and support Black students pursuing graduate degrees in STEM. Black students are often not provided the guidance they need in preparing for graduate school, nor are they provided the support once they are admitted into STEM graduate programs at PWIs (Garcia et al., 2021; Gibau, 2015; Griffin et al., 2018).

For HBCU graduates, who may not have the financial means to give back to their institutions during the early stages of their professional careers, contributing their time to help others is often seen as a fulfilling and welcome gesture (L. Clark et al., 2016; Hilton & McClain, 2014). Nance explained that being able to mentor students is one way to pay it forward, which could also contribute to the sustainability of HBCUs. She remarked, "I'm not necessarily positioned to give back financially as I would like, but I do give back. I mentor students. I go back to recruit. I give time when I cannot give finances. I think alumni giving back in ways that they can help and will help HBCUs be sustainable."

Similar to how Nance pays it forward by mentoring students through the HBCU-DAP program, Danielle Pleas, detailed how she and some of her former high school classmates encourage students to consider attending HBCUs, using mentoring as a recruitment approach. Pleas told us, "I currently work with students to encourage them [to attend an HBCU]. We created a mentoring program, a small mentoring program, where we provide mentoring for some of the juniors and seniors who are looking at the HBCUs that a lot of us attended for college. We try to encourage the kids to look at the opportunities that are provided at HBCUs." She added, "I feel like for me, it has come full circle a bit. Going back to the same high school, and mentoring and encouraging folks to give HBCUs a chance, because I can remember back when I graduated, the conversation was always, well, you do not want to go to an HBCU because it doesn't look like the real world, you know?" Pleas continued,

> I have friends that I went to high school with who now have children who are attending HBCUs and have reached out for help around looking for internships or looking for opportunities for graduate school. I try to be as helpful as possible, talk with their children, encourage them to continue their academic careers at HBCUs, provide them with any internship opportunities I may have or that I may know of. So, I think for me, mentorship means just being a bit of a conduit and a linkage and helping people link together and link with different organizations and opportunities.

Lynn Wooten, a North Carolina A&T State University graduate, explained that mentoring those within the community, especially "Black and brown folks," is an important aspect of her paying it forward. She shared during our interview that being able to mentor people from underrepresented backgrounds was something she learned to value as an undergraduate student and that also carried over into her time as a graduate student and faculty member. Wooten reflected,

> Every day of my life I try to pay forward what A&T gave me and usually intentionally it is mentoring everyone in my community, Black and brown folks. So, throughout when I got to Michigan and the PhD program, making sure as a teaching assistant that I really nurtured people from underrepresented backgrounds. When I went on to my first faculty

appointment in Florida and continuing throughout my career, if you look at the people whose dissertation committees I've been on when I was at Michigan, for example, two African American women with undergraduate degrees from A&T.

She added, "I want every student who touches me to be treated as good as A&T treated me and it's the way I want someone to treat my children because I truly believe that college, to be successful, takes a village."

Though some of those we interviewed did not attend an HBCU, their mentoring approach was influenced by mentors who attended an HBCU. These mentors made clear the importance of paying it forward. For example, Leah Hollis, a professor at Morgan State University, explained,

> I enjoy helping students find their pathway through. The way I was brought up with my mentors and in retrospect, I found that many of my mentors, even though they were faculty at PWIs, were products of HBCUs. They said you know, you do not pay me back. You pay it forward. And so, the mentoring that I have received over the years has brought me to some really great places. They also make sure you pay it forward. Oh, how can I thank you, Dr. Hollis? I am the one coming up behind you, that is how you do it. So, I believe in you pay it forward, just as somebody helped me through as well.

Hollis elaborated on her approach to mentoring by describing how it allows her to be creative in the guidance she provides to students. "I like the mentoring part because I see it as being creative, so somebody brings me their concern or issue and says, I am trying to get from A to B and with the mentee, so to speak, we are creating that pathway. I do not believe that I am sitting high in my toga and pouring knowledge into somebody, and they are writing on some scribe, and they scamper off and do something. I see mentoring more as participatory." Hollis continued, "I am there to respond to what their ideas and what their needs are and if by chance, they are straying into a direction that does not make sense, I help. Like you think you are going to be a history professor, but you are getting a degree in education. Well, I need to pull your coat and say you are not in the right program. So, in that sense, what I enjoy is the creative process in mentoring."

Trina Fletcher, a UAPB graduate, voiced the importance of staying connected to those you mentor over time. Fletcher explained that maintaining mentoring relationships was something she learned while an undergraduate student at UAPB: "Mentoring was fundamental for just everything for me. And it also made me value the importance of staying connected with people. For example, I did a research internship when I was at Norfolk State University and Swayley Black wrote my letter of recommendation six years later for my PhD program at Purdue University because I stayed in contact with her. UAPB taught me that. Stay connected with your mentors. Mentor up and mentor down." Fletcher recognized mentoring to be personal in nature and thus she made it a point to stay engaged with her mentors even though she had long since graduated from UAPB.

According to Lee et al. (2015), mentoring up involves empowering mentees to be active participants in their mentoring relationships by shifting the emphasis from the mentor's responsibilities in the mentor-mentee relationship to equal emphasis on the mentee's contributions. Conversely, mentoring down refers to maintaining the emphasis on the needs of the mentee. Fletcher, who is a professor at Florida International University, exemplifies mentoring up and down and shared the way she mentors down:

> There were students that I had in class who have now graduated, I still mentor them. Hey, how's it going? What jobs are you getting? Are you registered for the National Society of Black Engineers? I'm still sending the dean at UAPB emails about National Science Foundation grants. I'm emailing the vice president of research. I'm always mentoring up and down. To me, that's mentoring. And I also mentor Black and brown students at Florida International University in our college. So, I'm constantly in that space even though it looks a little bit different at FIU.

Much like Fletcher, Jeffery Miller, a Morris Brown College graduate, integrates the mentoring he learned at his alma mater into his work. Miller's occupation is that of certified relationship coach. He stated,

> I specialize in coaching men on how to be better lovers, husbands, partners, and fathers. And I've had several people from Morris Brown reach out to me that have gone through coaching services. And part of mentoring isn't just mentoring someone who's younger. It's also mentoring a peer, a man who may have been struggling with his communication style, a young lady who may have unresolved concerns about her relationship with her father. Mentoring for me has expanded a lot from younger people to people my age and a little older and I'm still able to effectively reference back to nearly every leadership lesson I learned as a drum major at Morris Brown.

For Miller, mentoring evolved from serving as a role model for those younger than him to helping others thrive through his business.

Familial Mentoring

It is widely known that HBCUs tend to provide more inclusive and supportive environments and a stronger sense of belonging for their students as compared with their PWI counterparts (Booker & Campbell-Whatley, 2018; Palmer & Gasman, 2008; K. L. Williams et al., 2022; Winkle-Wagner & McCoy, 2018). Many of those we interviewed shared stories of how the family-centered environment of their campuses contributed to their academic success and overall growth and development. They also described how the mentoring they received was familial in nature, with mentors expressing care and concern for them as a person as well as academically. This approach to mentoring is powerful due to the positive long-term outcomes for alumni after college, including increased well-being, employee engagement and more positive perceptions of their alma mater (Kendricks et al., 2013; Gallup & Strada Education Nework, 2018).

Isaac Addae, a faculty member at Tennessee State University (TSU) and graduate of both Tennessee State and Morgan State Universities, shed light on the importance of HBCU faculty serving as influential familial mentors:

> When I was at Alcorn State University, my dad's colleague, Dr. Napoleon Moses, became like my godfather. He took me under his wing, and I learned a lot from him, so much so that I call him my other dad. But he was just a faculty member who saw a young man who was talented, and he wanted to invest in me. When I got to Tennessee State University, the dean of engineering at the time, Dr. Decatur Rogers, same thing. He saw this kid who had a lot of potential, was a little bit arrogant, and took me under his wing.

Addae added, "He really shaped and molded me and helped me develop into a leader. When I got into the corporate world, I was prepared as a Black engineer because of having people like Dr. Moses and Dr. Rogers help shape and mold me."

Addae also recalled mentoring in his graduate student experience at Morgan State University:

> My dissertation chair, Dr. Christopher Masters. I mean, I cannot sing his praises enough because he taught me so much while going through that dissertation journey. And he was a big part of my being able to finish the program because while I was a PhD student, I was married, had a newborn child. I was working full-time as an engineer. I changed careers, left my program—started working at Tennessee State, and went through a divorce. And the whole time, Dr. Masters was there keeping me encouraged, keeping me focused, helping me understand, "hey, you are capable of developing great research. Just do not let all these things get in the way."

He continued, "I just think that at Black colleges, I find people that care. They just give a damn."

Addae is proud of his role as a faculty member and mentor, relaying to us: "My students often come to me and not to brag, but they come to me, and they say 'Professor Addae, you are one of the best teachers that I have had since I have been at TSU,' and they say that because they know that I care and that I want them to develop and be their best. And I think that's where Black colleges thrive." For Addae, his faculty recognized his talent and took time to invest in him. The time and attention they dedicated to mentor Addae, in addition to their caring nature, are what helped him become the engineer and leader he is today.

Trina Fletcher detailed how her mentor held her accountable:

> I just knew her as Dr. Benjamin, but this woman was number two [at UAPB]. She had her hand in everything. Looking back on it, by my senior year I was like the provost is texting me saying 'Where are you at?' My department chair, because I was in the STEM Academy . . . if I was late for class, he is on my butt. He may not be like that with every-body else, but for anybody in the STEM academy, they were on us. To me, that was mentoring, holding me responsible, teaching me time management skills, study skills and I still talk to my department chair to this day.

Fletcher's account highlights how HBCU faculty maintain elevated ex-pectations while also engaging in what is often described as a form of intrusive advising (Davis, 2015; Hadley, 2011; Sims, 2019; I. Williams et al., 2008). Intrusive advising differs from the traditional prescrip-tive and developmental models in that the faculty member or advi-sor makes the initial contact with the student (Hadley, 2011). This approach to advising can benefit students, especially those at risk, because they may not always know how to respond to unexpected occurrences. The goal of intrusive advising is to help students feel that the institution cares about them. Students who feel as though they belong at the institution tend to be more academically success-ful than those who do not feel a sense of connectedness (Hadley, 2011). In fact, according to a 2015 Gallup poll, roughly 60% of African American graduates of HBCUs commented that their professors cared about them as a person, compared with a mere 25% of African American graduates of PWIs (Seymour & Ray, 2015).

Antoine Alston, a professor at North Carolina A&T State Univer-sity, was candid in his description of the caring and holistic way he mentors students. With great enthusiasm, he told us, "You know, mentoring is so important. Mentoring involves somebody seeing something in you that you do not see in yourself and not being afraid to have that conversation with you and pushing you and saying you can do better. Mentoring has been a big part of my life. I sent 21 students on to graduate school—Black and White and Latino, 21 students to get PhDs at six different PWIs, from Purdue, Texas A&M, Michigan State, Florida, Iowa State, Mississippi State." Alston added, "My students are all over the place and I'm immensely proud of that. I have got students who are entrepreneurs, I got students who are teachers, at the US Department of Agriculture but mentoring is the biggest part of what you see at HBCUs."

Alston described all the ways in which he has helped support students outside the classroom and how he is committed to their overall well-being. Chuckling, he shared:

> That's old-school Black college right there, coming to get you out of bed, calling you, "where are you at?" or "what have you?" Or, like when I have career fairs, telling a recruiter before you come, I need you to see this student and I make sure that the students show up and they are dressed a certain way. We got them prepped, [we] drive them to the interview. Talking about mentoring, I have bought clothes. I have helped pay rent. I have helped buy books. I picked up people from the bus station and the airport. I have been to funerals. Whatever the occasion, I am not saying that to brag. I am just giving you the facts. Mentoring is more than just sitting there telling some people their class schedule. Mentoring is a holistic process of helping a student develop. That is the best way I can describe it.

Holistic mentoring, which includes supporting students' full lives beyond academics, is important in that it has a positive and long-lasting impact on college students' academic success (Crisp, 2010; Luedke, 2017; Luedke et al., 2019; McCoy et al., 2020). Alston's commitment to students is reflective of someone who believes in investing in students. For him, helping students thrive academically is only one aspect of his role as a mentor; he believes that making a difference goes beyond the four walls of a classroom and inserting himself into the lives of his students.

Mentoring can also extend well beyond the confines of an HBCU undergraduate education. Reynold Verret, president of Xavier University, shared "that a mentoring relationship normally does not end when a student graduates. There are those who were my students 20 years ago and they are still in touch sporadically in some way or other about where they are in their career or other life decisions. The notion that none of us is self-made. Mentoring taps on your shoulder and says, 'What have you been doing?' 'Where are you going?' and asks questions." Verret's description of the importance of mentoring even after students graduate, and his concern about their career and life trajectories, demonstrates the way mentoring relationships evolve over time. Much like a family, relationships at HBCUs are close, often caringly intrusive, and long term.

As shown in the experiences of HBCU graduates, not only is mentoring embedded in the culture of HBCU campuses, but the mentoring experiences of students carry over into paying it forward to others. Those we interviewed spoke with deep commitment to African American students and noted that mentoring was ingrained in them by HBCU faculty. For HBCU graduates who may not have the means to give back financially, they saw mentoring as both a form of service and a way to give back.

6

Understanding Philanthropic Support

Philanthropy and Historically Black Colleges and Universities have a complex relationship. On the one hand, without large-scale philanthropy, HBCUs would not exist as we know them. If it were not for the investments in HBCUs in the early nineteenth century by industrial philanthropists, these institutions might not have survived and educated the Black middle class that exists today (E. Anderson & Moss, 1999; J. D. Anderson, 1988; Watkins, 2001). At the same time, however, these philanthropists—including oil baron John D. Rockefeller Sr., steel magnate Andrew Carnegie, and railroad tycoon William Baldwin, among others—had ulterior motives, such as creating a semiskilled labor force for their companies. In philanthropic relationships, and in fundraising for colleges and universities, there are often trade-offs, and they can be dicey. When the topics of race and equity are introduced, the giving of money becomes even more complex (J. D. Anderson, 1988; Gasman, 2007a; Watkins, 2001).

As a result of the lack of power wielded by African Americans in the United States, often because of systemic efforts to disenfranchise

Black people, HBCUs have, for the most part, been in a position of having to ask White people, foundations, and corporations for money to support the large-scale education of Black people (J. D. Anderson, 1988; Gasman, 2007a; Watkins, 2001).[1] There have been some substantial efforts to bring together resources in support of HBCUs—the most well-known being the United Negro College Fund—but even this organization, created in 1944, was built with funds from White industrial philanthropists and only had its first African American chair of the board of trustees in 2021 (B. Adams, 2021; Gasman, 2007a). Why? Because African Americans do not have equitable access to wealth (Baradaran, 2017). In the twenty-first century, HBCUs have become more vocal, assertive, and savvy in their interactions with philanthropy. As we were writing this book, philanthropy was booming in HBCU communities, with philanthropist MacKenzie Scott bringing large-scale attention to HBCUs and motivating other philanthropists to give as well (Gasman et al., 2021).

The murder of George Floyd—shown around the world on televisions in nearly every home in 2020—was a wake-up call for many Americans, including philanthropists and those working within the foundation world. Those within the HBCU community are thrilled with the increased attention to these institutions but also nervous about whether it is a blip on the philanthropy landscape or a long-term commitment to the success of these venerable institutions. When we talked with Belle Wheelan, the president of Southern Association of Colleges and Schools, an organization that accredits all the HBCUs in the nation save a few, she shared, "I think today the perception of HBCUs is more positive than I've seen it in the 47 years I've been in higher education, if for no other reason than there's more money flowing to them right now and people only put their money where they think there's some value, you know, that will enhance it." She noted that it is time to capitalize on this attention: "I think right now is the time that [HBCUs] need to be building endowments. They need to be cultivating those deep pockets. They need to have a positive story to tell. They need to be focusing on student success activities, so that they have graduates who can then go get jobs in those companies, so that those companies will continue to support them." With a gleam in her eye, she continued,

> I think that HBCUs have the stage right now and the money that has come in from [MacKenzie Scott] and all the contributions that I call guilt money, you know, because it's in vogue to give money to people of color today. [HBCUs] need to do something with it and I tell them, I said don't use that money to go pay off all your bills. You take some of that money and you invest it so that you have it around for when times get tough, because [HBCUs are] not always going to be in the spotlight where people are going to want to continue to give them money, but you've got to have a good story to tell and those institutions that were given that large amount of money are our stronger HBCUs that potentially have a stronger story to tell but they can't just sit back on that right now. They must keep moving forward.

Robert Palmer, a graduate of Morgan State University and a faculty member at Howard University, has been studying HBCUs for nearly two decades. He agrees with Wheelan. From his perspective, he thinks that "right now we are in this period of kind of a racial reckoning, people are much more sympathetic to the plight of Black and brown people. Big donors, big corporations, people who are passionate about those issues are finding ways to give back and really help. But I think the larger question for me is what happens once we transcend this whole notion of this racial reckoning? Will those same corporations, or will other corporations give or continue to give? I don't know." Palmer believes that if HBCUs continue to tell their story and to talk about the ways in which they support and have an impact on the Black community and society at large, foundations and corporations will be much more willing to invest in HBCUs. But right now he thinks that we are in a period where people feel compelled to give because of Black Lives Matter and the murder of George Floyd. As he shared, "There's this intentionality to kind of feel a level of sympathy and people are trying to find the best way that they can to support Black and brown communities. And fortunately, they think the best way to support the

Black and brown communities is to invest in education, to invest in higher education, and HBCUs."

Michael Sorrell, president of Paul Quinn College, is "thrilled" that some HBCUs have received large donations. He is not convinced, however, that this level of support will continue or that it will move the needle in terms of changing the HBCU sector. According to Sorrell, the "investments aren't necessarily in the right place." He added, "On the surface, two million dollars sounds amazing. But if [HBCUs] have been dealing with inadequate capital investment resources for 20 years, that two million dollars is not the magic elixir. It doesn't fix the problem." According to the US Government Accountability Office (GAO, 2018; Thurgood Marshall College Fund, 2021), HBCUs have considerable deferred maintenance needs given the lack of capital investment made in them for decades. Among public HBCUs, for example, there is between $67 million and $81 million in deferred maintenance needs (GAO, 2018; Thurgood Marshall College Fund, 2021).

Sorrell believes that each HBCU needs a major benefactor who believes in the HBCU enough to donate and let the institution use the funds as the leaders deem most appropriate:

> Many higher education institutions got their footing because there was a benefactor, right? Like it was John D. Rockefeller, Cornelius Vanderbilt, right? Somebody said it's important to me that you succeed, so I'm going to stay with you, and I'm going to fund you continuously. So, what would move the needle is if the billionaire boys club, and the billionaire women's club said we're each going to pick a school, and then we are going to ride it out with that school. [Let's say if] MacKenzie Scott said, "You know what, Paul Quinn [College] is my school, and every year I'm going to make the investments necessary for Paul Quinn to have all the resources it needs to do [its work]." If [Amazon's Jeff] Bezos said, "I'm going to go invest in Spelman," right? If Bill Gates said, "I'm going to go invest in Morgan State"? If [Melinda] Gates said, "I'm going to go invest in Huston-Tillotson," right? Or let's say they pick two schools, and it's sort of like what churches do, when they tell you we need you to make the church one of your two philanthropic priorities. If they did that, that moves the needle. That changes the game.

Over the course of their history, HBCUs overall, and individual HBCUs, have received a few game-changing donations (Gasman, 2007a; Gasman & Bowman, 2010). As mentioned in Chapter 1, the Rockefeller-sponsored General Education Board donated—with strings attached—$63 million to Black colleges beginning in 1903, with the express purpose of training the formerly enslaved Black population in a semiskilled fashion (Goldberg & Shubinski, 2020). This influx of cash supported HBCUs across the nation, including many of the most well-known institutions, such as Dillard University, Spelman College, and Fisk University.

As mentioned in Chapter 1, the UNCF came to fruition in 1944, changing the way that private Black colleges raised money through consolidation. They banded together, under the leadership of Tuskegee Institute president Frederick D. Patterson, to secure large-scale funding for their entire group rather than competing with each other [Gasman, 2007a]). During the 1960s and 1970s, HBCUs saw a rise in corporate giving, especially to private institutions. These donations, however, paled in comparison with those that corporations gave to similar PWIs. White-led corporations were resistant in terms of their willingness to trust HBCU leaders with large donations owing to racist ideas about Black leadership (Gasman & Drezner, 2008).

In 1988, comedian and television sitcom actor Bill Cosby gave the largest gift ever to an HBCU—and it is still the largest gift given by an African American to an HBCU. He and his wife Camille gave $20 million to Spelman College on the eve of Johnnetta Cole's inauguration as president. Unfortunately, because of accusations against Cosby related to sexual assault, the college returned the gift in 2015. Another substantial donation to support HBCUs—albeit indirect—came from the Bill & Melinda Gates Foundation in 1999. The Gates Millennium Scholars Program, which is administered by the UNCF, has given just over $1.2 billion in scholarships to outstanding scholar leaders at colleges and universities across the nation (UNCF, 2020). Although the Gates money did not go directly to HBCUs, it helped sustain the UNCF more fully and increased its influence and longevity, which is important to the long-term viability of HBCUs overall, and especially private HBCUs.

In 2014, the Koch Brothers—David and Charles—donated $25 million to the UNCF for entrepreneurial and free-market-focused programs at HBCUs, creating the Koch Scholars Program. This donation came with controversy as the Koch brothers have long had a reputation for backing deeply conservative policies that have a negative impact on African Americans. They have supported efforts to disenfranchise Black voters through their backing of the American Legislative Exchange Council (J. Nichols, 2011).[2] In addition, the Koch brothers have given large amounts of money to the Tea Party, a Conservative fringe group, and other Far Right candidates who oppose many policies, initiatives, and laws that empower African Americans (Fenn, 2011; Gasman, 2014a).

From the beginning, with heavy support from John D. Rockefeller Jr., the UNCF has worked across party lines and has taken money from people of all political perspectives (Gasman, 2007a, 2014). It has often had little choice, given African Americans' lack of access to capital. In the 1970s, however, under the leadership of Vernon Jordan[3] and Christopher Edley Sr.,[4] the UNCF began to push back against the control that came bundled with White philanthropic support—for example, the organization needed the approval of Rockefeller's associates to write a check for more than $250. At this time, the UNCF took on a stronger position, began hiring more Black fundraisers, and launched an edgy Ad Council campaign—"A Mind Is a Terrible Thing to Waste"—that pushed back against American racism and the oppression of Black people (Gasman, 2007a, 2014). In 2017, the Thurgood Marshall College Fund (TMCF), which represents public HBCUs, also accepted a donation of $25.6 million from the Koch brothers; it, too, faced pushback by critics (Seltzer, 2017).

Another philanthropic gift, not given directly to an HBCU but one that raised the profile of HBCUs, was Robert Smith's[5] donation to Morehouse College graduates. The billionaire paid off $34 million in student loan debt for the 400 Black men graduating from the Atlanta-based institution in 2019. Smith's donation brought wide-scale attention to the large amounts of debt that Black students take on for an education as well as to HBCUs overall (Criss, 2019). Of note, African

American bachelor's degree recipients have an average of $52,000 in student loan debt. Nearly half of this debt is from student loans they take out to pursue graduate degrees upon completion of their undergraduate degrees (Hanson, 2022).

The year 2020 brought the largest influx of philanthropy to HBCUs in their history. Gifts came in from Michael Bloomberg ($100 million), Dominion Energy ($25 million), TikTok ($10 million), Google ($65 million), Netflix ($120 million), and, most prominently, MacKenzie Scott ($560 million).

Presidents of HBCUs were stunned by these donations—donations that led to more interest from foundations and corporations throughout the country. Mary Schmidt Campbell, president of Spelman College, recalled the donation from Netflix CEO Reed Hastings and his wife Patty Quillin with excitement in her voice:

> When Patty Quillin and Reed Hastings came to visit the Atlanta University Center, they walked all over the campus. They talked to students. They talked to faculty, etc. and they gave a very generous gift to Morehouse and to Spelman. Shortly after the George Floyd death, I get a call from Patty Quillin, and she says "We really feel that we need to increase our commitment. We think so highly of what you are doing, and we're going to make a commitment of $20 million."

According to Schmidt Campbell, "I fell on the floor. It's an eight-figure gift. She called back a day later and said 'we changed our mind. We're going to make it $40 million.' By now, my heart had dropped." She added,

> What impressed me profoundly is that when we did all the [publicity] for that gift, they took the stance that they were making this gift, and they gave all the reasons why Spelman and Morehouse merited it. But they said they were also making it because it was about time that White capital flowed to Black institutions. And I just thought I had never had a donor say that so emphatically who had so much influence.[6] He's a real influencer, to say that so emphatically.

Schmidt Campbell hopes that the Hastings' stance has had an influence on other corporate donors. In her words, "He put out there in the universe that we had as much merit, we were as deserving as any other college or university. That was one philanthropic gesture which I thought was extremely meaningful."

Perhaps the most stunning of all the recent donations to HBCUs are those by billionaire MacKenzie Scott, who gave $560 million to 23 HBCUs (Figure 1) as well as donations to the UNCF and TMCF (Gasman et al., 2021). The vastness of her gift and the message that accompanied it were unique and welcomed by HBCU leaders and supporters. In most cases, the Scott gifts were the largest in the histories of the HBCU recipients. What stunned most of the HBCU presidents receiving these donations was that there were no strings attached. She gave them the money and trusted the leaders to use it wisely and in a way that they saw fit. This is how Scott approaches her large-scale giving overall, which she has written about extensively in a series of *Medium* posts (Scott, 2020a, 2020b, 2021, 2022).

Scott's approach to philanthropic giving is data driven and places trust in the hands of organizational leaders. Before making her gifts, she and her team did extensive research. According to Scott, "I asked a team of advisors to help me accelerate my 2020 giving through immediate support to people suffering the economic effects of the [COVID-19] crisis. They took a data-driven approach to identify organizations with strong leadership teams and results, with special attention to those operating in communities facing high projected food insecurity, high measures of racial inequity, high local poverty rates, and low access to philanthropic capital" (Scott, 2020a).

Scott also sought the perspectives of experts across a variety of sectors in order to make informed decisions. As she writes, "The team sought suggestions and perspective from hundreds of field experts, funders, and non-profit leaders and volunteers with decades of experience. We leveraged this collective knowledge base in a collaboration that included hundreds of emails and phone interviews, and thousands of pages of data analysis on community needs, program

Institution	Amount
Alcorn State University	$25,000,000
Bowie State University	$25,000,000
Claflin University	$20,000,000
Clark Atlanta University	$15,000,000
Delaware State University	$20,000,000
Dillard University	$5,000,000
Elizabeth City State University	$15,000,000
Hampton University	$30,000,000
Howard University	$40,000,000
Lincoln University (PA)	$20,000,000
Morehouse College	$20,000,000
Morgan State University	$40,000,000
Norfolk State University	$40,000,000
North Carolina A&T State University	$45,000,000
Prairie View A&M University	$50,000,000
Spelman College	$20,000,000
Tougaloo College	$6,000,000
Tuskegee College	$20,000,000
University of Maryland Eastern Shore	$20,000,000
Virginia State University	$30,000,000
Voorhees College	$4,000,000
Winston-Salem State University	$30,000,000
Xavier University of Louisiana	$20,000,000

HBCU recipients of MacKenzie Scott donations.
Source: Scott (2020a, 2020b).

outcomes, and each non-profit's capacity to absorb and make effective use of funding" (Scott, 2020a). According to Scott, "We do this research and deeper diligence not only to identify organizations with high potential for impact, but also to pave the way for unsolicited and unexpected gifts given with full trust and no strings attached" (Scott, 2020a).

Scott gave the full amount of the donations up front, and as evidence of trust in her team's research and the HBCU recipients, she did not burden them with complicated reporting obligations: "Because our research is data-driven and rigorous, our giving process can be human and soft. Not only are non-profits chronically underfunded, they are also chronically diverted from their work by fundraising, and by burdensome reporting requirements that donors often place on them" (Scott, 2020a).

Scott's donations to HBCUs are nondiscretionary funds, so HBCUs can use them as they deem appropriate. Her approach to philanthropy provides "maximum flexibility," and she respects the strength of effective HBCU leadership: "All of these leaders and organizations have a track record of effective management and significant impact in their fields. I gave each a contribution and encouraged them to spend it on whatever they believe best serves their efforts" (Scott, 2022a). More recently, Scott has shied away from the attention she has received from her large-scale and unprecedented donations to HBCUs and has asked for the focus to be on the organizations—a nontraditional approach for a philanthropist.

When we talked to those inside the HBCU community and those who work extensively with HBCUs, they had a great deal to say about MacKenzie Scott's donations. According to Reynold Verret, president of Xavier University of Louisiana, "The MacKenzie Scott gift is a special example. There are many who are now thinking of HBCUs and learning about HBCUs and who never gave before. Even before MacKenzie Scott did her analysis, she mentioned that there is a certain return on investment that is quite phenomenal at institutions like ours." Verret also mentioned that in the past, donors would often give a small gift to HBCUs and a larger gift to nearby majority institutions. Research suggests that funders often use this approach because they do not value HBCUs in the same way that they do majority institutions, and they also do not believe that HBCUs will manage the funds appropriately (Gasman & Drezner, 2008). Verret is hoping this "old habit" has gone away. He believes that Scott "disturbed that equilibrium so that others are thinking, even some corporate sectors are realizing, that there's a sort of national need for HBCUs and that they serve in a very powerful way."

Armando Bengochea, a program officer at the Mellon Foundation who works closely with HBCUs, agrees with Verret, saying, "I think there is new attention to the whole sector of HBCUs. I think that foundations are increasingly aware, and I think there is a public awareness that there simply wasn't years ago about HBCUs. You hope it's not a fad." He added, "I don't have a critical word to say about MacKenzie Scott because she doesn't have to do anything that she's doing, and she's doing it all willingly. And she's only begun to give away her money. So, I think the other HBCUs hopefully can sit tight and hope that whoever the hell's advising her and doing the analysis continues to look at this sector."

John Wilson, former executive director of the White House Initiative on HBCUs during President Barack Obama's administration, is skeptical about the continued support by philanthropists. In his words, "Right now, I don't suspect that the indications are substantial enough to confidently declare that this will be a new era. It certainly is a moment, but I wonder, like others, that had not George Floyd been killed, would we have had this moment?" He added, "In order for this to be sustainable, then certain things have to happen in the philanthropic community and in the HBCU community." To our question of what needs to happen in order for a climate of ongoing philanthropic support of HBCUs to be created, Wilson responded, "We can make sure that we give the donors a good return on their investment. We can use the investment well enough for the donors to say, 'Hey, these other 20 did X, but you did Y. That's interesting. Let's have another conversation!' That means you just enhanced your image of being investment worthy. That has always been within the province of HBCU control."

On the other hand, Wilson also hopes that these large donations—like MacKenzie Scott's—are "contagious" in the philanthropic community. He added,

Yes, it may have been triggered by George Floyd, but it cannot be sustained by George Floyd. It should be sustained by what HBCUs do now to ensure that many philanthropists around the country and world know that HBCUs are indeed worthy of major investments. Make no mistake, I join others in appreciating those gifts a great deal. I just hope they continue, in order to help measurably close the gap between HBCUs and others. Harvard and others raise daily what some HBCUs raise in a year.[7]

David Wilson, president of Morgan State University in Baltimore, Maryland, is more optimistic about the impact of Scott's donations, with a few caveats: "I do think that the MacKenzie Scott gifts have the potential to open a fire hydrant of philanthropy and to direct it toward many HBCUs. I think for those HBCUs to be the recipient of those philanthropic investments, they must pay attention to, based on what Ms. Scott wrote in her blog, the things that she paid attention to— stability of leadership, effective management systems, a commitment to justice, equity, and equality." He added "that she has paved the way and I think it is incumbent upon us then to make the case to other potential donors of the worthiness of a place like Morgan State for other transformational gifts." Wilson, whose institution received $40 million from Scott, is already seeing change and can "enter some spaces" that were not open to him before. He also made it clear that he does not plan on spending the Scott funds. Rather, "we are interested in investing it and using the interest off the investment to enable us to support our targeted priorities in perpetuity. I hope that other HBCU colleagues who are receiving the transformational gifts don't just see it as an opportunity to spend, but they see it as an opportunity to invest, because those things don't happen every single day."

Virginia State University, where Makola Abdullah is president, received $30 million from Scott. He perceives Scott's donation as a kind of "vetting" of HBCUs:

If you were holding onto $200,000 because you were concerned about whether we'd be able to spend it okay, then MacKenzie Scott gave us $30 million. It's kind of like well, she thought we were okay to catch $30 million. Maybe it's okay if we catch a million from you or $200 grand. So, I think she changed, for many of our institutions, the ability to have that money, for her to believe that we could and should spend it wisely for the impact of our students. It really helped other donors say, "Maybe we can trust Virginia State and maybe unrestricted or less restricted is better than more restricted."

Abdullah added, "And it has helped us be able to ask. I mean, if I turn around and ask somebody for a million dollars now, they don't blink. They don't always give it to me, but they know that I've got $30 million, so I'm used to asking for real dollars. So, it really helped our fundraising game and [our ability to] go to different folks we couldn't go to before."

Abdullah also thinks that HBCUs that have received the Scott money are benefiting from the cushion that the money allows:

> It gave us the kind of cushion that has us moving differently related to finance. When we got $30 million of unrestricted money, it's like having a nice bit of savings and not having to worry about your checking account all the time. And so, the level of freedom and flexibility it's given us in terms of relieving the level of stress. Do we need to make cuts for the spring semester? It's given us some cushion to be able to prioritize, to strategize, to dream and not to worry about the smaller bumps in the road, financial bumps in the road that typically happen at an institution that, as an HBCU, we're usually right on top of all our financial challenges. It really liberated the staff to begin to think differently.

For those presidents who did not receive a donation from Scott, there were unintentional effects, such as a feeling of their institutions being labeled "unworthy." According to Roslyn Artis, president of Benedict College, the donations gave some leaders "pause." She reminded us of past predictions of a third of HBCUs dying off (something that W. E. B. Du Bois predicted long ago).[8] Artis is also concerned about what happens after the historic influx of philanthropic dollars. "The challenge is when people come back and say, 'See, I told you. We gave them all this money and their graduation rates haven't improved.' One, we're [in] the middle of a pandemic, and two, it takes time to effect change. If we could change it overnight, I can assure you I would have done it." Artis explained that "you can't change graduation rates in one or two years. It's a longitudinal process. It's an input problem." Artis worries that this concentrated focus of philanthropy, which she is grateful for and would not turn down, will result in an "I told you." She urges caution, noting that "we must begin to sensitize people as to realistic expectations."

Aaron Walton, president of Cheyney University, agrees that those institutions that received the Scott donation will be under scrutiny in terms of how they use the funds, and their use or assumed misuse will have an impact on all HBCUs. According to Walton, "It's not what you earn, it's how you use what you earn. Let's say that universities are given a ton of money. If it's not used prudently and judiciously, there's an old saying that 'water will seek its level.' It must promote and propel the university to take it to the next step. It can't be to maintain, it must be to advance because maintenance means that you are stuck in place, which means that you're not moving forward." Walton elaborated,

I think [the Scott donations] have tremendous potential to advance the universities if used properly. Some look at it as if it's the time to take the foot off the pedal because when you get an infusion of capital like that, it can be tempting to ease up, and take your focus off an area in which you need to be diligent. Right? So, it has positioned some of the HBCUs to move to the next level and I would hope that they would take full advantage of the investment that these individuals are making.

Walton feels that his institution is in the right position to receive funds from Scott and other philanthropists, but he cautioned,

I think the culture must be prepared for a MacKenzie Scott call. Money doesn't change your culture, just your financial position. You are who you are. You could have money and still be lacking in some of the qualities and attributes that you need to have. And you can be not as wealthy and have those attributes. Right? It has a lot to do with that internal makeup and who you are and what you're made of to begin with. These things are add-ons, they just add to what you already have going for you, but they're not a substitute for what you do, or don't have. But I will take the money if someone wants to give it to us. I could put it to good use.

Although Jackson State University was not a recipient of Scott's donations, Thomas Hudson, the president, is excited about the impact of the influx of money to HBCU campuses:

They are large and they're largely unrestricted, which shows the level of trust that unfortunately, a lot of people don't always have in HBCUs. She gave this amount of dollars and said I trust you to do what you need to do to make the type of impact that we want these dollars to make and that is so important, because Jackson State University, like many HBCUs, we're very dynamic. We have a lot of needs. Yes, we want to emphasize STEM. That's the way the world is going. We want to make an impact in that area. We also want to emphasize education. We want to emphasize social justice. We want to make an impact in public health, which is a big area that Jackson State University is pushing and in order to do that, you need the type of dollars that will allow you to give scholarships, to hire faculty, to support faculty in their research through release time, through reduced course loads and things like that. When you get that large amount of dollars unrestricted, it gives you the flexibility to really place those dollars where [they're] most needed and to make a real impact. That part is so important.

Hudson added, "I applaud MacKenzie Scott, and I applaud those schools that have been able to receive those philanthropic contributions, because it's going to really make a great impact on them, in accordance with their mission and what they want to do. That's something that we really need to push going forward as HBCUs, making sure when you give gifts to universities, they have the ability and the flexibility to use those gifts where they would be best suited."

While the donations from Scott and from others have been game-changing for the HBCUs receiving them, Bill Moses of the Kresge Foundation worries about the HBCUs that are not attracting the attention of this new philanthropy: "For all the good news of some HBCUs getting significant gifts, the challenge of course, is that not every HBCU has been getting those gifts, and so how do we help HBCUs [overall] flourish?" As a foundation, Moses noted, his organization is asking the question: "How do we stay strategically supportive?"

Attracting Funders and Philanthropists

To garner philanthropic funds, HBCUs must be skilled at attracting them, and that job is in the hands of the president, by and large. The most effective strategy is to tell a comprehensive and riveting story about one's institution and have a deep knowledge of institutional data (Gasman et al., 2013). We are amid what Philip Piety (2013) calls the "educational data moment," in which colleges and universities are collecting analytics on nearly everything to increase student outcomes. According to Conrad et al. (2013), "Data-driven decision-making can help institutions understand complex educational processes, collaborate with others and design programs and policies that best meet the needs of students" (p. 1). Makola Abdullah, of Virginia State University, considers himself the "number one cheerleader" for his institution, and he uses data as he cheers. As he shared, "We're beginning to have a lot more success with that now. I try to get out as often as I can and run my mouth as the number one cheerleader, as the brand ambassador for Virginia State University, whether it's social media or in person. My job is to continue to tell people how great VSU is and to explain to them all and to tell the stories of the students and how they can support the students." Abdullah includes students in donor engagements because he knows how powerful their voices are in securing funding. He told us that "when the students get into the room, it's a wrap. When they start telling their stories, it's just a wrap." Abdullah relies on the fundraising staff at Virginia State to write proposals and to set him up for success. Interestingly, Abdullah shared, the institution has received quite a few donations from people who are not connected to Virginia State; instead, "they went online and just decided that they wanted to support the institution."

Roslyn Artis, president of Benedict College, tries to convey a solid return on investment to prospective donors. She isn't "looking for a donation." In Artis's words,

> I believe in return-on-investment conversations. I'm looking for an investment, and I speak in those terms when I'm talking to potential investors, right? What are you going to get out of it? There's a business case for investing in these institutions. We are suppliers of talent. We don't produce widgets, we produce human capacity, and so if you are looking for high-quality, diverse talent, an investment in our institution is the shortest way to achieve those goals, and so we're looking for partners. We look for a mutually beneficial symbiotic relationship. We want partners to be on our advisory councils.

She added,

> If our curricula are not meeting the needs of industry, we want you to tell us that. We can take it. You need to tell me that you don't think we're heavy enough in data analytics, and we can make those curricular modifications with your support. If we don't have state-of-the-art equipment for our students to lean on, how then can they come into your places of work, ready to work on state-of-the-art equipment? So, by investing in first-rate equipment, current technology, software, etc., you ensure that your workforce is well-trained upon completion.

She reiterated that she is looking for investors and partners and that return-on-investment language tends to appeal to those "partners and friends" from whom she has realized fairly significant philanthropic investments.

Agreeing with Artis, Thomas Hudson, of Jackson State University, said that "you must show your institution as a good investment. Anyone, whether they're giving, whether they're trying to work with you through partnerships, through fundraising, in whatever context you encountered them, they are looking to see, okay, will I get a return on this investment I'm making in you? And so, showing return on investment for us is showing outputs, showing our strategic plan, showing our dedication to improving our work in certain areas."

Hudson added that he capitalizes on some of his institution's most important accomplishments by "showing the number of graduates overall and the number of first-generation students that we brought in and showing how [a donor's] contribution can not only contribute to that [success], but also enhance [it]." Hudson repeatedly asks donors (especially corporations or foundations), "How can we help you achieve your goals? If your goal is diversity, how can we work with our career services and work within the programs to help you bring the diversity that you're seeking to your organization? How can we be research partners? How can we work with you, especially when you're talking with foundations, those conversations are generally geared towards a specific challenge that they want to address." Hudson believes that success comes from demonstrating that the HBCU can be a good partner and a worthy investment.

Ruth Simmons, president of Prairie View A&M University, thinks that philanthropists will only invest in an exemplary product, not an inferior one: "The key to philanthropy is pretty simple, basically. Who wants to support an inferior product? Nobody. And so, the secret to philanthropy is not what a development office does. There's no development office good enough to raise money for an inferior institution. None. So, what does one do? The first task of fundraising is to tell the story of what you're doing well. And this is true, by the way, no matter where you are." As we were talking with Simmons, she recalled her presidency at Brown University:

> I remember when I first started at Brown, this is exactly what I said at Brown. It's not up to the development office to raise money. It's up to all of us to make the quality of what we're doing clear. And that means you've got to tell the story of the kind of research that you're doing. You have to tell the story of how you're helping students. You have to tell the story of how you're transforming lives. And our stories are powerful. And so, a lot of the money we raise comes because somebody read a story in the newspaper about something we did.

Simmons told us about one such instance while she was at Brown: "We decided that we would create a center for race and justice. And a phone call came, I'm going to give you a million dollars for that. So, the most powerful way to attract funding is by being acutely aware that, first, the underlying quality of what you're doing has to be made apparent." Simmons also stressed the importance of a communications team that can "advance stories" and share the "wonderful work that's going on." From Simmons's perspective, advancing stories "is without question the only way to raise the best kind of money."

Simmons also believes that in order to maintain philanthropic interest and sustain HBCUs, it is necessary to make strategic use of philanthropic dollars. In discussing the gifts from MacKenzie Scott, she said,

> Here's the thing. If you look across the spectrum of how people are handling their gifts, you'll see quite a variety, no doubt. In our case, I've continued to say the most important thing about what we do for our students is to improve the quality of what we're able to offer them, period. And so, we've deployed the money solely for those purposes, for more faculty, for improved financial aid, for research funds for faculty, all the core needs of the university, nothing for ancillary things.

Simmons admitted that some people on the Prairie View A&M University campus have had a hard time with her approach and that "this has been very frustrating to people because everybody has needs." When people ask, "Why couldn't I get some of that for my program?" she says

> The answer is very simple. And that is one rarely gets a gift of that kind, and when you do get a gift of that kind, you want to use it to secure the future of the institution. There's no other way to think about it. So, most of the money we put in endowment, which means that the financial aid is endowed. The faculty support is endowed and so forth. There's one portion of it that we took to support a building project because this particular program is the greatest source of visibility for the university, so that seemed like a good investment. But otherwise, it needs to be there for students to come 100 years from now, and that's something that is very important.

Simmons is convinced that strong leadership is essential for attracting funders and for the long-term sustainability of HBCUs. As she conveyed to us,

We talk a lot about strategic planning, strategic thinking, but I find that very few people do that well, actually. It's kind of a catch word. But what we should be doing in our community is thinking about the small list of things that really will get us to the next level. It is never a list of 100 things. It's always a small list. And then we should drive that to a fare-thee-well, and that is to me, this is why I go back to taking the time to mature as leaders because I actually got to watch that process in other institutions and was totally transformed by that kind of thinking.

Simmons reiterated, "And because I had a chance to see that [process] and participate in that [process] as I was coming along, I came to understand the value of being able to focus on a small number of things that could drive equality."

To have the best product, Simmons made faculty development her priority when she took on the leadership role at Prairie View A&M University. She let the campus constituents know that the faculty teaching load had to be reduced; she had to "right-size the faculty in terms of the number of tenured track faculty versus adjuncts." She also had to increase research support for faculty.

Louis Sullivan, former president of the Morehouse School of Medicine, agrees with Simmons in terms of having the best product—something for donors to invest in. As president, he presented the institution's strongest ideas to philanthropists. According to Sullivan, "We would go to philanthropists to tell them what we were doing, why it was important, and we would want them to work with us and to participate and to help support this effort and give them reasons why." He added that "you have to really be persistent in your ideas, but it was really to show a return on investment. Someone who has the resources, why should they give some of those resources to you as opposed to any of several other opportunities that they have to use those resources elsewhere? So, it was really that constant research, developing concepts and really working to really make sure that we developed a first-rate product from that investment that would be the thing that guided us." Sullivan worked with his faculty to generate powerful, "audacious ideas."

Walter Kimbrough, president of Dillard University, said his approach to garnering funding includes "trying to share as much good news about the things that are happening, because I realize, even particularly through social media, there are a lot of funders that pay attention to you." He added that "we have to keep getting out the information [related to] the creative things we're doing, and make sure that that's being covered, so when people start doing their due diligence about the institution, they start to read these things and be like, 'Oh, I didn't know about Dillard in physics or Dillard in film' and those kinds of things, and that's what gets people excited." As an example, Kimbrough stated that under his leadership, Dillard announced a "million-dollar grant from the Kellogg [Foundation] for a Center for Racial Justice." Kimbrough often uses outside evaluators to increase the validity and credibility of the work Dillard is doing. As he shared,

> We want to make sure that when they're researching, trying to figure out if this is a good investment, they see a lot of the work that we're doing. So, it's about getting that information out, I think, and I like a lot of data driven information, and particularly from outside validators. When I talk about our physics program, I'm using the data from the American Institute of Physics that compiles this, and they even did a report to talk about how we diversify physics, and Dillard is mentioned throughout that report.[9] So those are the outside validators that I can take to the [potential donors] to say people recognize the work that we're doing here, and it's good work, and it's worthy to be supported.

John Wilson, executive director of the White House Initiative on Historically Black Colleges and Universities during the Obama administration, came into his position with the intention of increasing philanthropic giving and relationships with HBCUs. He told us, "While I think it's important to maintain that core mission of optimizing federal HBCU funding, I thought we needed to do something different with the White House as a pulpit, a bully pulpit. We need to embrace the private philanthropic community and have conversations with them. So basically, I came in with my eye on the philanthropic community, trying to change that conversation." Wilson admitted that not everyone in the HBCU community liked his approach, sharing,

> I got into trouble as a result, because there are a number of HBCU presidents who told me, "Your job is to make sure Barack Obama, the first Black president, gives us about $3 billion." I said, "You know what? We can try that. I understand your desire, but if you notice when he came aboard, the economy was broken. So, pushing billions to HBCUs is going to be difficult while he's trying to fix things, or, as he said, take the car out of the ditch." At any rate, the shift my team and I were making was not always appreciated by some of the leaders in HBCUs, but I made it anyway.

For HBCUs that have gone through difficult periods, Aaron Walton, president of Cheyney University, suggests trying "friend raising" before moving to fundraising. He told us, "Coming out of corporate, I believe in return on investment. There was no way with some of the optics that existed at Cheyney that anyone was willing to make a meaningful investment until they were confident that it was going to exist. You don't invest in something that you don't think is going to exist. Right?" He continued, "Initially we've had to rely on relationships. confidence is beginning to be restored, giving us the ability to go out and ask people to support us from a financial position."

When we asked Walton about Cheyney not receiving funding from MacKenzie Scott, he said that the university "had not been in a place where perhaps we were on the radar screen for a MacKenzie Scott and some other [philanthropists]. If they did their homework and they saw some of the things that Cheyney used to be and are not aware of what Cheyney has become, it would have been a challenge [to donate to the institution]. I got a lot of questions from the alumni. 'Well, why don't we get money from MacKenzie Scott?' Walton is realistic about what is needed to attract donors, stating emphatically, "Let's take a time-out. First, we must position ourselves to be worthy of people making an investment. The first thing I'm going to say is you need to make an investment in your university. Rather than ask someone else to make an investment in your university. If someone else sees you make an investment in your university it must be worth something to someone, and maybe they will make an investment." He added, "There is no traction from individuals who want to say, just give it to me because I exist. I'm saying give it to me because I have earned it. Cheyney is earning the respect of philanthropists and foundations, and that's the only way that I want that money, is to earn it." With the increased interest in HBCUs on the part of philanthropists, corporations, and foundations, HBCU leaders have shifted their messages to one of investment in a high-quality education that is necessary for the diversification and strengthening of the nation (Baskerville, 2021).

Foundation Perspectives on HBCU Fundraising and Philanthropic Contributions

In recent years, foundations have become more interested in and supportive of HBCUs. Two foundations that have had long-term relationships with HBCUs are the Kresge Foundation in Michigan and the Mellon Foundation in New York. To understand how these foundations view and interact with HBCUs, we talked with two individuals— Bill Moses at the Kresge Foundation and Armando Bengochea at the Mellon Foundation—who have worked on numerous foundation-sponsored initiatives with HBCUs.

When Bill Moses came to the Kresge Foundation, the funder mainly supported the construction of facilities. The Kresge name is on countless buildings at colleges and universities across the nation, including some HBCUs. According to Moses, "Eventually the Kresge Board decided that we should do something for HBCUs, which resulted in an $18 million initiative to strengthen HBCU fundraising capacity." The initiative focused on Xavier University, Dillard University, Johnson C. Smith University, Bethune-Cookman University and Meharry Medical School. Although Moses had worked with HBCUs in previous professional roles, he became much more familiar with them through the HBCU Initiative: "Since then, I've had the good fortune of hiring HBCU graduates and people who have [received] training at HBCUs. So, I have a lot of confidence and faith in the quality of HBCUs and the promise of HBCUs and their graduates." When the Kresge Foundation first began working with HBCUs, according to Moses, "there was an internalized narrative that HBCUs couldn't raise money, given the lack of resources they traditionally had, and the kind of opportunities that their graduates historically had." Moses clarified, noting, "I don't want to dismiss the effect of racism on HBCUs, but I think the [Kresge HBCU] Initiative[10] showed that with the right tools, training, and support, HBCUs could raise relatively significant funds. The Kresge HBCU Initiative, which ran from about 1999 to about 2005, proved that HBCUs could be very effective in fundraising." He added, "Spelman had done it, but it was seen as maybe a lightning strike, as opposed to a generalizable trend." Moses also shared that "the other thing that the HBCU Initiative did was that many of the institutions that we supported ended up becoming much more effective, and often in some cases, changing the dynamic of who the leading HBCUs were over time. They developed the tools that allowed them to be, frankly, beneficiaries of people like MacKenzie Scott years later."

At the conclusion of the HBCU Initiative, the Kresge Foundation turned its attention toward the UNCF. "We had supported the UNCF since the 1940s," Moses said, "but in a very small way." During the 1940s, Kresge was not shoulder to shoulder with the Rockefeller philanthropies or the other, bigger, older mainstream foundations that supported the creation of the UNCF in 1944. Recently, however, the Kresge Foundation provided several million dollars to the UNCF's Institute for Capacity Building (ICB). The ICB looks at a variety of areas, such as enrollment management, but the Kresge Foundation mostly supported fundraising capacity building, and that allowed strength in fundraising to expand beyond the five institutions that the original Kresge HBCU Initiative had focused on, and to the whole UNCF system of colleges. All of UNCF's member schools benefited from the fundraising training. Moses recalled, "I think it was Claflin University that credited our support for their success, and the ICB really helped institutions build some of that fundraising muscle. It also helped to create a cadre of African American development directors, which I think was critically important, so that you had both the technical skills and the ability to raise money at HBCUs, and a growing cadre of African American fundraising professionals in the field."

Moses believes that supporting HBCUs, other Minority Serving Institutions (MSIs), and community colleges is essential because these institutions serve low-income and first-generation college students, as well as students of color (Conrad & Gasman, 2015). From his perspective,

> The challenge has been while MSIs, community colleges, HBCUs, and public institutions have the enrollment and often a mission to serve our focus students, they don't always serve them as well as we'd like them to. Spelman is amazing. Delaware State is amazing. Morehouse is amazing. Prairie View is amazing; Paul Quinn is amazing. But the issue is how do we make sure that all colleges can live up to their mission and their students' dreams? That includes things like strengthening fundraising, strengthening the board, and strengthening the back-office operations.

To attract funders, Moses thinks that HBCUs should emphasize their quality and their disproportionate impact on educating African Americans, particularly in certain fields like STEM and the professions (Gasman & Nguyen, 2019). "I think that it's important to emphasize HBCUs' role and their importance for not just the African American community, but the entire community in the cities in which they're located, and that it's important for those local donors and leaders to realize how important those local HBCUs are and not just to focus energy on the PWIs that have traditionally gotten big donors' energy and attention." Moses reminded us of a lesson he learned years ago: "If you claim you're committed to social justice, or you claim you're committed to diversity, equity and inclusion, if you claim you're committed to supporting the African American community and addressing historical wrongs and structural racism, then you should be supporting HBCUs." He continued,

I just don't have confidence that you can change highly elite institutions to become more supportive of lower-income people and students of color. Are they better than they were? Yes. We're seeing the percentage of Pell Grant students increase to above 20 percent at some highly selective institutions, which was unheard of 10 years ago, but that's not the same as HBCUs, which have Pell Grant numbers in the [high] sixties or seventies or eighties. The fact is that highly selective institutions can have cultures that can sometimes be hostile to students of color or to low-income students. They can be hostile to people who aren't, frankly, to the manor born.

According to Anthony Carnevale and Martin Van Der Werf (2017), most highly selective colleges and universities admit less than 20% of Pell Grant–eligible students, whereas MSIs and other mainly open-access institutions have percentages of Pell Grant–eligible students ranging from 45% to 90%.

When we asked Moses about the more recent influx of federal and philanthropic dollars to HBCUs, he suggested that HBCU boards and presidents

look at those resources and see them as once-in-a-lifetime opportunities to address whatever the challenges they see on their campus. Ideally, they should not treat these funds as just today's income, but really say this is special funding above and beyond ordinary income. Are there certain things HBCUs could do to strengthen the institution, whether that's upgrading facilities, upgrading faculty, better enrollment management, better outreach, or looking into partnerships with other institutions, either HBCUs or PWIs? They could use these resources to serve students, of course, or maybe strengthen their endowment. I would hope they make sure that they use that money for something that will be lasting, and that the legacy of this moment, as horrible as it has been, can be turned into something more positive.

As a foundation leader, Moses sees three issues that HBCUs need to address. First, HBCUs must ensure that their boards "are strong and capable of leading complex institutions into the twenty-first century."

Second, HBCUs must "demonstrate to potential students how valuable it is to go to an HBCU." And third, with the caveat that it might not be possible, "HBCUs [need] to figure out how to make their institutions more affordable, which is a challenge." "You know," he said, "the reason some of the most elite institutions in this country are affordable is because they have gigantic endowments that dwarf [even the Kresge Foundation's endowment]. The fact is that when you can't discount much, what seemed like a pretty good sticker price may not be a very competitive out of the showroom price, as they say in car dealerships." Moses continued,

> We see a lot of students going to HBCUs and then dropping out after a year or two. Not because they couldn't cut it academically, but because they couldn't cut it financially. So, I think that's an important thing to do, and families, they're sacrificing their mortgages and they're taking two jobs and things like that to try to get their child a degree, which attests to the commitment that [African American] families have to their children's education. At the same time, there's got to be a way to make that more sustainable. That is a challenge.

Like Moses, Armando Bengochea of the Mellon Foundation has worked with HBCUs for a considerable time, especially in his role with the Mellon Mays Undergraduate Fellowship (MMUF). The MMUF program, which encourages undergraduate students to pursue PhDs in the humanities, engages a small cadre of HBCUs among its members.[11] According to Bengochea, "The Mellon Foundation has had a very long grantmaking relationship with HBCUs, which literally goes back to the two original foundations that merged to create the Mellon Foundation, the Avalon Foundation and the Old Dominion Foundation. They were making grants to Hampton Institute. So, there's a long history."

The relationship between the Mellon Foundation and HBCUs has grown over time. Initially, the foundation worked with only a small number of private liberal arts HBCUs. Bengochea, in his position as senior program officer, convinced the foundation that they should be working with public HBCUs as well. Mellon has supported roughly 15 HBCUs as part of the MMUF program and another group through the foundation's faculty development activities. Describing the relationships that have developed between HBCUs and the foundation, Bengochea stated, "The foundation's history and certainly before I got there was much more about individual relationships with individual grantees. So, there [wasn't really] an approach to the HBCUs in which we said now we're only going to fund this." He shared that for a long time there was funding for what was called "the internationalization of the curriculum." In his words, "A lot of HBCUs found themselves feeling like, 'Hey, our students can't study abroad. They can't afford to,' and [HBCUs] don't have sufficient resources necessarily for the sort of new academic obsession with globalization." The Mellon Foundation made numerous grants that helped enable institutions to do internationalization work. Bengochea noted that "if there's any initiative at all now, it's that we're just very concerned about the provision of faculty development opportunities. We're aware that no one else in the humanities is funding faculty development at HBCU[s]." As he explained, faculty development includes "the opportunity to take international seminars together and visit one another's institutions as residential scholars or any number of other things, holding teaching and learning institutes during the summer. These are institutions that don't have pre-tenure sabbaticals and don't have any of the kind of research and teaching supports that we take for granted at wealthier institutions. They're too busy teaching. So, that's pretty much the sort of niche that we've carved out, I think, via the other funders in the sector." Bengochea added, "I think we're seeking to provide folks with an opportunity to stay in touch with their field, improve their teaching metrics, whatever it is they're telling us that is necessary at a given time."

Bengochea suggests that HBCUs can improve their engagement of foundations and individual philanthropists by forming relationships with foundation relations staff—even one individual. "There are HBCUs, even well-known ones, who every time we knock on their door about a grant, we're talking to a different individual. Often there isn't someone who is 100% dedicated to foundation relations. And having someone who gets to know us and is always pinging us and saying, hey, we've seen the Mellon Foundation's doing this and that, and I can show you why we're really the people you ought to be talking to about whatever it is, social justice outcomes—[that's important]." One of the reasons HBCUs often do not have dedicated corporate and foundation staff in their development offices is that they lack the fundraising infrastructure that most PWIs have and benefit from in terms of securing funds (Gasman, 2009).

The Future of Philanthropic Funding of HBCUs

Former Morehouse College president John Wilson has worked in fundraising most of his career—and has the personality for it. He shared with us the following:

> You must get out there. You must have the right conversations with the right people. I spent a lot of time in Silicon Valley. It used to be the case that if you were doing the right thing as a college president, you were in New York, Wall Street, the financial sector. Now it is Silicon Valley. I spent a lot of time out there getting to know people at Apple, Google, all the key places out there. I ran into only one other HBCU leader while I was out there. As a matter of fact, this person was on his way out of a meeting with Apple's Tim Cook when I was on my way into a meeting. And that was Johnny Taylor, former president of the Thurgood Marshall College Fund. I think it was maybe two months after I saw him with Tim Cook, when Apple gave a check for $40 million to the Thurgood Marshall College Fund.

He stressed that "you must get in front of the right people in the philanthropic community. It is very clear to me that in order to get in front of them, you must have a sense of confidence about the topic. You must have a sense that you are worthy to be in front of them, to have this discussion about this HBCU. I was very confident that the Morehouse brand could get me into any room in the philanthropic community, very confident about that."

Martin Lemelle, vice president of finance at Grambling State University, thinks that HBCUs must be "ready" for increased philanthropic support. More specifically, he said, "[we have] to do some internal work, so that we're prepared when the MacKenzie Scott gift happens, whether that's on the front end—[receiving a donation], positioning yourself so when the opportunity does happen, the lens is expanded outside of what traditionally may be your core powerhouse or top brand recognition HBCUs." He added, "Where we have to grow in the HBCU environment is positioning ourselves in front of those types of philanthropic organizations and persons, and then creating our internal processes to ensure that it's sustained." Being ready and exuding confidence in the education one's institution is offering are at the heart of securing philanthropic contributions.

The Power of Alumni Giving

Alumni giving is another important aspect of philanthropy to HBCUs. But because of a lack of assets among African American families, frustration with some aspects of their HBCU experience, and the absence of a culture of giving while undergraduates, many alumni of HBCUs do not give back, despite loving their alma mater (Gasman & Bowman, 2012). Over the past three decades, alumni giving has increased, but it still hovers around 12% for private HBCUs and 9% for public HBCUs (Gasman, 2021; Norwood, 2018).

Among those alumni who do give back to their alma maters, the passion for their HBCU is strong. According to Jeffrey Miller, an alumnus of Morris Brown College and a member of its board of trustees,

> Part of that passion though is giving back to Morris Brown. The house that I live in, I wouldn't have gotten [it] or the job I have, I wouldn't have gotten that. Everything that I have around my family, my children, my granddaughter, I wouldn't have any of that stuff were it not for Morris Brown. I wouldn't have met my wife at the time were it not for Morris Brown. And so, this is just part of paying back a debt that you can never repay. It's the best I can do to repay it.

Despite his passion for HBCUs and his willingness to give back, Miller is aware of the low alumni giving rates at HBCUs and regularly suggests that his classmates and all HBCU graduates should give back. As he shared, the best way to strengthen HBCUs is "to contribute to the HBCU financially because alumni participation rates at HBCUs are very, very low. Claflin is leading the way. There's a lot of room for growth at all the other HBCUs and it's all about giving." He also urges alumni to add their HBCU alma mater to their will. "Take care of your family first and if there's anything that you can leave to the HBCU, leave it. One of our prominent alumni, she left Morris Brown in her will and took care of her family, and it was quite a financial windfall that came to Morris Brown to really help us balance the books." Miller suggests that in addition to giving financially, HBCU alumni should give of their time:

> If you can contribute some type of time to your HBCU in a way that aligns with what the HBCU allows, do it. Now, don't go and try to make your own rules. Follow the established rules. Stay within the guidelines and if you can give time to your HBCU, give it because when they go away, we don't get a new one. They don't come back. And so, it's incumbent upon us as alumni to make sure we're doing more every month than we did the previous month to support our HBCUs.

Damon Williams, a Xavier University graduate who believes in giving back to his alma mater, shared, "I think we must open those wallets and give back. For those [who] are not able to give back financially, because we do know that everyone's not able to give back, even though I think we could be giving back something. Whatever your institution, the year that it was founded, if it's eight, whatever, have all the graduates give back $8, $40, whatever it is. Start the process." Williams also encourages alumni to give their time to HBCUs: "I think a lot of times that there's so much excellence in the alumni group that we could be peer mentors. We can go on campus and sit on a panel." Williams believes that giving back includes advocating for HBCUs daily in the various roles that alumni play in larger society. "We can advocate at the office. In the boardrooms, where we sit on boards. We have a place of privilege, sitting at a seat at the table. So, are we educating individuals on HBCUs? Are we educating individuals on why they were founded, why they exist, these types of things?" Williams added, "We just got to work with our schools. We got to give back, we got to give feedback when surveys come out. When we don't see that something's right, we got to be on those alumni boards. I'm not saying that it always must be negative or constructive but show the institution you're engaged. You want to add, you want to be involved, and I think it's responsible we talk about this as we elevate ourselves."

Antoine Alston, an alumnus of North Carolina A&T State University, expects alumni to give back. Chuckling, he told us, "Look, dig in your pocket and write a check. When you get out of here and you make it and after you've been out a couple of years and you made it, write a check, and pay it forward. Reach back to the school that gave [to] you." More specifically, Alston believes that HBCU graduates have an obligation to reach back and help someone else succeed:

I've said this about some folks I know, that when they got up to the top, they put an out of order sign on the elevator that says no more folks allowed on the elevator. They didn't send it back down. That's been one major issue. You must be willing to reach back to the next generation or the people behind you. So, alumni need to be able to write checks, but also be willing to come back and speak to the classes, be willing to hire these students, advocate for these students. When you get a job at that big corporation, don't be afraid to open your mouth and say, well, have you considered going back to Florida A&M or [North Carolina] A&T or Alabama State or Central State or wherever, and hiring students. Be an advocate within your organization for your alma mater. Don't get all quiet and clam up, you know? Be an advocate, speak, open your mouth. Have a little backbone about yourself. There's that old saying, don't have a wishbone where your backbone should be, okay? So, reach in your pocket, write a check sometime, advocate for your school.

He added with enthusiasm, "In other words, make yourself available to your alma mater and that's as simple as I can put it."

Historian and Stillman College graduate James Anderson is also committed to giving back to his alma mater and is doing so as a member of the board of trustees. As Anderson shared,

I'm learning to be a trustee. They invited me to be a trustee. They also inducted me into the Stillman College Hall of Fame. But I've always felt that if there is anything that I could give back to Stillman, I would not hesitate to do so. I wish I was a billionaire and could just really help Stillman in so many ways, but this was one way that I can help. I'm really honored to be in this role, but I'm also willing to roll up my sleeves and work as hard as I can to keep Stillman strong.

With a commitment to equity, Anderson added,

I think about kids from the Black Belt of Alabama, from other places in Mississippi, who sometimes have not thought about going to college, like I didn't. I didn't have a chance, but you get to Stillman, and it remakes your life and so being able to serve as a trustee and being some kind of steward of what happens, I'm really focused more on students and what happens to students at Stillman and I always wished that I could give a whole lot more than I can, in terms of time and effort and resources.

Lynn Wooten believes that she must pay forward her profound experience at North Carolina A&T State University. She knows not only that giving money to one's alma mater is essential but also that time and service make a difference. As she relayed to us, "Go back to your campus or mentor someone from your campus. Share your talent and your time in any way that you can. When [North Carolina] A&T calls, I can't say no because A&T was so good to me and so I still give back." In the same vein as Damon Williams, Wooten believes in sharing the HBCU story:

Everybody talks about treasure, talent, and time, but the other thing we forget about is testimony. Every time you see my bio, I talk about my A&T experience. I try to be a live testimony for what A&T did for me and what A&T did for others. You might not be able to give your treasure, time, or talent, but you do have connections and you have ties. Going back to testimonies and ties, sometimes I'll just say to people "Do you have A&T on your LinkedIn profile." Let's be proud. Let people know you've gone to A&T.

A long-term connection is important to Martin Lemelle, an alumnus of Grambling State University:

I'd venture to say that a lot of us are still in the process of getting to a mature state, and so being able to do [something for your alma mater] is essential, and you start to create this connection with the alumni population that leads to the offering of their talent. Alumni who want to come back and work for the institution, offering their time through volunteerism or serving on particular boards, corporate advisory boards, or institutional program boards. And then yes, getting them to ultimately invest in the institution. Alumni have expressed a lot of interest in mentorship recently and wanting to have this shadow or pilot program for students who may be interested in their fields, and so what is the apparatus to do that, because alumni are leading busy and active lives.

Lemelle acknowledged that some alumni will not give back because they had a bad experience at their HBCU: "If they have a pain point connecting with the institution, that creates a bad experience, and then we lose the opportunity to connect with them."

From Thomas Hudson's perspective as both an alumnus and president of Jackson State University, all alumni of HBCUs should "get involved with your giving, get involved with your time." He also stressed to us that lending your connections to your alma mater is essential, especially if you work for a large company. Hudson believes that everyone should give, regardless of income—even giving a small amount is important in his eyes. Research shows that if people start giving, no matter the amount, they will continue giving and will increase the amount that they give (Gasman & Bowman, 2012). As he shared, "It's not how much you give. It's not about waiting until you have enough money to start an endowment. It's that making JSU a part of your monthly bills. I'm going to start with $25 a month. I'm going to start with $10 a month."

Acknowledging that HBCUs do not have a history of instilling a culture of philanthropic giving in their students while on campus, Hudson told us,

As a young alumnus, I wasn't really taught to [give back]. It's not how much you give, it's that you're counting. We will have to do a better job of really training our alumni to understand that from day one, once you get that degree, make JSU a part of, make giving to the university just a part of your monthly giving, your monthly expenses. It can be as low as $5 a month, that gets you counted, gets you on the record. When we look for philanthropic support and foundation support, they often, without exception, want to know how much of your own alumni are giving? They look at your giving rates, even when they're vetting you and you don't realize it. They're looking at the alumni giving rates. They're looking at how much your alumni invest back into the university and that's one of the best ways to really attract that larger support.

It is important to ensure that those attending HBCUs understand that giving is essential, if not paramount, to the success of HBCUs overall. Trina Fletcher, an alumnus of the University of Arkansas at Pine Bluff, believes that HBCUs must develop a culture of philanthropy:

We have got to start talking to students about giving back to the institution while they are at the institution. [There] should be a required class [about] giving back, whether it's service, money, etc. and we need to talk about financial literacy because it's all a cycle. Our kids are not good with money. They're taking out loans they don't need, and this is a cycle. If alumni are not giving back, that is a big contributor of the long-term sustainability of our institutions so that we're not relying on government money, state funds, etc.

Walter Kimbrough, president of Dillard University, often writes about alumni giving and philanthropy. He believes it is important for HBCU alumni to give to their schools, regardless of the amount. "I keep telling people, it's not the amount, everybody's got to give and get in the habit." He reminded us, however, that the low alumni giving rates at HBCUs are complicated:

I think sometimes HBCUs are criticized a little unfairly because people will say, well, your alumni giving rates and alumni giving amount isn't what it should be. [Studies] indicate that African Americans are a very generous group, but the school is coming behind church.[12] I had a conversation with somebody who was like, look, I'm a preacher's kid, if they're active, and there are a lot of HBCU alum[ni] who are very active in their church, they tithe first, and then they give something to the school. So [if] you factor that in, I think we still do very well, but there is a broader sense of philanthropy, and it starts with the church and then the school and other things are after that.

While serving as president, Kimbrough has seen his alumni giving rate increase—hovering around 25%, which is strong. He has found ways to incentivize alumni giving. For example, "for Giving Tuesday,[13] we have a major donor who this year is doing a half a million-dollar match, and he wants us to really target new donors or people who are going to increase their donations. So, when you tell an alumnus, I can double your money off the top, people buy into that. It is easy for them to say, yes, I want to participate." Kimbrough added, "I think a lot of people say, well, I want to give back to my institution, and you know, I think it is good to do some volunteering, or I want to talk to students. It is better if you can give the student an internship that is paid for. Those kinds of things that are tangible, because it not only provides the student with the experience, but then it provides them with some financial support as well."

To increase and sustain alumni giving, Armando Bengochea of the Mellon Foundation believes that HBCUs "need to develop their donor bases and make sure that they have the most highly professionalized alumni relations and development office programs." In his words, "There was a time not so long ago when it was the moan that HBCUs were sort of behind the eight ball in terms of building those operations, that they were relying way too much on just some charismatic president." Although he knows that HBCUs lack resources to build these types of operations, he shared that he's "optimistic, especially considering other new philanthropy and the new visibility of HBCU graduates, and the new public discourse valorizing HBCUs."

To build alumni giving and his institution's alumni database, Kevin James, president of Morris Brown College, used social media. As he candidly shared,

> When I was named president, I got a million Facebook requests that day, because people wanted to know, well, who is our new leader? I started a Dr. Kevin E. James page, where I could get unlimited followers and people could watch me and I started using that page to talk to my alumni daily. And so, I use social media strategically with my alumni base because they were the ones who were giving. They were the ones who at the end of the day were the direct folk who were interested in Morris Brown not closing, because I believe everyone else had given up on Morris Brown.

James regularly posts videos detailing the state of the college, positive happenings, and his vision. Not only is he able to engage alumni, but he can quell rumors about the stability of the institution, whose situation was precarious for many years.[14]

Reynold Verret, the president of Xavier University, understands that alumni giving can be complicated and that it is tied to the wealth of African American families. "I think alumni have the capacity to give, but given that many of our alumni do not come from wealthy families, the history and capacity for giving is not there because of the lack of generational wealth." He noted that there is "new wealth," but regardless of race or ethnicity, new wealth is not as philanthropic as intergenerational wealth (Valley, 2020). Verret believes the best way "to increase alumni giving is to model how to give moderately at first, then more." He said, "We have new alumni within the first five to 10 years of graduation—they will be giving more later in life. Some older alumni do appreciate that they are leaving a legacy."

Looking for productive ways for HBCU alumni to love their institutions, Makola Abdullah, president of Virginia State University, relayed to us, "People love Virginia State. I mean, they love it. That love is real. They love, love, love Virginia State. And I know part of what happens is that they want that love to be reciprocated. They want the university to love them in a way that they love the institution, and I am not sure that we understand, well, I know that we do not always have the resources to do it." He continued,

We have to figure it out because if we do not, what we run the risk of is people who love the institution so much feeling as if the institution does not love them [back]. And now, you have a problem. And I think that is when you start getting disgruntled alum[ni]. You start getting letters. When they feel like I have all this knowledge, I have all this love for Virginia State and you are not tapping into it in a way that could benefit [the institution]. I can help Virginia State and you are not using me, and we just have not figured out a good way to do that.

For some alumni, such as historian and Florida A&M University graduate Ibram X. Kendi, what they learn during their time at an HBCU motivates them to not only give back to their alma mater but also build institutions that benefit African American people beyond HBCUs. As Kendi shared with us,

I think going to an HBCU and having and literally operating or enrolling within a Black institution in a society where Black institutions and communities have been under attack, but just being exposed to really how effective and important a Black institution can be really, I think for me, enhanced my commitment to institution building and just the role and the importance of institution building because you get that from just knowing the tradition and history of HBCUs which, of course, are some of the most important, not only Black or even antiracist institutions that have been built. So, I think that has parlayed me to consistently think about building institutions whether inside of organizations or outside.

Philanthropic giving is vital to the future of HBCUs. Without it, HBCUs cannot move forward in substantial and sustainable ways. Although individuals, corporations, and foundations tend to give most of their philanthropic contributions to PWIs, HBCUs offer a significant return on investment. They increase the socioeconomic mobility of African American students, adding to the strength of the economy. They also play an outsize and vital role in lifting and supporting African American communities (as will be discussed in Chapter 7). Yes, philanthropic gifts to wealthy PWIs assist the few low-income students who attend them, but gifts to HBCUs propel large numbers of low- and middle-income students forward and toward their career and life aspirations. As Walter Kimbrough has asked for over a decade, what would happen if, rather than giving $400 million to Harvard or Columbia, philanthropists began giving to all the HBCUs in the nation? By giving to 23 of them, MacKenzie Scott has provided an example for other philanthropists to follow (Kimbrough, 2015).

7

Building Community

I think HBCUs are not simply in a community. They are of the community. So, they reflect the communities that they serve, the families and the people in the communities around us tend to be a part of.

—ROSLYN ARTIS, President, Benedict College

I think that we do understand that as our HBCUs move, so does the community in our area. And that's why it's important that we take responsibility for that and try to build as best we can and develop the community and have more economic development on our campus.

—MAKOLA ABDULLAH, President, Virginia State University

For more than 150 years, Historically Black Colleges and Universities have been economic engines in their local and regional communities and across the nation (Gasman & Commodore, 2014; UNCF, 2018). Their impact is reflected in various economic and community development projects that fuel job growth, workforce development, and training opportunities and collectively contribute to a better quality of life for residents. More importantly, HBCUs purposefully focus on the economic development of Black communities (Bevins et al., 2021; Freeman & Cohen, 2001; Gallo & Davis, 2009; UNCF, 2018).

A 2018 UNCF report, *HBCUs Punching Above Their Weight: A State Level Analysis of Historically Black College and University Enrollment and Graduation*, highlighted two key national-level findings about HBCUs: (1) they annually generate 134,090 jobs and $14.8 billion in total economic impact for their local and regional economies, and (2) on average, their graduates each year can expect substantial earnings totaling $130 billion over their lifetimes (UNCF, 2018). Across the 21 states and territories where HBCUs are located, they provide an average of 6,385 jobs annually in each state and generate an average of $704.7 million in total economic impact (UNCF, 2018). Additionally, many HBCUs are in regions of the country where overall economic activity has been lagging, making the colleges' economic contributions to those communities even more essential (UNCF, 2017). Each dollar spent on, or by, an HBCU and its students has important "ripple effects" across a much larger area. That means heightened economic activity, more jobs, stronger growth, and stronger communities (UNCF, 2017). The impact of HBCUs can be realized through the contributions they make to empower communities through their cultural, civic, and intellectual engagement efforts (Freeman & Cohen, 2001; Gasman et al., 2015; McMickens, 2012; M. P. Smith, 2017).

To better understand the role HBCUs have in community and economic development, it is necessary to describe the complementary nature of these terms. Community development is taking collective action, and the result of that action can be in any or all realms: physical, environmental, cultural, social, political, economic, and so on (Phillips & Pittman, 2009). In contrast, economic development is the intentional practice of improving a community's economic well-being and quality of life. It includes a broad range of activities to attract, create, and retain jobs and to foster a resilient, pro-growth tax base and an inclusive economy. The practice of economic development consists of a collaborative effort among industry, government, and various community stakeholders (International Economic Development Council, n.d.). Definitions of community and economic development are clearly parallel: community development produces assets for improving the quality of life and business climate, while economic development mobilizes these assets to realize benefits for the community (Pittman et al., 2009).

HBCUs as Anchor Institutions

Anchor institutions have a significant infrastructure investment in a specific community, which makes them unlikely to move (Fulbright-Anderson et al., 2001). H. L. Taylor and Luter (2013) refer to anchor institutions as those entities that have four distinguishing characteristics: (1) spatial immobility, (2) corporate status, (3) size, and (4) the anchor mission (social purpose, democracy, and justice). Universities are often referred to as anchor institutions because they, "by reason of mission, invested capital, or relationships to customers or employees, are geographically tied to a certain location" (Webber & Karlström, 2009, p. 4). As such, they have a strong economic interest in the health of their surrounding communities. HBCUs have been anchor institutions in their communities long before the term became trendy. Roslyn Artis, president of Benedict College, conveyed poignantly the significance of HBCUs to local communities: "HBCUs serve their communities, by understanding that they must be engines of economic growth and prosperity, and they must oftentimes get out there and lead in such a way that they are hearing the voices of the community and they are understanding. I do think HBCUs do this better than any [other university]." As an example, under its previous president, Benedict College was aggressive in terms of community development. The college has a community development corporation, and affordable housing has been part of Benedict's story with the institution buying up dilapidated properties, clearing the area, and building housing for families.

Martin Lemelle, executive vice president and chief operating officer of Grambling State University, emphasized the value of a strong partnership between a community and its university:

> You know that the town-gown relationship is very important, particularly for Grambling, when the city's population is really based on the university. So, without the university's impact here, economic development in Grambling really comes to a halt, and so they must be great partners. We must think about the needs, whether it's campus policing and the community orientation aspect, public health, when we started the crisis intervention plans for COVID-19, we had to think about our student population obviously, but also the impact it would have on our more senior community in Grambling, and so those conversations must be active. They must be connected.

He continued,

> Certainly, there's the talent aspect of having team members relocate here and recruiting them to be a part of the city and the parish and the greater Grambling-Rustin community. And then if you think about metropolitan areas, like a Morgan State in Baltimore and how that development and infusing what talent looks like for the city of Baltimore, with a population of African Americans often, who are underserved and lacking some opportunity, what does Morgan represent as a beacon for young Black and brown kids growing up in Baltimore? There's so much beauty to having a university and understanding its context within a city or a town.

Referencing the economic contributions of HBCUs within local communities, Isaac Addae, a graduate of Tennessee State University, stated,

> Most, if not all, Black colleges are embedded in a Black community and the institutions have a significant economic impact. One, through employment. People from the local community, faculty, and staff are employed at the institution. That is a huge factor in terms of the local economy. And then once the students are on campus, they are spending their money in that local community as well. So, businesses benefit

from student spending. That's another level of economic impact. And then, of course, things like homecoming and football games and whenever people travel to campus for events, there's that spillover effect on the local community. So, to me, Black colleges are the lifeblood of the community that they sit in.

David Wilson, president of Morgan State University, shared his commitment to ensuring that the local community experienced economic growth and prosperity at the same time his institution was thriving. Because the university anchors the community in economic prosperity, he explained to us,

> HBCUs understand that as they rise, communities around their campuses must rise with them, or else they become, if you will, a kind of island. And so here at Morgan, when I arrived, we paid a lot of attention to the neighborhoods that abut the campus and what has happened? Why aren't there shops and restaurants and amenities in this area? This is a desert and so as you know, I have been successful, going to Annapolis and getting $90 million for this building, $90 million for this building, $120 for this one and $140 for this one and all of these new facilities arising on the campus, and we are transforming ourselves from a capital perspective.

Wilson continued, "During my 11-year presidency now, we have just eclipsed $1 billion in capital investments here. I would say you would not find another HBCU in the country that is even close to that. Who knows, maybe [North Carolina A&T], I know what we have here, and we have no deserts. So then, we had to make sure that we were bringing our communities along with us."[1] The work that Wilson and others are doing to enhance the economic impact of HBCUs in local communities—and beyond—takes time and only works if the HBCU listens to those in the community. As Wilson shared his approach, he spoke with a deep love for the Baltimore community that surrounds Morgan State:

> It has taken me eight years to make sure that the community's voice was heard in a major economic development project. The campus will anchor a supermarket, shops and restaurants, eateries, and amenities that

this community has not seen in 60 years. HBCUs serve their communities by understanding that they must be engines of economic growth and prosperity and they must get out there and lead in that but lead in such a way that they are hearing the voices of the community and they are understanding, and I do think HBCUs do this better.

Producing local business owners is one way that HBCUs have made a significant economic impact in their communities. As Jeffrey Miller, graduate of Morris Brown College, explains, "Several of my peers who got to Morris Brown in 1988 are business owners now. They have been working on their business plans since they got to school. Some of them are on their fifth iteration of a business, having built the businesses and sold the businesses several times over. And so, really putting people together so they can maximize their potential, that is something else that HBCUs do."

For those we interviewed, it was clear that the HBCU and the local community should have a reciprocal relationship. The extent to which the economic needs of the local community are met hinges on how HBCUs invest time in engaging residents in various aspects of decision-making processes and economic growth.

Contributions as Land-Grant Institutions

As we conducted the research for this book, it was interesting to hear accounts from those who had close affiliations with or led Black Land Grant universities, also known as 1890 institutions. These individuals described how community engagement manifests itself through the land-grant mission of the institution. For example, Harold Martin, chancellor at North Carolina A&T State University, described the role of his institution in meeting the needs of the region and state:

We have an incredible partnership with almost every business sector of Greensboro, and the county we are in and region we serve. We are fortunate to be a land-grant institution. We were created with the expectation that we would understand the needs of our region, our business needs of our state, and we would create and foster academic programs and research and outreach driven to meet those needs and serve those needs through the role of our faculty and our staff and our students as well.

For Martin, being a land-grant institution means you have an obligation to focus outwardly on the needs of local, state, and regional stakeholders.

Others we talked with also expressed how the land-grant mission helps to foster a deep commitment to community engagement. Alton Thompson, executive director for the Association of 1890 Research Directors, stated, "The 1890 Land Grant Universities that I worked for have a formalized extension program, outreach, and engagement program as part of their federal mission. I think through outreach, education, and community involvement, the 1890s have been particularly sensitive to the needs of community residents." He continued, "And typically, when I was dean of agriculture, I really got to be involved with the North Carolina Extension Service both in North Carolina as well as the South as well as the Midwest. And the community, the extension service, also has advisory groups. And those advisory groups consist of community leaders. I really got to know the people in the community that we serve and as we design programs for these areas; the people in the community are involved in designing programs." Thompson considers the role that extension, outreach, and engagement play in the land-grant mission to be at the heart of community engagement efforts, especially as it relates to being sensitive to the needs of residents.

Ruth Simmons, president of Prairie View A&M University, agrees with Martin and Thompson regarding the unique role of land-grant institutions. "As you know," she said, "land-grant institutions, 1890s, have a very distinctive mission. The wonderful thing about the land-grant mission is the creation of institutions that while educational, focus on helping communities, solving real problems in those communities, and the premise being that we can [do even more] as universities [than] provide the intellectual power for the country." Most of these institutions are in rural areas; however, Simmons told us that her institution has shifted its focus to working more with urban communities:

We have done something in terms of our recent kind of version of our land-grant mission, and that is we have decided to focus in part on the urban community. And we've created a program where our college of agriculture, our business and nursing colleges, and our criminal justice college go into urban centers to provide services on-site that include nutrition information. It includes diabetes information. It includes planting urban gardens. It includes financial literacy instruction. It includes providing advice to communities about how to deal with adolescent delinquency.

Simmons continued,

The land-grant purpose is really to be out there helping on the ground as it were, not in the ivory tower where we set ourselves apart and try to solve problems from a purely intellectual basis but rather human-to-human, trying to do the things that will help communities thrive. So, that's a very gratifying aspect of being at a place like Prairie View A&M University, the fact that you have those two dimensions. You can do research projects in the laboratory. You can do a very fine scholarship that doesn't require much other than you sit at your computer and work on resource materials and so forth. But you can also go out and deal with community issues and make a big difference in doing that.

Simmons's account of the importance of being a land grant and ensuring that her institution helps communities thrive was a common refrain among those we interviewed. Her words exemplify the dual nature of land-grant institutions—that is, their focus on the practical nature of helping communities through engagement efforts as well as through intellectual activities that are carried out via research conducted by faculty.

Contributions to Workforce Development

Historically Black Colleges and Universities have had a long and successful history of contributing to the nation's workforce development efforts, especially within the STEM and teacher education fields

(Archibald & Estreet, 2017; Engerman et al., 2021 James et al., 2020; Malhotraet al., 2018; Nelson & Lang-Lindsey, 2020; K. C. Smith et al., 2021). HBCUs contribute primarily through the diversity they provide to employers. Several individuals we interviewed mentioned the ways in which HBCUs contribute to local, state, and regional workforce development, as well as the impact that HBCUs have in creating jobs and providing technical training for youth and adults. For example, as Harold Martin told us, "North Carolina A&T began to expand the investments in the academic programs across our university to enhance the reputational focus on addressing the growing needs of the region, producing outstanding teachers for school systems, enhancing success of academic programs through K–12, building out STEM and STEM relationships with the corporate industries in the local community and across the state." He added, "We also supported the College of Business to address the emerging needs tied to entrepreneurship and producing graduates who are prepared for entrepreneurial pursuits. It is also worth mentioning that we addressed the growing demand for healthcare providers, [producing] outstanding nurses within the region and state."

North Carolina A&T has also become a driving force for economic growth in the region. According to Martin, "We have become, in the minds of our business leaders and political leaders of our region and our state, the leading public university for our region in driving economic growth and prosperity for the future of our community in the region. And that's the position we want to be [in] henceforth, and so we're excited about the role we play." From our conversation with Martin, it was clear that North Carolina A&T plays a considerable role in diversifying the workforce in Greensboro and beyond: "Diversity became the core role that we were going to play in helping to build out highly competent, diverse, well-prepared graduates across these areas that were essential to the growing needs of our community. And that's what we do exceedingly well across those critical areas of importance to our university and to our community." As Alton Thompson, a professor at North Carolina A&T, explained, "Workforce development in terms of diversity, equity, and inclusion is really a significant contribution that HBCUs make to society. I think the future for the spirit of the US and the advancement of US depends on having a commitment to diversity, equity, and inclusion." He elaborated, "I think HBCUs really are, I guess, a paragon of excellence in terms of a source of diversity, equity, and inclusion. I also think for our country to reach its full potential, we should be serving marginalized populations and people of low-income backgrounds."

Rick Gallot, president of Grambling State University, shared sentiments like those of Harold Martin regarding his institution's workforce development efforts. He told us, "We've got a workforce of about 500 faculty and staff, so we certainly provide a lot of jobs for this area." Gallot emphasized that Grambling's workforce development efforts have resulted from the institution being the only one in Louisiana that offers a bachelor's degree in cybersecurity, which contributes to increased diversity within this field. These efforts also made it possible for Grambling to form partnerships with other institutions and businesses. He stated,

> We have a long history in terms of production of African American computer science graduates. We have become a part of what we call the Cyber Corridor along Interstate 20 that has linked up Louisiana Tech, Grambling, the Cyber Innovation Center in Bossier City, Shreveport, and which is the home of Barksdale Air Force base, and so there is a lot of cyber-related activity going on here along Interstate 20 in North Louisiana, and we are a part of it. So, we are proud to be a part of training the workforce and diversifying the workforce in cybersecurity.

Communities benefit when HBCU graduates return to their hometowns, as these individuals can contribute to economic growth and development. As Alton Thompson, a North Carolina A&T State University graduate, explained, "There are a lot of HBCU students sent back to their community, which contributes to their local economic development. And I read a report that stated that the economic impact of HBCUs is about $14.8 billion.[2] When you think about the economic impact of $14.8 billion, it really adds a lot to local and regional economies. HBCUs contribute to economic development in a large way and really help this country in a significant way as well."

Looking toward the future, Isaac Addae spoke of the innovation that takes place on HBCU campuses and how these institutions are fertile ground for venture capitalists:

We launched the HBCU Impact Capital because we noticed that there was a lot of energy around HBCUs that stems from 2020 and the push for racial equity after George Floyd's death. However, a lot of the energy that was directed toward HBCUs was more about financial contributions to endowments and scholarships and building centers on campus for entrepreneurship. We also noticed that the venture capital community was investing in Black college campuses, but their focus was trying to get more students to come work for venture capital funds.

Addae continued, "My partner Trey and I understand the power of scaling Black businesses and we don't see much of a venture capital focus on Black colleges and the business ideas that potentially exist there. So, the focus for our fund is to shine a light on Black colleges and help people understand that there is innovation taking place on these campuses and that venture capitalists should invest and help create and launch businesses coming from the whole Black college ecosystem." Building African American capital can lead to increased opportunities for African American communities, including a livelier and engaging civic and cultural life for young and old.

Civic, Cultural, and Intellectual Engagement

One of the main contributions of HBCUs has been to empower individuals culturally and civically in African American communities (Freeman & Cohen, 2001; Gasman et al., 2015). Michael Nettles, former senior vice president at the Educational Testing Service, believes HBCUs do significant civic engagement and are positioned to represent the political interests of residents through workforce development and job creation:

I think that HBCUs have provided a presence in communities where they are located that enhances the political opportunities of people and the economic and social opportunities of their communities. HBCUs can represent their communities in governors' mansions, in legislators. They bring experts, scholars, professionals, who can advocate for their communities. They provide economic support for the communities where they exist. I mean, people have jobs in those communities. So HBCUs being there, whether it is professional jobs, or you know, average blue-collar jobs, and that contributes to the economic viability of the communities where they exist.

I think one of the things that I have always seen, particularly at both places being in urban environments, is the campus could be like a living room for meaningful conversations. It's neutral grounds to have those meaningful conversations for the broader community, and really provide some of that intellectual sustainment for the broader community.

He added,

I think all colleges or universities are engaged particularly in the community service aspect and getting students to be involved in internship opportunities and all of that, but to be sort of that living room for the community to have conversations, a place to have political debates.

Dillard University exemplifies the commitment to open dialogue and political debate that Nettles mentions and that is central to the purpose of HBCUs. As Kimbrough stressed, "Dillard has had a ton of [debates], gubernatorial, mayoral, it's the neutral ground. I think that's a really good role to play, and it sort of feeds into the intellectual climate of the campus, to provide those things." HBCUs provide much-needed opportunities for local communities to engage in civic discourse and other forms of intellectual empowerment.

Belle Wheelan, president of the Southern Association of Colleges and Schools, holds a view like Kimbrough's. She emphasized how the engagement of HBCU presidents carries over into the community: "I think many of the presidents are in the Rotary Clubs, the Lions Clubs, the Chambers of Commerce, the bank boards, the school boards, all the kinds of civic engagement that is expected of a college president and so they're able to bring a perspective to the community that the community might not have." Referring to North Carolina A&T State University's and Benedict College's contributions in the local community, Wheelan said, "I'm sure Chancellor Martin has changed the culture in the community through his involvement, as well as President Artis of Benedict College and all the other institutions that are in that area. They can pick the brain of the Black intelligentsia in their local communities where those communities that don't have an HBCU don't have that luxury."

Offering an example of how institutions within the Atlanta University Center helped create a strong and vibrant Black community in Atlanta, Louis Sullivan noted,

> HBCUs make many contributions to their surrounding community, and I will use this matter as an example. You know the Black community in Atlanta is a very vibrant, very strong community. A major reason for that is the schools in the Atlanta University Center because the graduates of those schools become business leaders in Atlanta, become physicians, become lawyers, civil rights leaders. And fortunately, we also have an enlightened majority community in Atlanta. We have had great mayors such as Ivan Allen Jr.[3] and others, so that the race relations in Atlanta are really quite positive and I think are just as strong and positive as any place in the country. They are not perfect because we still have problems in Atlanta, but that is the truth for Atlanta.

He continued,

> The homes that the African Americans have in Atlanta have always been very good homes because in the years of segregation when Black people could not get home mortgages, Atlanta had the Atlanta Life Insurance Company.[4] [Atlanta Life] supported mutual federal savings and loans, [and] a mutual savings bank. Black banks provided mortgages back in the '40s for Black people when White banks were not giving them. So, Black people were able to get mortgages for their homes. They also had many businesses, real estate, insurance, drug stores, and others. So, the

people who developed these businesses and who ran them were mainly graduates of the schools in the Atlanta University Center, not only Morehouse College, but Spelman College, Clark College [now Clark Atlanta], and Morris Brown College, as well.

HBCUs also make profound cultural contributions to local communities. For example, Gallot spoke of how Grambling "serve[s] as a cultural center when you think about plays and concerts and other events and activities that the public and others in the area have an opportunity to participate in. It is a cultural center for this area as well, and again, we are in Grambling, Louisiana, which is a 99% African American city. So that again is part of what we do." He continued,

> Some of the other things that we do, and certainly as a kid growing up in this community, I was a beneficiary of learning to swim in the university pool. That was something that we all did during the summer. There was a certain time of day during the summers that the local community could come and swim in the pool. Football games and athletic events are a big, big draw for the area. Those are just some of the things that we contribute to the area.

Gallot's description made clear that Grambling's efforts in providing cultural activities for the local community helped contribute to a better quality of life for its citizens. Wheelan agrees with Gallot, stating,

> In addition to the money that they contribute with the payroll and money that [employees] spend within their communities, I think HBCUs are a place for people to come and experience life. Not just the students that they have but their local communities come to the concerts and the athletic events and the debates and all the social events that they have and so there is a connection, a town-gown connection. I think that's very strong and not just with the African Americans in their local communities but any and everybody and their local communities, they can come and experience that HBCU life.

Like Wheelan, Louis Sullivan spoke of the ways that HBCUs provide cultural engagement opportunities for local communities:

HBCUs add to the cultural life of a community with art shows, with music, with drama. Then I would also add that on a national scale, Black colleges are important because they embody the history, the culture, the aspirations of the Black community. They represent in this institutional sense the Black community because I believe that in our pluralistic society, if you have institutions that also embody your values and your culture, that really helps to inform the other parts of your community about you, who you are as an individual and your values.

Sullivan believes that Black colleges contribute to the vitality of our country as a democratic, pluralistic society. He also views Black colleges as having a holistic impact on the nation through their civic, cultural, and intellectual engagement efforts. It is because of these efforts that HBCUs are such powerful institutions.

Demographic and intellectual diversity benefits communities. With that idea in mind, Aaron Walton, president of Cheyney University, is forthright in his views on how HBCUs add to the cultural life of the surrounding community: "HBCUs introduce their surrounding communities to talent that would not actually be a part of them if the HBCU did not exist. So HBCUs can draw individuals from a wide range of geographies both nationally and internationally, particularly individuals seeking a specific type of experience that an HBCU can provide. I feel anytime you infuse a community with a variety of thoughts, exposure, and experiences, it benefits that community because they are not living on an island." Walton added, "They have other experiences that can become part of their environment, and that makes for a better community. The types of students that HBCUs attract, the influences that they can have, both on the community with the students that are there and vice versa, all have an impact on the surrounding community." Walton shared how Cheyney students help out in their community by participating in civic organizations and volunteering for service projects. Like Walton, Brittni Brown, a graduate of the University of Arkansas at Pine Bluff, believes that the communities around HBCUs benefit from their intellectual diversity: "I think they benefit from the expertise of the faculty and staff that reside in those places, from the smallest things of inviting a speaker to a classroom, to also being able to engage in research and other initiatives . . . that allows the folks from the institution or the university to work with people firsthand in those communities."

Antoine Alston, a professor at North Carolina A&T State University, describes HBCUs as a "place of strength" and a "centerpiece of intellectual thought." He explained,

> Anywhere you have a college, you really have elevated the stature of that community. You know, Black colleges were usually built on the Black side of town and so we are very important to this side of town. We are in East Greensboro and so no matter where you go, Black colleges are really the heart of where they're at. They really are the centerpiece of intellectual thought, cultural enrichment, economic development, economic empowerment, a place of strength. And when I say strength, it is a place where the community can come and voice their opinion about things, where we have forums on different things, and it just provides a lot.

For Alston, HBCUs are a major source of cultural and intellectual empowerment for local communities and enrich communities in numerous ways.

Community Engagement

Historically Black Colleges and Universities have a rich history of engagement with their local communities and strong connections with their residents (Akintobi et al., 2021; Gasman et al., 2015; Lomax, 2006; Maddux et al., 2006; Pasque et al., 2005). Those we interviewed shared numerous stories of the positive relationships between their HBCUs and residents of the local communities. For Michael Sorrell, president of Paul Quinn College, meeting the needs of the local community is at the core of the college's purpose: "We have very clearly embraced this idea that the heart, the purpose and the soul of HBCUs is to lift, to fight and to inspire, and that is what we try to do." Sorrell described how his institution addresses the social needs of residents:

We understand that there are lots of people out there that do not like [our community outreach and activism], right? We do not care, because we are not doing it for them, we are doing it for a higher purpose. So, for us, I mean, when the city was derelict in [its] duties, when the pandemic first started, we fought the indifference that they had, and forced them to give us the resources to run a COVID-19 testing center on our campus. We did a food drive because people were hungry.

He added, "We remade our school during the pandemic so that we could be even more to this community. We are now home to two schools. I mean, we have a K–12 school, and we have an international baccalaureate [school], 6th to 12th grade. We have very clearly embraced this idea that the heart, the purpose, and the soul of HBCUs is to lift, to fight and to inspire, and that is what we try to do."

Trust is essential between HBCUs and their local communities. David Wilson, president of Morgan State University, told us that HBCUs

rarely will violate that trust. And so first, that's a huge way in which HBCUs serve the community, if research is coming out of Morgan, that speaks to lead paint in Baltimore, or speaks to environmental issues in Baltimore, or speaks to public safety issues, the community is more likely to embrace that evidence-based research coming out of Morgan, believe it or not, than it would be embracing [research] coming out of Johns Hopkins [University] and it's because of the trust piece. HBCUs serve the[ir] communities by understanding the trust communities place in them and being careful not ever to violate that.

Marquita Qualls, a graduate of Tennessee State University, shared with us the historical contributions tied to community engagement:

I have [experience with] two HBCUs. For both, they are really beacons in the community. For Tougaloo, if you are familiar with Tougaloo and you know Tougaloo's[5] history and their role in the civil rights and freedom movements along the way. Tougaloo has just been that place where people know and can go to and respect in the community. There is a beautiful chapel on Tougaloo's campus where people will have their weddings and events, but just to feel a part of Tougaloo. Once you go inside the gates and are part of Tougaloo, you feel the history, and you can feel a part of its contribution to Mississippi's history in terms [of], as I said, the civil rights and the freedom movement, just as well as just being able to understand that this is the place that produces so many of our local doctors and local lawyers who continue to this day to serve that community. So, there is that outreach and there is a connection there.

Offering several examples of Benedict College's history of community engagement and commitment to addressing social issues, Roslyn Artis sees HBCUs as "more than places of higher learning. They are places for a community to gather and engage and for critical questions to be answered, and in some instances, where the necessities are provided." Artis elaborated, "I think HBCUs are not simply in a community. They are of the community. So, they reflect the communities that they serve, the families and the people in the communities around us tend to be a part of. We are cornerstone institutions in many respects, much like churches in the Black community. We're part of the community. And so goes the schools, so goes the community." She described how Benedict performed an important service during the pandemic:

> Most recently during COVID, we of course have been a testing site in this community, where people were afraid of testing and most assuredly vaccinations. They look to Benedict for guidance. We are the place they could get, not only tested, but we distributed supplies during the height of the pandemic. We were handing out toilet paper, right? We were handing out personal protective equipment to the community. We did a drive-through, kind of just pop your trunk and we will fill it with supplies.

Artis continued to speak about Benedict's commitment to the ideal of social responsibility within the local community. She explained, "What I forgot were the stories, the individual stories. When we now know that 31% of Benedict students are housing insecure. Think about that 31%. A third of the kids on this campus do not have a stable home environment, so they're crashing on a couch or the floor. They don't have a place to call home. That wreaks havoc on your ability to focus on your academics, and so we learned about a lot of those during COVID-19." Benedict College's students are not alone in their quest for basic needs. According to a 2019 report from the Hope Center at Temple University, of the nearly 86,000 students who completed a survey administered by the center, 45% were food insecure and 56% were housing insecure, with 17% noting periods of homelessness while in college (Goldrick-Rab et al., 2019).

Sierra Nance, a graduate of Winston Salem State University, mentioned that the visibility of HBCUs in the community serves to inspire future generations of students to pursue a college education: "They foster community. My HBCU sat in the middle of Dr. Martin Luther King Jr. Boulevard, in the city. So, homecoming, like any events that we have on campus, was always open to the community. We did a lot of community drives, like our nursing school was one of the top nursing schools in the city, and in the state. They also did mobile clinics for the surrounding community." Nance believes that the mere existence of HBCUs in a community does much to foster opportunity for young people. "When I went to North Carolina for school, I met students [who] were from North Carolina—and there are like 11 HBCUs in North Carolina, so they grew up knowing that they wanted to go to an HBCU as children. I think that's important, just their visibility alone fostered access to higher education for students that grow up around HBCUs."

Like Nance, Brittini Brown believes that HBCUs serve as aspirational and inspirational models of educational excellence:

I think they also benefit from, and this is one of the things that I think is probably most important, is that the kids that grow up in those places, they always get to know what it looks like to see a person who's been to college. There are so many people who I've met or encountered who said I never met a person who went to college, or I've never met a college graduate, or there's not one in my family. And so, when you have these cities that are smaller towns, that don't have a lot of huge infrastructure in them, those students automatically get a firsthand look at what it looks like to see a person who looks like them, who is going to college or has achieved a college education, and so I think access doesn't seem out of reach for those students, and just knowing what is possible I think is huge. I think that is one of the really big contributions [that HBCUs make].

HBCUs are cornerstones within communities. Makola Abdullah, president of Virginia State University, offered several examples of how his faculty engages with the local community, commenting that it was impossible to count the number of relationships that the university had with the local community:

> I know certainly about Virginia State, but I think HBCUs are the lynch-pin for the community. Here's the best way I can describe it. There was a time when I tried to get somebody to capture all the relationships that we had with the school district of Petersburg, and we had to stop. We couldn't do it. We couldn't get a list of everything because we got faculty members working with students. We have faculty members working with teachers. We have faculty members working with principals. We have faculty members working with the district. We got deans in differ-ent colleges working with faculty. I mean, it was so engrained and so connected that it was almost impossible to capture all the relationships that we have in Petersburg and in the surrounding community. And then so much of what people do is personal and on their own.

He continued, "So, you've got people who aren't working officially for Virginia State, but their brand and their volunteer activities out-side of VSU is still VSU while they do the work that they do in the community."

HBCUs improve the quality of life of their surrounding communi-ties through community development and involvement. Thomas Hud-son, president of Jackson State University, says of the university:

> We're within the fabric of the community. It's a safe place in a lot of re-spects. For some people it's the walking trail, it's your community event space. We, in this COVID environment, we are offering vaccines. You know, we've been a pillar in terms of helping in that effort. So really

HBCUs are woven into the fabric of the community. We live here, we work here, we eat here, we spend money here and we educate the surrounding community. I don't have to remind you that there's a high school, there is a middle school. There's an elementary school, all within a one-mile radius of the university and we service all those entities in different ways."

For Hudson, Jackson State is a fixture within the community and reaches residents in numerous ways, thus contributing to a stronger bond with the institution.

Jeffrey Miller, a Morris Brown College graduate and board of trustee member of the small college, described the impact of HBCUs on educating future generations of students and instilling in them a spirit of wanting to give back to their communities: "The first thing is being a place of employment. There's a multiplier effect around an HBCU. Paul Quinn as an example, when they went and established an oasis in a food desert, that's a multiplier effect for the community. Michael Sorrell, president of Paul Quinn College, believes that education can jump-start the socioeconomic mobility of people who grow up in long-neglected neighborhoods and that is what compelled him to lead Paul Quinn." From Miller's perspective, as an urban institution, Paul Quinn has remained responsive to the campus and community needs by investing in its infrastructure to address chronic issues affecting the area.

Paul Quinn has a vision for becoming an engine for social change in the community, transforming the lives of residents in its under-resourced neighborhood (Vanderburgh-Wertz, 2013; Castro-Samayoa & Gasman, 2018; C. Tatum, 2019). One notable example of the college's commitment to the local community is the development in 2010 of the "We Over Me" urban farm on its former football grounds. In recognition of the lack of healthy food options in the neighborhood surrounding Paul Quinn, the farm has three goals: (1) help address the lack of affordable, healthy food options available to economically depressed areas in the City of Dallas, (2) create a replicable model for achieving sustainable urban redevelopment built around providing safe food options to economically depressed communities, and (3) create a facility that will deliver preventive health care focusing on nutrition and exercise to the underserved community surrounding the college (Duke University, 2013). The farm donates 10% of the produce it grows to neighborhood charities, runs a pick and purchase program for residents, and sells the rest at farmers markets and to the college's cafeteria and local restaurants. The farm also provides agricultural education to students and community members while offering valuable work opportunities to students.

Our discussions with important HBCU stakeholders revealed the breadth and depth of HBCUs' efforts to bolster local economies, lead community development efforts, and organize cultural, civic, and intellectual activities for the benefit of local citizens. HBCUs have the power to transform local communities and improve the quality of life of a city, state, and the nation.

8

Challenges and Calls to Action

The power and contributions of Historically Black Colleges and Universities are immense and profound even amid their obstacles. HBCUs face numerous challenges, including customer service concerns, leadership instability and preparation, board ineffectiveness, low graduation rates, financial instability and subsequent threats to long-term sustainability, and the need to tell better HBCU institutional stories. As we have shared, we talked to people across the HBCU landscape, and although they are hopeful and resolute in their belief in the power of HBCUs, they are also aware of the challenges that these institutions encounter—some of which are faced by other types of institutions. Regardless, they are important to address because the long-term sustainability of HBCUs is essential.

Tackling Customer Service Concerns

Years ago, Dillard University president Walter Kimbrough referred to financial aid, the bursar, and the registrar as the Bermuda Triangle within HBCUs (Gasman & Bowman, 2010; Wilcox et al., 2014). He noted that the customer service complaints in these three areas—and beyond—were systemic at HBCUs and were one reason that HBCU alumni often refused to give back to their institutions. Research demonstrates that Kimbrough's hunch is valid (Gasman & Anderson-Thompkins, 2003; Gasman & Bowman, 2010). Outside of not being asked to give, the top reason that HBCU alumni do not give back to their alma maters is the customer service they received while a student and often as an alumnus (Gasman & Anderson-Thompkins, 2003; Gasman & Bowman, 2011).

Although all colleges and universities experience inefficiencies and negative commentary related to service functions, HBCUs are particularly plagued by such lore. Social media, especially Twitter, TikTok, and Instagram memes, have added a new dimension to the issue. These images can do damage in terms of student recruitment and fundraising. From the perspective of Martin Lemelle, vice president of finance & business services at Grambling State University, "You see the memes, right—'I just went through *The Hunger Games*[1] with the HBCU financial aid office.' It's this nostalgia and endurance that everybody talks about with some sense of pride, but as a chief operating officer at an HBCU, I don't want that experience." Lemelle wants students to be able to "pick up their phone and get everything that they need." He added, "I want them to proactively know those options that are available to them so that they have a great experience." He would like to see more HBCUs invest in automated systems that provide customer service functions, sharing,

> A lot of folks have gone to embedding automated chat features into their websites, to high traffic areas. Now, instead of talking about the last call that came into the president's office about an air conditioner being out in a student's room, I have a queue of intelligent data that these are the top 10 questions that happen on move-in day for example. I can go to the air conditioner vendor and say, 'You missed 20 rooms out of these 200. Now let's talk about my contract.' When you think about the student experience first, it starts to have an impact on everything else, your bottom line, the way your team functions.

According to Thomas Hudson, president of Jackson State University,

> We have to make sure from a customer service standpoint, not to make it hard for [students] to become a part of us. [We] must eliminate the institutional barriers to entrance, meaning get rid of the stories that I had, that my friends had about waiting in long lines and how long it takes to get to us and really being more customer service–oriented. If you come to us and we make it so difficult for you to become a part of us, you will go somewhere else.

He added,

> One of the reasons the for-profit institutions exploded was because they made it so easy for you to become a part of them. We need to make it easier for you to become a part of an HBCU. That means our processes must improve. That means our response rates must improve. That means we must act like 'Hey, we want you to come here.' We must borrow some of the techniques from some of these other institutions that make it a welcoming, easier environment for you to come. We know once you get here, you'll find a great nurturing environment that will again help you become who you're meant to be, but I can't keep putting barriers to your entry to the point where we're losing 3 out of every 10 persons who want to come here, because we've made it so difficult for them.

For-profit institutions attract students with savvy marketing and by spending a considerable amount of money on high-touch and high-tech customer service (Vazquez-Martinez & Hansen, 2020). Unfortunately, they do not have high graduation rates, especially for Black students. In 2021, the average for-profit college and university graduation rate for African American students was a mere 14.2%, well below the performance of HBCUs (Nietzel, 2021).

Most of the issues related to poor customer service at HBCUs are a result of a lack of resources—and often one individual doing the job of several people (Gasman & Bowman, 2010). There are immense disparities between HBCUs and Predominantly White Institutions in terms of resources. Robert Palmer, a professor at Howard University, experienced this firsthand while a student at Morgan State University. Having attended a PWI for his undergraduate degree, Palmer had a point of comparison. "I did get a sense of the resource disparity [between] PWIs and HBCUs. I remember when I attended a PWI, when I went to a computer lab, there was always someone working there and there was always paper available. At Morgan at the time, even though they had computer labs, you couldn't find someone working, so that was frustrating if you had a question and needed some assistance, or there would be issues with paper and the long lines." He added, "I [also] wasn't used to standing in a line for five hours to access financial aid at [my] previous institution, [but] that was my experience attending an HBCU. Morgan [had] this whole culture around 'this is the way things are.' I was not used to that. At Morgan it was kind of like a term of endearment. It's called the Morgan Way." Palmer has found the same attitude at Howard: "I think Howard is a great institution. But like every institution, there are problems. There's this culture of kind of accepting the way things have always been done."

Palmer also shared his frustration with having to micromanage people to get them to do their jobs: "When you have to email someone five times, to get them to respond to your email, or to get them to do their job, and that to me is very frustrating, because I'm very proactive. I'm very efficient. I like to get things done and so having to email someone, one person five times to have them even acknowledge my email, that becomes very frustrating." But despite being frustrated with inefficiencies, Palmer said, "I had a chance to see just how powerful, how motivational, and how culturally nourishing it was to be at an institution where people looked like me and supported my success."

Leah Hollis, a professor at Morgan State University, has had similar experiences and thinks these frustrations are common across HBCUs. According to Hollis, "No matter who I speak to as an HBCU graduate, most [people] talk about the lack of customer service. So, if you got to go to the bursar's office, if you've got to add or drop a class, if there's something you must do on the way to facilitate your next academic year, that is like pulling teeth." Like Palmer, she also understands these frustrations as a faculty member, noting "sometimes I find myself calling three and four and five and six times to get something done. I never had that experience with PWIs." Hollis shares Lemelle's feeling of "nostalgia and endurance that everybody talks about with some sense of pride." She said that at first she thought it was just her experience. But when she started talking to cousins and relatives, all of whom love their HBCUs, they would say, "If I could get through such and such a service, I can go anywhere." Like Kimbrough, Hollis finds the lack of customer service to be a detriment to progress, enrollment, and alumni giving at HBCUs. She shared with frustration,

> I don't know what that is, that you have a phone number to call financial aid, but it rings off the hook all day. If you've got a question about parking, there is a number, but nobody's over there. But if you walk over to the building, they're over there, I find that disconcerting. Students are trying to get through and we put up obstacles because we don't answer emails and don't answer phone calls. I don't think it's any specific HBCU. I hear [this experience] from HBCU graduates regardless [of the institution]. We've got to clean that up.

Of note, as we were writing this book, Howard University was in a standoff with students who were frustrated with the dire condition of residence halls, including mold in the walls and a lack of COVID-19 testing for the residents. Students occupied the Blackburn University Center for nearly a month and slept in tents outside the building. They demanded immediate change, and most of their power came from an effective social media campaign that engaged alumni across the nation (Franklin, 2021).

These customer service inefficiencies must be resolved as they hurt HBCUs in myriad ways. Although students and alumni have every right to complain and to speak up for their rights as consumers, some HBCU leaders worry about the very public nature of these complaints. Grambling University president Rick Gallot painfully shared that

The advent of social media has created a venue for even your own alumni to just trash the school. They go on and there's too much grass growing at the stadium that you're not going to use for six months, and so then that becomes a big deal. And again, it's not unique to Grambling. I see a lot of other schools whose alums, I mean they just go all out of their way to talk about all the negative things going on, in a public way, and it just, it's unnecessary, and you're already fighting all these other significant fights, and then having to just deal with the noise. And of course, that contributes to instability in fundraising, in recruiting, things like that. 'Oh, I'm not sending my kid to that school.' Those kinds of things that again, come from within our own family.

Gallot would prefer that those with complaints speak to him directly instead of "airing dirty laundry publicly." He said, "It almost pains me to talk about it, but I think at some point we've got to have a real conversation about this, and that it is from our own people." During many of our interviews, we learned that issues related to customer service were a barrier to increasing student enrollments—or, even worse, poor customer service left a bad impression on graduates, which often contributed to them not wanting to support their alma maters, financially or otherwise. It was promising to hear that among those we interviewed, especially the HBCU presidents, many were making customer service a top priority.

Leadership Instability and What Leaders Need in Order to Lead

As we talked with those in HBCU communities, we often asked what are the greatest challenges that HBCUs face. Inevitably, the answer was leadership. From current presidents to alumni to funders, concerns about the sustainability and quality of leadership surfaced. Robert Palmer, an expert on HBCUs, shared, "I don't want to paint HBCUs as if they're all the same, because there are many very strong leaders at HBCUs, but there are HBCUs that have experienced rapid turnover in leadership and that causes a problem. It actually threatens the stability of institutions, when a president is not able to carry out their vision and implement their plan for improving the institution." Walter Kimbrough has been tracking presidential turnover at HBCUs for nearly a decade and remains concerned about the impact of unstable leadership on HBCUs in the long term (Harris, 2017; Kimbrough, 2014).

Those bringing concerns to the fore were also focused on the unique skills that HBCU presidents will need for their institutions to thrive in the future. Presidents leading state-funded and state-affiliated HBCUs must be savvy in their interactions and communications with elected leaders. Rick Gallot thinks "one thing that is very needed is someone who has got political acumen, and not just politics like elected officials, but of course, for those of us that are at public institutions, you've got to be able to have some level of credibility and access to elected officials. So, me being personal friends with the governor certainly helps Grambling State University." As revealed by those we interviewed, leadership instability can have long-term implications for most any institution; however, HBCUs often feel the negative effects from this to a far greater degree. Leadership instability, which often results from presidential turnover, can be traced back to governing boards choosing the wrong individuals to lead. Unlike PWIs, which can often recover at a much faster rate, HBCUs that experience multiple instances of presidential turnover often struggle for years. Hence, it goes without saying that choosing the right leader should be a top priority for governing boards, campus communities, and external stakeholders.

Not only must leaders understand state and local politics, but an understanding of institutional politics and culture within HBCUs is important as well. According to Belle Wheelan, president of the Southern Association of Colleges and Schools,

> The first thing [presidents] need to do is to be politically astute, and not [just about] national politics but internal, institutional politics. You need to understand how to care for and feed your board. Who needs more attention? How do you get them to understand that you're the

president and here is what you want to do, and this is how it goes along with the policies that you all have established. Many presidents will go in with a split board [meaning not everyone voted for them]. And [they have] to spend a lot of time nurturing those [who did not vote for them], to bring them on board or at least to make sure [they don't] lose any of those who had supported [them]. That's a tough thing to do, when you've got an institution to lead and yet you have to sit over here and make sure that you're not losing the people who hired you, that's a tough thing to do. And so, understanding those politics before you get in there, I think, is very important, and sometimes people don't.

Wheelan added,

I've seen a lot of presidents, across higher education who are just caught up in the fact that I'm president. I get a car. I get a house. I get a big salary. Yeah, but there's a whole lot of strings pulling all of that and they aren't aware of that when they go into it. They don't stop and think that, yeah, I got in on a five to four votes but what does that mean, and do I really want to accept this job, knowing that half the board doesn't want me here in the first place? So that's one thing, one skill that they need, I think, is how to read the politics of the institution.

Jeffrey Miller, an alumnus of Morris Brown College and a member of the institution's board of trustees, agrees that presidents must have a certain amount of savviness. This attribute is especially needed when an institution is facing a dire situation. Miller said that "presidents need to be very savvy with how to influence people. They must have really strong interpersonal skills, very good communication skills and just be a dynamic leader, somebody that can come in and really, really get things going and motivate people to want to be a part of the team." He shared a story about Kevin James, the young and energetic president of Morris Brown College, who found a way to repair a fire-damaged campus building despite having a lapsed insurance policy. Miller recalled, "I said to him, 'That's pretty doggone amazing that before we could marshal the troops, you already had people lined up bartering service, volunteering.' That's the type of innovation that was needed in that moment and that type of creativity, that type of desire to get it done, that's something that all HBCUs need to have going forward."

Being able to navigate politics is key to effective leadership as is understanding the business aspects of the academy given the complicated nature of today's colleges and universities. Presidents—and especially those leading institutions like HBCUs, which are constantly under the microscope—need to have a firm understanding of budgets and finance. According to Belle Wheelan, who in her role at SACS regularly sees HBCUs struggling with financial issues,

> You need to be able to understand your budget, understand the finances, don't just trust your CFO to tell you this is how much money you have. You need to understand where that money is coming from, where that money is going. How can you grow that money? Where can you go to get a line of credit if you need one? It's something that just must be attended to, and presidents are notorious for and again, across higher education, of spending time raising money, working the legislature, and losing sight of what is going on in their own institutions.

She added, "Presidents have to know how to balance the internal and external forces that are coming at you, and you cannot spend all your time on the road. I think, because the finances, the governance and decreasing enrollments or the politics are the things that can pull you down. Those are the skill sets that you need to be able to be successful."

Aaron Walton, president of Cheyney University of Pennsylvania, sees higher education as a business and makes no apologies about his perspective. He was tasked by the State of Pennsylvania to resurrect Cheyney when it was near death (Hill, 2017). As Walton put it,

> [Presidents] have to have tremendous business acumen. There's no question, education is a business. If I were not convinced about that before I came to Cheyney, I am now convinced that education is a business. And if you don't have business discipline and an appreciation for the business model, you are not going to be as successful as you could be. So, I think that HBCUs have those types of leaders and there are some

who are forging ahead. But many are not. They're not forging ahead. They're just maintaining or just able to survive. And that's only a matter of time.

In his role as president of Grambling State University, Rick Gallot feels like the "mayor of a small town," noting, "We've got a police department, we've got a water system I've got to operate. There's human resources, there's all these competing components at times. I think having a team of folks who can help to run the business enterprise is so important. If you look at HBCUs [that] have struggled, often, finances are at the root, or the lack of finances is at the root of many other problems that end up flowing from that." One of the major outcomes of HBCUs' lack of fiscal responsibility is that it can contribute to a loss of accreditation. Additional factors that can lead to HBCUs losing accreditation include campus turmoil, failure to provide appropriate responses and support in follow-up and progress reports, noncompliance with federal programs, lack of financial stability, mounting debt, and difficulty with processing financial aid (Fester et al., 2012).

Thomas Hudson, the president of Jackson State University, agrees that understanding the business of leading an HBCU is necessary to be successful, and he sees it as connected to students' success and faculty retention: "Understanding the business of higher education means making sure your financial house is in order, making sure you're always making investments there. Making sure that you have created the place and the space for students to come in and thrive and for professors to come in and really help those students thrive. So really understanding, first and foremost, the business of higher education and what that means for your institution and what your institution needs are in that area." The need for HBCU leadership to have some depth of understanding of and experience with budgets and finance is critically important for the growth and sustainability of their institutions. The ever-increasing demand to better meet the needs of students, expand program offerings, address campus infrastructure issues, and enhance technological innovation will require

HBCU presidents to think boldly about how to best position their institutions for the future.

A Focus on Students

To move HBCUs to new levels, sustain their futures, and attract donors, presidents must focus on student success. According to Hudson, a president must ensure that "each person on campus knows their part on that continuum to make sure that students have a smooth pipeline and a smooth transition from first contact to degree completion." He believes that every aspect of the campus is tied to student success. Likewise, Spelman College president Mary Schmidt Campbell said that

> students have to leave knowing that they are active players in creating a future. If a college is doing its job, the students and faculty in that college should be helping to create that future in the same way that Stacey Abrams walked out of here and said, "I'm going to change the electoral landscape in the United States." She didn't say I'm going to prepare myself to change that. [She said] "I am going to change it." So, that dynamic and that dynamism I find so much alive here on HBCU campuses. We have this imaginative, inventive spirit that is everything whether it's a college education or politics, medicine, law, music, or art.

Believing that his success as president is linked to his putting students first, Michael Sorrell of Paul Quinn College told us that "you have to love the students." He also feels that HBCUs need to offer a different message to their students—one of building wealth and the importance of wealth building in Black communities:

> We need to have honest conversations about the need for them to become wealthy. We don't do that. I often tell people, whoever is president of Paul Quinn College 20 years from now is really going to like me a lot, right? Because they will have the benefit of students who came through during my tenure that had it beaten into their heads that you have an obligation to create generational wealth, right? It doesn't make you a

sellout. It makes you brilliant. It makes you brilliant because [students] have these noble goals. Everyone wants to start a nonprofit. How are you going to start a nonprofit when you have no profit? Right? And the reason they want to start nonprofits is because that's what they've seen in their community, and what it's really saying is, I want to be in charge, and I want to do something good. I'm like, that's great. But I need you to look at this from a generational context.

Sorrell added, "You must treat poverty as something to migrate out of, like it's generational, and we tell the students, your job is to make money, so that the next generation has choices. That's just the way it is. You don't get to pursue your fantasy. You get to be the person who stops the cycle, and that is perhaps the greatest gift that you can ever give your family. I think we must have that conversation honestly, in a transparent fashion."

Sorrell also believes that HBCUs must make sure students know that it is OK to make mistakes and that messing up is normal:

The other thing we do is don't talk about our messiness, right? Like we like to pretend as if we had it all together forever, and that's not, that's not authentic. Like the students need to hear, I messed up too. This is how I messed up. This is what I learned from it. I'm not going to paint a picture that's unrealistic and you know, all pardon my language, but own your shit. Right? Like own it, and from there, help [students] have a different story.

Martin Lemelle, of Grambling State University, believes that "leaders going forward have to have a [student-oriented] mindset. They must lead with a sense of compassion for students and an understanding of the student experience." He continued, "You know, the days of Dean X just said it and that's the way [it is], that doesn't fly, particularly in the student affairs context with Title IX and equity issues. We must be compliant and responsible, and we have to have [a student-focused] mindset." Addressing the needs of students should be the foremost goal of all institutions. Our interviews revealed that a focus that centers students and their academic accomplishments is what will enable HBCUs to reach new levels of success and increase the likelihood of sustainability.

Personal Qualities

People we talked with for this book, especially those in leadership positions at HBCUs, were candid about the individual and personal qualities that HBCU presidents need to ensure the sustainability of these venerable institutions. Reynold Verret, president of Xavier University, shared that humility is important—specifically, "humility in the sense that the HBCU president has to have several talents. Be able to communicate, interact with people, diverse people, all those things that are important, but humility is to attract and recruit bright people on [their] team. And humility in that I would want people on my team who are as bright or brighter than me." He wants members of his team to let him know if they think he is wrong, noting that presidents should not be on a pedestal. He stressed that presidents want to get the "best out of people" and that the only way a president can navigate "uncertain water" is through humility and flexibility of thinking.

Ruth Simmons, president of Prairie View A&M University, advises leaders who want to be president to "mature into leadership." Regarding her journey, she said,

> I wasn't in a hurry for personal reasons. I was not on a fast track, and I didn't want to be on a fast track. . . . Too many people today are convinced they're ready for the multifarious responsibilities of presidencies before they actually are ready. Some can learn on the job, it's true, but not everyone. There's obviously a suite of qualities and abilities that you need in order to serve your institution well. . . . I would say that people need to take the time to mature into the leadership role so that they get the finance piece, so that they get the academic piece, so they get the student affairs piece, and so forth. They need that in order not to buckle when they have difficulties.

Louis Sullivan, former president of Morehouse School of Medicine, agrees: "An individual who is well grounded and quite knowledgeable in his or her field" is essential in the presidency. He added, "You are heading an academic institution. Your life should be an expression of what an academic institution should be like. So, really, the field can be quite broad. It can be mathematics or music or anything in between, but first of all, you should have that."

Sullivan also believes that being secure in oneself is key to effective leadership at HBCUs—that is, someone "who is open to different perspectives, who respects his or her fellow man, who encourages open and honest and rigorous debate and is inclusive. I believe the leader should be one who leads with collaboration, who inspires good debate, [and] good discussion." He added that leaders of HBCUs should "be able to deal with uncertainty given the volatile landscape of higher education and the world, and the racial dynamics in the country." In situations such as the recent COVID-19 pandemic, Sullivan said that HBCU presidents must have the ability to educate and reassure people amid fear and misinformation around science and health:

> The lack of understanding of science was revealed with a number of people. So, our university presidents and their leaders really are the kinds of individuals we look to, to help us work through new experiences in a way that we minimize the negatives from the disruption. But we build on that so that we come out of this a stronger society on the other end. [College and] university presidents all over the country have a similar kind of opportunity and experience to really influence the lives of our future leaders. So, if we're successful in having good presidents, that will help us have good quality leaders in all aspects of our society.

Leaders outside the world of HBCUs, such as the Kresge Foundation's Bill Moses, agree that it is essential for presidents to have a strong academic background in their discipline. "I think [presidents] are going to need to have really solid grounding in the academic field that they began in, so they can be the kind of scholar or represent that kind of scholarship in the institution, even if they have plenty of other things to do." Moses agrees that in addition to this academic strength, other skills are also essential: "I think that they need to have solid management skills. They need to have a strong relationship with their board. They need to be able to raise significant amounts of money, both from their alumni and from within the African American community, but also more broadly. They need to see HBCUs as educational institutions, but also as cultural, social foundations."

Serving as an HBCU president requires that a leader interact with those within the institution as well as with external stakeholders. Thus, authentically connecting with the public is critically important. It is also important for presidents to garner respect from their leadership teams as they are charged with supporting the president's institutional vision. Presidents who lack humility and a collaborative mindset and who lead in a more autocratic fashion will lose traction with faculty, governing boards, staff, and students. HBCU presidents who possess the personal qualities of a visionary leader and who inspire people will bode well for the future of individual HBCUs and HBCUs overall.

Board Ineffectiveness

In conversations about HBCUs with anyone—from presidents to faculty to alumni to outsiders—boards of trustees are often mentioned as an issue (Commodore, 2015; Gasman, 2016; Nelms, 2021; Owens & Commodore, 2018; I. Taylor, 2020). Discussions regularly focus on board ineffectiveness, board interference, and the conservativeness of boards. Who is on an HBCU board and why they are on the board are important questions. It is essential to have a diversity of individuals in terms of area of expertise, experience, race, gender, and affiliation with the institution. All too often HBCU boards have a majority of clergy and alumni, in addition to individuals with little wealth or little access to wealth. This formula does not work (Nelms, 2021; Powell, 2020). In addition, it is vital to have individuals on the board who are interested in doing the work of the board and not merely being on the board. In the words of Jeffrey Miller, a trustee at Morris Brown College, "I've seen some board members serve who are all about 'Hey, I'm on the board. I'm a board member. I get to do this, that and the other.' And no, that's not what it's about."

Another issue with boards pertains to listening too closely to alumni; these individuals, who are part of the institution's past, often want it to remain the same rather than move forward (Ezzell & Schexnider, 2010). According to Belle Wheelan,

> You have a lot of [HBCU] board members that, more so than in many other segments of higher education, listen to their alum[ni] about not wanting to change things. In a lot of other institutions, alum[ni] can give them money to make changes happen. But with HBCUs, I have found that there are more alumni who don't have a lot of money to give but they want everything to stay the way it was when they were there. So, I tell presidents all the time, you tell them thank you so much for your suggestion, but till you give me a check for $25,000, I don't give a flying fig what you have to say and that's tough to do, because you don't want to cut off your nose to spite your face. There is an alumni member on most HBCU boards, [and] there's that direct pipeline into what is going on and so there's a loud vocal voice there that's not always constructive and I have just found that more with HBCUs than I have other segments of higher education.

According to Ruth Simmons of Prairie View A&M, "When boards are ineffective in choosing leadership, then they're impatient when leaders are learning. And so, leaders are often terminated because boards are dissatisfied with their progress, and yet they appointed them." She added,

> Here's the speech that I give to boards of trustees when they say, "Well, what do you think of this candidate?" I'll say, first of all, "I'm sure you know that that candidate does not have a depth of experience for this position. [But] I'm not concerned about that person. I'm concerned about you as a board. Do you know what you're getting into? Are you willing to take on the process of shaping this person into a powerful leadership role? Are you ready for that?" So, boards are often frankly responsible for not being ready for that.

Walter Kimbrough, president of Dillard University, agrees with Ruth Simmons. He thinks it is important to ensure that HBCU presidents are prepared and highly qualified, but he also thinks that the HBCU sector needs "to spend a lot more time with governance, because 9 times out of 10, when I see folks who are unsuccessful, it was because it was not a good fit when they were selected, or the board is dysfunctional. It's not necessarily that the person did not have a certain set of skills." He continued,

> I mean sometimes you get somebody in, and they don't have the right skill set but you watch sometimes, I just look on the side and I see people coming in and I'm just like that's not a good fit. It's not going to last. I've told people who have looked at some presidencies and asked me about a place. I [said] that is not a good fit. Do not go there. They've got some issues, and the person does it anyway and it doesn't work out. I hate to be right, but I have been, every time somebody has asked me, and I told them not to do something and they did it, it did not last more than two years.

Some HBCU presidents have the opportunity to work with stellar board chairs and boards of trustees. Mary Schmidt Campbell, president of Spelman College, was fortunate to begin her role with Rosalind Brewer as the chair of the Spelman board of trustees. Brewer, a Spelman alumna (discussed in Chapter 4), who at the time was the CEO of Sam's Club, understood the role of the board of trustees, and that made Campbell's job significantly easier. Campbell described Brewer as "unbelievably extraordinary," saying "I've got a Black woman Spelman alumna who's a CEO of a major company." Seeing the opportunities, Campbell said to her board chair, "The president leads the conversation with the community so that a vision emerges from the community. There has to be real faculty consultation. Staff need an opportunity to contribute. Student perspective is imperative. The board of trustees has to embrace and endorse that vision for the college." She recalled,

> I said once that strategic vision is adopted, that strategic vision becomes the covenant between the board and the president. So, I don't have to wake up in the morning and wonder whether my board wants to know why I'm spending so much time trying to raise scholarship dollars. [It's]

because we have decided that's the absolute number one priority for Spelman College. The board would never have to wake up one morning and say why is Mary trying to build a new arts building. Well, because that's one of the essential pillars that's in our strategic vision.

Our interviews revealed that many problems facing HBCUs can be traced to board ineffectiveness, and when boards become stronger and more efficient, HBCUs do as well (Schexnider, 2017).

Low Graduation Rates

Historically Black Colleges and Universities as a group have an average six-year graduation rate of 35%, which is lower than the national six-year college graduation rate for African Americans, which hovers at 42% (National Center for Educational Statistics, 2021). Many individual HBCUs have graduation rates that are above the national average for African Americans, such as Hampton University (54%) and Morehouse College (55%), and some HBCUs, like Spelman College (71%) and Howard University (63%), boast some of the highest graduation rates in the country, especially given the percentage of Pell Grant-eligible students they enroll.

Graduation rates have long plagued HBCUs because these institutions educate large numbers of low-income students—nearly 70% of HBCU students are eligible for Pell Grants, which means these schools enroll the highest number of low-income students in the nation (Nathenson et al., 2019; Wood, 2021). All too often the graduation rates of HBCUs are compared with those of majority institutions that enroll very few low-income students—including Ivy League institutions that, up until recently, typically enrolled less than 10% of Pell Grant-eligible students. In the past few years, because of intensive calls for justice, these highly selective institutions have had percentages that hover around 20% ("Some colleges," 2019; "Economic diversity," 2021). The socioeconomic status of students matters because students from low-income families are less likely to graduate and more likely to drop out, stop out and return later, or take longer than six years to graduate, which is the typical measure of graduation rates (Conrad & Gasman, 2015). HBCUs have had a mission to educate low-income students since their beginnings, and as we saw in Chapter 3, they play a substantial role in moving students from the lowest incomes to the middle class. Thus, because of their mission, HBCUs will continue to struggle with graduation rates (Nathenson et al., 2019).

Perhaps graduation rates are not the best measure of success for HBCU performance. According to Makola Abdullah, president of Virginia State University, "Number one, we need an entirely different metric, and the metric has to be simple. One of the big challenges with graduation rates is you are always putting them into context. Our graduation rate, I'll say, is mid-30s or low 40s, but for a school like ours with the Pell eligibility rate, if you rank the schools in my bracket, we're actually doing very well. There aren't schools that have over 70% Pell eligibility that have a graduation rate over 50%." Abdullah added, "When my secretary of education [says] I'd like to see you at 60%, I'm like that's a damn miracle. Did you know no one's there? No one's there. So, if you want me to not have the students I have, I can do that. I can get rid of all my kids and just get rich kids and I can graduate at 60%, or I can be an access school, and do it at 42%." Because most policy makers, even those in higher education more broadly, do not understand the link between income and graduation rates, Abdullah said, "you have to explain it. And even when you explain it and you do it well, people go okay and then right after you leave the room, they [say] these graduation rates are too low. Why are they at the bottom of the list?"

Thomas Hudson has similar concerns:

> When you look at the graduation rates, particularly with your public HBCUs, the six-year rate, it's going to at some point become more and more of a story and more and more of a deterrent, in terms of, okay, if we're going to invest the large amount of dollars in these HBCUs that we do, then what is a realistic return and what is a realistic ask, in terms of improving some of these outcomes? I'll just be transparent. Jackson State's six-year graduation rate is about 43%, which is not horrible for a

public HBCU, but I flipped the numbers and I do this in my alumni meetings, and I did this in my state of the university. You flip that around, should anyone be satisfied when about 6 out of 10 of your students come in and do not receive their diplomas within six years? So, should that be the end? Absolutely not.

Hudson added,

> When you look at student debt, which is a big topic of conversation, a lot of that conversation is centered on your for-profit institutions. At some point, that conversation can and will shift to HBCUs, since we are in the spotlight and say, "Well, hey, what about some of these HBCUs that have 20%, 30%, six-year [graduation] rates? You know, aren't they a part of this conversation as well, since one of the biggest drivers of student debt is those who do not receive their degrees and therefore cannot make the type of living that allows them to pay off their debt." So, we must up our game, for lack of a better word.

Historically, graduation rates have been used as a proxy for institutional value. Some of those we interviewed shared that a system focused on alternate measures of success—one that recognizes service to low-income and first-generation students—should be considered, as it would allow HBCUs to highlight their successes in educating students, especially those from diverse backgrounds.

Finances and Long-Term Sustainability

Historically Black Colleges and Universities face considerable challenges regarding their finances and long-term sustainability. Although the current landscape is looking brighter in terms of private foundation, corporate, and individual philanthropy as well as government investment, the long-term situation and sustainability for HBCUs are less certain (Parks, 2022). Makola Abdullah, president of Virginia State University, said that "we are in a renaissance of sorts right now, [and that] private philanthropy, federal government, state government particularly in Virginia are all looking to invest in HBCUs.

How well will we be prepared for the end of this renaissance? We've got to get ready for that now, when those monies aren't there anymore, and we still are responsible for educating the next generation of best and brightest folks."

For Kevin James, president of Morris Brown College, which has been struggling since the late 1990s owing to misuse of federal financial aid funds and mismanagement, a strong financial picture is key to the survival of HBCUs (Gasman, 2007c). In his words, "My goal here at Morris Brown was to turn the financial picture around. For us to become a candidate for accreditation, one of the major components was financial stability, to show that we were stable. Clean audits, process, procedure in the finance department and it was critically important for us, because we lost our accreditation due to financial mismanagement and financial instability." He added that "it was very, very important for us to really, really put down deep roots and show that we were stable in [terms of finances]." While we were writing this book, Morris Brown College, under James's leadership, regained federal approval to accept federal financial aid dollars, is financially stable, and has been approved for accreditation by the Transnational Association of Christian Colleges and Schools (Whitford, 2021).

Belle Wheelan of SACS agrees with James's assessment, noting that most of the accreditation issues for HBCUs are related to their finances: "HBCUs tend to live from paycheck to paycheck and you can't run an institution like that, because you've got to have some money there so in case a catastrophe happens, you can keep the doors open. And so, they're not getting funded well from the state if it's a public institution or because they don't have that [large] endowment on which to fall back if they're a private institution, any little catastrophe that comes along crushes them financially." From the perspective of Bill Moses of the Kresge Foundation, the recent influx of philanthropic and federal support can serve to strengthen HBCUs and thus help them maintain accreditation. He noted, "The question is will HBCUs use [the current financial] opportunity to fix long-term problems and serve the students in the immediate crisis in a way that serves their institutions well going forward. This time of prosperity for

HBCUs could be a fundamental shift or it could just be the high-water mark for a couple of years."

For Dillard University president Walter Kimbrough, "it starts with the finances. I just describe [HBCUs] as underresourced institutions that serve an underresourced population. To me, when I see the challenges that the institutions face, that's where it begins." Kimbrough regularly balances putting more money in his financial aid budget for students and repairing a building's roof. Many colleges and universities have the resources to address both issues, but HBCUs regularly must choose between them. In most cases, HBCU leaders choose financial aid for students. According to Kimbrough, "I know for us, we put more money into student financial aid, so yeah, you might have a little bit more deferred maintenance, but I'm thinking, I can put off on this roof a little bit, and let me graduate students, with as [little] amount of debt as you can have." Of course, many colleges and universities defer maintenance issues as well, but not at the level of HBCUs (GAO, 2018; Thurgood Marshall College Fund, 2021). In many instances, deferred maintenance persists and goes unaddressed because HBCUs must prioritize financial emergencies or because funding constraints prevent them from addressing maintenance issues (GAO, 2018). In addition to delaying maintenance, HBCUs also shelve training, infrastructure upgrades, and other non-academic initiatives, which leads to inequities in facilities, services, staffing, and faculty professional development compared with other institutions.

Armando Bengochea, of the Mellon Foundation, has worked extensively with HBCUs for decades and worries about their underlying financial model. He shared that "the main challenge they face is that they can't afford their undergraduate student body. This is the big problem. Even a place like Spelman, which has several hundred million dollars in endowment, is one dramatically failed class entering—in terms of not hitting their enrollment targets—from going into major crisis." Bengochea said this problem is not limited to HBCUs: "HBCUs share that problem or fate with lots of predominantly White, private liberal arts colleges, but colleges that are mostly

White institutions don't have anything [close to the] share of Pell-eligible students [that HBCUs have]." As Bengochea explained,

> HBCUs must be able to afford to continue to construct a class without a lot of the resources that other institutions bring to bear. So, I worry most about enrollment swings. Right now, we're in an up period [based on the crisis in American society around race]. We're now experiencing a moment in which HBCUs are getting more students to apply and getting a greater share of those Black students who traditionally go elsewhere. And so, I think the big problem is just how do you diversify the pool of candidates for admission so that your [tuition] discount rate is not as lopsided as theirs are? That's I think a big worry.[2]

Howard University professor Robert Palmer shares Bengochea's concerns about enrollment. He noted that, based on his research, "there are a number of HBCUs that are, they're losing students. Their enrollment is very low, and students—Black students—certainly have other options now. So, working hard, to appeal to those students, providing a quality campus experience and making sure that the HBCUs keep their tuition and fees in a range that's going to support students who attend those institutions [is essential]." Jim Montoya of the College Board, an organization that engages with HBCUs regularly, also noted that enrollment is a significant challenge (Lundy-Wagner, 2015). He stated:

> Clearly, enrollment continues to be an issue, particularly given the fact that so many HBCUs are tuition-driven in terms of their revenue. Not only are many HBCUs tuition driven, but changes in enrollment can also significantly affect revenue. So, enrollment is an area where the College Board and HBCUs have a chance to work collaboratively. In 2020, we held our first annual HBCU enrollment leaders convening. And while we've had the HBCU conference, this is very specific to issues related to enrollment, knowing that if you ask most of our colleagues at HBCUs what is one of the biggest enrollment challenges you face as an institution, it's exposure. And this is a moment, I think we would all agree, where HBCUs are being looked to as an opportunity to embrace

greater numbers of students, and being recognized, as they should be, for the amazing contributions they have made and are making to broader society. So, we held our first annual HBCU Enrollment Conference, and we just had our second one. We talked very specifically about the impact of COVID on evaluating students' applications at HBCUs.

Enrollment at HBCUs has held stable for decades with some fluctuation. According to the National Center for Educational Statistics (2021), while African American student enrollment at HBCUs increased by 11% between 1976 and 2020, the total number of African American students enrolled in colleges and universities more than doubled during that same period. As a result, the percentage of African American students enrolled at HBCUs fell from 18% in 1976 to 8% in 2014. More recently in 2020, it increased to 9%.

Bengochea also worries about the long-term sustainability of HBCUs because White Americans do not understand them in ways that they should. Owing to our color-blind society—one in which race is not a factor—some White people cannot comprehend the need for HBCUs in a world that they think should be focused on integration and assimilation (DiAngelo, 2018; Kendi, 2019). He noted,

I can't tell you the number of civilians, nonacademics, who are surprised that there are still colleges that Black students go to. And their reaction to that is based on the insidiousness of color-blind ideology. They object. They think wait a minute. Why should government dollars be supporting institutions that only Black students go to? And you can tell them all you want, that anybody can apply, and anyone can go to an HBCU. It doesn't seem convincing to them. But I am concerned that [White] Americans just don't know about HBCUs, and when they learn about it, they're not sure what to think in part because of color blindness.

Bill Moses of the Kresge Foundation sees a challenge for HBCUs in terms of their location, as it pertains to enrollment: "One structural challenge for HBCUs is that many of them are small liberal arts colleges, or small public institutions, in isolated places. And that's always been true, but the model is harder to sustain today than it once was.

And this is not a criticism of the institutions. They are who they are. They are where they were founded, but it means it's much more challenging to get them through this difficult period." Clay (2012) noted that for HBCUs located in rural areas, geographic isolation is more of a problem, taking a toll on students and faculty alike, especially when they seek to attract young people from urban environments. Physical isolation also interferes with faculty recruitment because rural areas offer fewer employment opportunities for spouses and fewer educational options for children.

Believing that long-term sustainability is linked to the types of degrees and programs that HBCUs offer, Thomas Hudson, president of Jackson State University, stated, "We have to show that we offer the type of programs, the type of degrees that students are seeking [today]." According to Ruth Simmons, to be a higher education choice for African Americans, "we need to be excellent institutions in every regard. That means that we don't have the luxury of doing things in a less than excellent way. We have to build our faculties. We have to build our resources. We have to be the best possible places that we can be. If we are, the students will come because it is all about choosing a place that will be offering you everything that you need as a student, and that need is going to be there." Simmons expanded on this, pointing to the support that HBCUs can provide to students:

It's hard for me to imagine a world in which individual students won't want the kind of support they need to thrive. As human beings, that support is vital. Without it, we can falter. We can even fail. And so, the support is everything. And so, I can't imagine a day when an HBCU determines that it doesn't want to be the kind of place that offers that support to students. If [HBCUs] offer that support in the context of an excellent education, I think parents will continue to say I want my child to go there.

Agreeing with Hudson, Simmons added, "By far, in my view, above everything else, HBCUs have to have the right programs. They have to have the right faculty. They have to have the right resources. Without that, they will not be sustainable."

David Wilson, president of Morgan State University, also believes that having strong degree programs is essential to the long-term success of HBCUs: "I think it starts with ensuring that you have the right menu of academic degree programs, that are in alignment with where the country is and where you see the country going for the next 30 years or so. And a lot of times, those are not those academic degree programs that have been in existence for 75 years." He added,

> I do think that sometimes HBCUs struggle with changing something from the past and I think this piece is a major challenge for sustainability. We must put in place more interdisciplinary degree programs, and we must listen to employers. We have to listen to graduate schools more. There is no harm in being more like Carnegie Mellon, or like Stanford, where you go there and you get a major, science, technology, and society, where they brought together these three academic areas. Can you find an HBCU where you can get a degree like that? That's what we're working on at Morgan, but we've got to be more innovative in the academic growth space.

Belle Wheelan, president of SACS, agrees with the focus on degree programs. From her perspective, HBCUs benefit when they focus on their strengths:

> HBCUs need to stop trying to be everything to everybody. It's okay to be good at developing teachers or it's okay to be good at developing lawyers or it's okay to be good in developing welders, but you can't necessarily do all of those at once. Because number one, you don't have the faculty to do it. You don't have the facilities to do it, you just don't. Putting in an athletic team because everybody else has got one. There's nothing anywhere that says you've got to have an athletic team to be a strong institution but that's the perception, that I've got to do that and they're losing more money. I mean, even Alabama, bless their hearts, with the championships that they have won, they're not making a lot of money on anything but football and yet they've got to [support] all those other sports. And so, you've got to be able to say no sometimes and to say, here is our mission. We're going to stay within our mission. We're not going

to expand our mission but we're going to follow our mission and you're going to know North Carolina A&T for this, for example, and this is what we're going to do, and we don't ever have to be good at anything else other than this.

Another area that is linked to sustainability is infrastructure. As mentioned by others, there are myriad issues related to deferred maintenance. According to David Wilson, "I think because of the age of the campuses and the decades that have passed without any kind of serious investment in infrastructure and the upkeep of the buildings and the important things that are below ground that you don't see, now I think the foundation upon which many of those buildings rest is not stable and I think serious attention has to be paid to infrastructure." Wilson added,

> We need to modernize our campuses to make sure that when students have the choice and they have [narrowed] it now down to five schools, of which one or two of those schools may be HBCUs, but they can't go, I'm in Baltimore, so they can't go to Hopkins and go like, oh, wow! And then come to Morgan and go like Jesus Christ, who would want to go there? And so, you have to kind of understand your competition and then modernize your campus in a way where there's not this huge separation between the rest of higher education and you.

According to Susan Adams and Hank Tucker (2022), *Forbes* magazine investigative journalists, public land-grant HBCUs have been underfunded by at least $12.8 billion over the past three decades. Owing to systemic racism, states have failed to match federal allotments to these HBCUs, adding to their infrastructure and deferred maintenance issues.

Aaron Walton, president of Cheyney University, agrees that

> There's been tremendous lack of attention to HBCU physical plants. I think a lot of forethought went into establishing the organization and the buildings, but the amount of work that needs to be done to make them stay current, relevant, and up to date has been absent, and that continues to be a challenge because it's like plugging up the hole, when

you fix something over here, you have another leak on the other side. That impedes your ability to be as focused on what you should, and that's the education of the students. Attempting to address a myriad of other issues diminishes your focus and takes valuable time away from the primary issue, student success.

The long-term sustainability of HBCUs depends in large part on the ability of presidents to focus on the most significant needs of the institution, such as increasing its financial stability, addressing infrastructure issues, boosting student enrollments, and expanding degree programs. Importantly, all these areas are interrelated, and so it is critical that presidents address them in such a way that will allow the institutions to better meet the needs of future generations of students.

Telling the Institutional Story

As we talked with people for this book, we heard over and over how important it is for HBCUs to better tell their own stories and to use data and evidence in these narratives. According to Roslyn Artis, president of Benedict College,

> We have a PR problem. I think the big challenge is the HBCU public relations problem, and that is the assumption and the narrative often perpetuated even by us, that HBCUs are less than, that HBCUs are the place you go if you don't have another choice, that HBCUs are poor, they're broken, they're behind, they're dated. They're all those things that sometimes we even accidentally perpetuate. We have got to reframe the narrative around HBCUs as first-choice institutions for the robust, full-bodied experience they provide, and the outcomes that we are able to achieve in terms of quality of life and graduate satisfaction and overall gains postgraduation for our students. We got to start within the HBCU community, really reframing the way we talk about these institutions.

Artis gave a powerful example: "I do not permit my students to say just Benedict [in terms of where they go to college]. What do you mean, just Benedict? Are you insane? Like it is an honor and a privilege to be at Benedict, and don't you forget that. And so, we correct that, lovingly correct, right, misstatements of the value of this institution, and I think that impacts everything else." Artis sees the public relations problem as one linked to HBCUs' challenges in terms of raising money. She explained, "Of course we're challenged for money. Why? Because we have a PR problem. You cannot raise money. People give to winners: people give to things that they think are successful and strong. We know that institutions that are perceived to be higher quality, more successful, better outfits, tend to attract greater donations." Research confirms Artis's premise, showing that, throughout history, philanthropists have wanted to be associated with successful organizations, especially in the realm of HBCUs (Gasman, 2004, 2007a; Gasman & Epstein, 2004).

Artis expanded on her ideas and talked more specifically about the students:

> Students aren't going to choose to attend an institution where the narrative is they don't have strong networks. You're not going to get a good job. They're not highly respected. You won't get into graduate school. We've got to change the narrative around HBCUs. We have got to reframe the narrative and begin to cast these institutions in a more positive light. I think the data is our friend in that regard. We've been punching above our weight for generations, and rather than apologize for our existence, I think we need to amplify the importance and the value of these institutions.

Rick Gallot, president of Grambling State University, feels similarly to Artis. He thinks that one of the challenges for HBCUs is that they are seen as "substandard, that students who come here can't go anywhere else, that the HBCUs are the institutions of last resort, when we're not." Gallot himself had a scholarship offer to attend Dartmouth, but because he always wanted to be in a marching band, he chose Grambling State University. In his words, "We have a lot of students who have scholarships and offers to go to all sorts of schools, but they choose to come here for a reason, and they choose to go to Howard and to Hampton and FAMU."

From the perspective of Morgan State University president David Wilson,

> We need to reclaim our narrative and not allow others to paint [HBCUs] as a set of institutions where students go who can't go anyplace else. I think that is so unfortunate and I think that is a major challenge and I think we need to correct that, because if we don't correct that, the students who are coming out of our institutions, they could be carrying this kind of label, which is, oh, but you only went there because you couldn't go anyplace else and therefore you may not be as good as somebody who had all these options, which is nonsense.

He added, "I have been extremely careful here at Morgan not to perpetuate [this idea]. My students here at Morgan have done very well. I'm on a panel, I don't care who it is, president of MIT or the president at Cal Berkeley and I'll say to them, my students bring something to this enterprise that your students don't bring, and your students bring something that my students don't bring, but neither one is superior to the other."

Armando Bengochea of the Mellon Foundation agrees that telling the HBCU story is essential and recommends using data. "I think it's [about] putting your best data first. Know what your institutional outcomes are. What are your institutional effectiveness metrics? Why are you a great place? And make sure you have the data to generate the story because foundations are interested in institutions that are going to be successful going forward and can show what their trajectory is." He continued,

> There's been a lot of conversation and speculation in the last decade or two about the use of institutional data at HBCUs, how prepared they are to know that part of themselves. There's nothing more important than being able to show that picture. So, I think investing in their institutional data capacity, there are a lot of leaders, Walter Kimbrough and some others that are good at this. And again, the accreditors make them generate that data. But how well you use that data and how well you create stories about yourself is another part of having data capacity.

In recent years, with the influx of monies from MacKenzie Scott, it has become clear that philanthropists are looking closely at institutional data and are drawn to colleges and universities that can tell a compelling story, including a convincing leadership story (Gasman et al., 2021).

When Reynold Verret arrived at Xavier University as president, he inherited a great institution that had been led to acclaim by Norman Francis for 50 years. During Francis's tenure as president, Xavier's enrollment tripled, the endowment increased significantly, and the university became the leading producer of Black undergraduates who completed medical school. Xavier also has a long-standing national reputation for excellence in placing the most Black students in medical schools and graduating the most Black biologists, chemists, physicists, and pharmacists. But Verret noticed that some of the good work of Xavier was not as well known. As he explained, "One of the first things I noticed is that we have been deficient in telling our story." He noted that Xavier has plenty of stories to tell and that it needs to share the good work more often and more widely.

Verret explained how he became convinced of the importance of sharing the institutional story. Shortly after becoming president, he received a check for $40,000.

> It was a cold check that arrived in a letter to the president. I opened it at four o'clock in the afternoon, maybe five o'clock in New York City. There was a note in it. The note basically said, "I want to thank you. I read an article about your institution. I want to let you know how much we appreciate reading it." So, I gave them a call and this person was a significant philanthropist in the Northeast. I'm speaking to him and his wife, we're having a lovely conversation because I called him, it was five, six o'clock around dinnertime. And at the end of the conversation, he says, "You know Mr. President, what may surprise you is that we never heard of [Xavier]."

Verret said this experience, and several others like it, "was enough to slap you on the head and say, 'ha.' It is a feeling that since we know our story, everyone else must know it." He added, "We have been quite intentional, making sure people hear what we are doing and have done."

Kevin James, president of Morris Brown College, uses social media extensively to bring attention to the institution. As he shared,

A very huge component of how I was able to get people to believe that [turning Morris Brown College around] was possible was through social media. [It] was not this is what I'm going to do but let me show you what we did today. That's what I do strategically, purposefully, two to five times a day. I used social media strategically to show everyone what we were doing, and they bought into it, because they could see it and so things would go viral.

Worried that the HBCU narrative is often dictated by those outside the HBCU community rather than those working inside these institutions, Kent Wallace, a physics professor at Fisk University, told us,

We have to tell our story much better. I understand that sometimes that comes down to resources. I'm not saying this in an accusatory way, but it is an observation that I think that the narrative of what an HBCU is, sometimes that narrative gets set by people outside the institution that don't necessarily even know about the institution. People challenging that there is racism, turning a blind eye to it, saying, "We don't need HBCUs. You can go to a majority institution now, the need for an HBCU doesn't exist anymore." That is not the case. Look at these voting bills that are being passed.[3] You might as well say that we're in the Jim Crow era all over again. So, I think one of the biggest challenges that we face is our perceptions of our scholarship and our academic abilities, and the abilities of our students. That's a challenge. And mind you, it's a perception.

The challenges discussed in this chapter should serve as the impetus for a call to action among the HBCU community. Those we interviewed shared concerns that much work remains to be done if these institutions are to be sustainable for the long term. Their future necessitates that we address the challenges in ways that reflect bold and effective leadership, innovative thinking, a commitment to excellence, and collaborative spirit. Using these ideals to guide our collective efforts will ensure HBCUs continue to serve future generations of students.

9

Opportunities to Sustain the Future

We must be careful not to assume that our past is our future.
Very often we sit on our legacies and say we did this 70 years ago.
That's not your future, that's your past. So, you do stand on your
past, but basically you need to shape your future and not rest too
greatly on your past without thinking deeply about your future
circumstances.

—REYNOLD VERRET, President, Xavier University of Louisiana

Imagine for a minute if Historically Black Colleges and Universities
had all the resources they need to thrive and that they deserve given
how they have worked for over a century to build the African
American middle class and propel African Americans to success.
Imagine if HBCUs were able to offer robust scholarships to their
students and to properly pay their faculty members. HBCUs have
substantial power and strength that can be life-changing for students, communities, and constituents, and an investment in them is
vital to the future of higher education as well as the lives of all African Americans.

In this concluding chapter, we highlight some of the opportunities that we believe can be capitalized on as HBCUs grow and prosper in the twenty-first century. These include the outsize role that HBCUs play, and can continue to play, in preparing African American students for graduate school (especially at Predominantly White Institutions); the potential of the faculty at HBCUs (for research, advising, and model teaching) if invested in properly; the opportunity for creating more research-focused HBCUs; the possibility of being out in front on free-speech issues; the potential to support Black women in leadership roles; and the modeling of true diversity, equity, and inclusion for higher education. All these opportunities are rooted in the conversations we had with those working in, shaped by, and working closely with HBCUs.

Incubators of Talent

Historically Black Colleges and Universities are incubators for greatness and play a significant role in preparing students for graduate school. This role, along with HBCUs' record of accomplishments, should be built up and should be part of the institutional story that HBCUs tell. HBCUs pour into students, nurturing them and providing the support to enhance their self-esteem. As historian and Florida A&M University graduate Ibram X. Kendi explained in Chapter 4,

> I think that [in] attending an HBCU and then going to a Predominantly White Institution for grad[uate] school, I felt that not only was I very well trained academically, but even trained sort of socially in the sense. I was able to develop a very strong sense of who I was and myself. When I went to graduate school, I [was] able to better manage this sort of overwhelmingly White space. I wasn't as concerned about what people thought about me because I knew I had a very strong sense of what I thought about myself.

Kendi was able to navigate Temple University in Philadelphia for his PhD because of the foundation built at Florida A&M University and the self-confidence instilled in him by faculty and peers.

Prairie View A&M University president Ruth Simmons, who graduated from Dillard, attended Harvard University for her PhD. As she shared in Chapter 4,

> Harvard was pretty uncomfortable with me. They didn't know what to do with me. They said because surely there would be no career for somebody like me in the academic life. Why? Because I was studying French, and what was an African American doing studying French? It didn't fit for them. Nevertheless, I was paying my own way. And so, I was there, and I finished my PhD in four years. And I always say that I was able to do that because my HBCU skilled me for what I was going to endure at Harvard.

Kendi and Simmons are just two examples of the countless highly successful African Americans who benefited greatly from their undergraduate HBCU experience in their pursuit of advanced degrees. HBCUs can capitalize on their talent in this area through structured pathways and partnerships at both HBCUs that offer graduate programs and majority institutions. They can also serve as role models for other colleges and universities that are focused on preparing their African American students for graduate school. As Armando Bengochea of the Mellon Foundation shared, "I think by definition, of course, HBCUs set out to train a certain kind of population—a historically subjugated and relatively excluded population of students. And thus, they do all they can to ensure the conditions under which those students can rise to become leaders and become upwardly mobile. So, they, as a result, I think, do a lot of work to make the conditions for a multiracial American democracy possible."

Among HBCUs you have a community of institutions that cultivate the talents of students and prepare them for a lifetime of success. More importantly, HBCUs help produce a pool of Black talent that might otherwise not have reached their potential or tapped into their greatness because of the oppressive nature of trying to "survive" at a PWI. We think it is fair to question whether Stacey Abrams, Ibram X. Kendi, Ruth Simmons, or Lynn Wooten would be who they are today had they not attended an HBCU. An HBCU should, at the very least, be an option for Black students when making their college choice.

Tapping Faculty Potential

One of the reasons that HBCU students feel secure, as well as prepared for graduate school, is the faculty, which is rich in talent and the most diverse in the nation (Esmieu, 2019). There is even greater potential if an HBCU fully invests in its faculty in regard to their professional development. As Ruth Simmons, president of Prairie View A&M University, remarked earlier, the first thing she did when she got to the Texas-based university was to let everyone know that "the single most important thing for us to do is faculty development, period. Reduce the faculty teaching load. Right-size the faculty in terms of the number of tenured-track faculty versus adjuncts. Provide research support for faculty." Although some of the Prairie View campus constituents did not fully understand her approach at first, she convinced them that the quality of the academic enterprise is the most critical point of evidence in terms of graduation, retention, accreditation, fundraising, and long-term stability.

In his role at the Mellon Foundation, Armando Bengochea works extensively with HBCUs and has for decades, and so he understands how hard HBCU faculty work. Their teaching loads can be as high as 8–10 courses a year, which is considerably higher than the 4–6 courses per year load that is typical at most PWIs. This difference is due to the resource inequities, as well as an overarching focus on teaching over research on many HBCU campuses. According to Bengochea, "We can talk forever about the fact that most of these faculty are teaching 4–4, 4–5, 5–5 loads, and so their structural conditions don't make it possible for the faculty to become great contributing scholars in their field. . . . They are invisible to higher education, especially to the top tiers." That said, Bengochea knows that HBCU faculty "know their students well because they study teaching and learning. And studying teaching and learning is not something that is of enormous value in the private and public elite [colleges and universities]. It's just not.

HBCU faculty are often in the forefront of work around teaching and learning, and I think it's important to wake up to that broadly for higher education as an important contribution that the academy makes in general in society."

Tied to the idea of investing in faculty potential at HBCUs, it is essential that African Americans believe in the value of HBCU faculty and what they can contribute to students and the institution at large. From Makola Abdullah's perspective,

> Black people must believe in Black folks' institutions. It's really just that simple. The ice is not always colder. Faculty at HBCUs have always been as educated, as knowledgeable with the same exact degrees as faculty at PWIs. Not only that . . . we are mostly a teaching institution, but we've also required those same individuals to actually teach, not teaching assistants. We're putting PhDs in the classroom to teach our kids. We use the same books. We're accredited by the same organizations. The idea of whether we provide a quality education to me is a foregone conclusion and . . . I'm not even going to debate it because . . . there's no basis in which to say that HBCUs aren't viable or aren't quality.

As majority institutions work to diversify their faculties after centuries of injustice, HBCUs will have a harder time competing for African American faculty because of a lack of financial resources. On the other hand, HBCUs offer much to attract African American faculty. HBCUs can create working environments that uplift and celebrate African American faculty in the truest sense, but this will take considerable effort. HBCUs have always had remarkably diverse faculties (Esmieu, 2019), yet they have become less and less African American in recent years. According to Antoine Alston, a faculty member at North Carolina A&T State University,

> We are having a hard time attracting a cadre of high-quality African American faculty. And when I say that I'm talking about native-born African American faculty. We have a big cadre of international-born [Black] faculty, which is great. But when you're talking about Black institutions, parents want to send their students here for a reason. They want them to

be taught by folks who not only look like them, but also have their experiences, and understand the communities where they're coming from. And it is hard to attract Black PhDs because if you come to an HBCU, you're going to have a higher teaching load. Your salary is going to be lower, and we're still expecting you to do all this and still make tenure.

Despite what many may see as less than ideal conditions owing to the volume of work expected of HBCU faculty, being able to work with faculty, staff, and students who look like them is a powerful mechanism that does not exist at PWIs. Hence, HBCUs provide opportunities for Black faculty to work in spaces that offer a greater sense of belonging, which can subsequently lead to increased job satisfaction.

Ruth Simmons shared a thought-provoking comment with us that speaks to the potential of Black college faculty:

> We have been highly imitative of White institutions. Instead of enjoying the distinct advantage of having a room of our own, we've imitated others and, as a consequence, we have underdeveloped the knowledge that we should have been creating for centuries. And so, now, one of the great advantages for us, if we assume that responsibility, is to do right by the history of African Americans in this country. And while much good scholarship has been done across the world in regard to African American life and history and culture, there is still a lot to uncover. Keep in mind that so much across the centuries was deliberately hidden because it was a shameful history, and just trying to uncover what transpired so that we'll be better informed is an ongoing process [and] I think we're still at the very beginning of uncovering those stories. So, the second purpose I think is to value and research and to collect and to protect the truth about African American history and culture.

HBCUs are places that center Black culture in ways that are affirming for faculty, staff, and students. What results from this type of environment and culture are opportunities for HBCUs to further their leadership in producing knowledge that highlights the contributions of Black scholars and the impact of their work in addressing the needs of Black communities.

A Greater Emphasis on Research

As we were writing this book, several HBCU presidents were participating in national conversations related to moving their institutions
to "Research 1" status—or becoming "research intensive universities" according to the Carnegie Classification system, which catego-
rizes institutions based on their research productivity. Although
most HBCUs have traditionally had a teaching focus, there are some—
especially the larger public universities—that offer graduate degrees
and PhDs and secure significant external funding. David Wilson, the
president of Morgan State University, is intensely focused on his institution becoming the first HBCU to secure Research 1 status (Mangan, 2022). According to Wilson, "Morgan is talking about [moving] to
an R1. Howard, I believe [is] doing the same thing. There are several
HBCUs and a lot of cash out there to enhance capacity at HBCUs for
researchers, with the [National Institutes of Health], [National Science Foundation], US Department of Education, US Department of
Energy, unfortunately probably because of George Floyd but none-
theless, there's more interest in cultivating HBCU research." Despite
this enthusiasm, Wilson realizes that there will be some growing
pains at HBCUs because of the historical teaching mission and what
faculty are used to in terms of their current workloads.

According to Leah Hollis, a faculty member at Morgan State University, "If you're part of a newer guard [of faculty], you're jumping
in with two feet [in terms of research] and have an opportunity to
really advance. You got to push a little bit, because HBCUs across the
board generally don't have as much funds, but you can set your agenda
and do well. But you must multitask like crazy because our course
loads are higher." Hollis understands that research institutions are different from teaching institutions and that the road for some HBCUs to
become research-intensive institutions will be challenging. She noted,

There's this one pathway to those more traditional markers of research
excellence and then you have, I'll call them the former guard. As you
know, HBCUs were mainly teaching institutions. So, if you have a core

of faculty that has been there 30, 40 years and they came as teaching faculty, to suddenly switch gears on them, now you're expected to get a grant. You're expected to publish, but you still have a four and five course load and we're still not paying you [enough] and you don't have a [research assistant]. Oh yeah and you have to build your lab. There is this cultural tension that I'm picking up between what we aspire to be and leaving behind the traditions of being a teaching college. And during that kind of transition, you've got static.

Hollis sees a difference in the newer faculty, sharing,

I conducted a writing workshop last year out of the provost office. These were the new guard of faculty. They're rocking and rolling; they're writing grant proposals or looking for opportunities. That was the purpose, and they were all newer to Morgan, I would say in the last 10 years. And some of them commented, well, I've got a couple people who sit on my review committees, and they've been here for 30 years. So, they really don't dig me publishing for a year and applying for a grant while they're about teaching and understandably so, because that's what they were brought in for.

As Hollis lamented,

That tension, I think can be disheartening, because it's certainly not the Wakanda[1] experience when you get into that kind of tension. It can motivate you, if you're particularly competitive and say, oh, so here's the brass ring and if somebody from the former guard is going to tie me down, I'm just going to go for the brass ring and not worry about it. So, it also depends on the motivation of a faculty member about whether you are going to acquiesce to the former guard or are you going to set yourself up to progress with the aspiring guard? I don't want to use old and new, but just the culture is changing and it's tough.

Hollis spoke of an issue that will require deep and difficult conversations. For HBCUs that aspire to achieve Research 1 status, faculty, staff, and students will need to come together and discuss in authentic ways what it will take to move their institutions to the next level.

Thomas Hudson, the president of Jackson State University, is also interested in his university becoming a Research 1 institution. He shared,

> It's great to see the [recent] investment in HBCUs, but the fact is there are no Research 1, Carnegie-designated HBCUs. [This is] the reason that a lot of times we can't invest in the faculty in a way that supports that great research that gets you to that level. Our faculty, we'll bring you in and you might have great potential but we're going to load you down with classes. We're going to load you on committees. In some departments [there's] only one or two of you and that's not conducive to the type of research and the type of time and investment needed to do the type of research that moves us up the ladder. So that's one of the things that we have to do better.

Speaking about the impact of the large donations to HBCUs from philanthropist MacKenzie Scott, Hudson stated, "If you're a Research 2^2 institution and you received a contribution from MacKenzie Scott, if you're not using a portion of that to support faculty in a way that allows them to then invest increasingly of their time in research, with the goal of moving you up to that Research 1 status, you're really missing the boat. That is paramount to what we need."

As we have shared throughout this book, HBCUs were born out of the desire to serve and uplift Black people. Thus, the desire to reach Research 1 status aligns with HBCUs' long and storied history of yearning to provide African Americans with opportunities. Likewise, this aspiration allows for a reimagining of what a twenty-first-century HBCU can be.

Leading on Free Speech

Across the nation, issues of free speech are at the forefront of our discussions, with controversies taking place on the right and the left (Haidt, 2022; Schrecker, 2021). These have played out on college campuses with administrators taking various stances on free speech for faculty, staff, and students and academic freedom for faculty. HBCUs have a considerable history of both protecting personal freedoms and, at times, succumbing to outside forces (Gasman, 1999; Williamson-Lott, 2008). In the current climate, HBCUs can be out in front on issues of free speech. From the perspective of Louis Sullivan, former president of Morehouse School of Medicine, the board of trustees of an HBCU must ensure that free speech and academic freedom are upheld:

> Having such concepts as academic freedom and having an environment where you bring forth ideas that are different or maybe in conflict [is essential]. Working through [these conflicts] so that you have freedom of expression, development of ideas, all of that enriches our society. But you must have an environment that has a culture that is open to that [disagreement], that you have free and open and honest debate. That makes society stronger if you have that. So, you must have a governing board that really helps to see that the environment of the institution supports [academic freedom].

Walter Kimbrough, president of Dillard University, agrees: "I think historically HBCUs have wrestled with ideas of speech, and I think the challenge people have is that if you start limiting speech, the people that get hurt the most are the marginalized people, and that's what I really fear." He added, "When people say we don't want this person to speak. Well, the person that you like, they're going to come after them next. So, I think you must be a defender for all those ideas to have a place." Kimbrough sees HBCUs as places where much-needed conversations can take place—even those that can move African Americans forward but might be delicate in nature: "I think HBCUs are a place where you can have some conversations the broader community is not going to have. It doesn't mean that they're controversial or anything. It's just a place to have that conversation." But he also thinks that HBCU communities need to push themselves to engage other voices—even those they might not agree with. According to Kimbrough, "I think that if we're going to be an intellectual institution, you have to have some different kinds of ideas that come in and that challenge the students. I think another knock on HBCUs that people always say is, 'Oh, it's not the real world.' I want our students to be involved, to hear the real-world issues, no matter what they are. So, you're talking politics, liberal or conservative. They need to hear ideas that might make them uncomfortable." He continued,

> I heard Cornell West say it best a couple of years ago. [We] keep talking about safe spaces. What we really need are unsettled spaces. We need to unsettle people, to get them to think and have this cognitive dissonance. I subscribe to that. I think that historically there have been sometimes when HBCUs have provided that, but I think within their actions, they've been a place to make sure that different ideas are able to be expressed to the broader community. I just think that's just very important. But like I said, there've been, you know, the politics, particularly during the civil rights movement, there were HBCUs that penalized students for being involved in civil rights[3], that's an issue, too. So, you know, we have to defend all kinds of speech, the things that we like and that we don't like.

As the nation curtails speech, HBCUs are places where free expression and speech can flourish, demonstrating the diversity of thought among Black people and preparing African American students to engage with and challenge both those ideas they agree with and those they abhor once they graduate.

Propelling Black Women into Leadership Roles

For far too long, Black women have been ignored in society and even within the Historically Black College and University setting (J. B. Cole & Guy-Sheftall, 2003; Gasman, 2007b). They have been overlooked and victims of intense racism as well as sexism across racial communities. In recent years, however, we have seen an increase in the number of Black women leading HBCUs (as we are writing, 22 of the 105 presidents are women) and participating in leadership programs aimed at increasing access to presidential leadership (Gasman, 2020; A. Washington & Gasman, 2018). Women HBCU presidential leaders from Mary Schmidt Campbell to Ruth Simmons to Roslyn Artis are changing the landscape for future presidents, paving the way for their brave and revolutionary leadership. As Schmidt Campbell has told Black women, "Claim your time, claim your ground. The consequence of not, is that you are not able to bring your whole self into the room. And that's what I want every woman who graduates from Spelman to feel after she graduates. Even as she opens herself to different points of view that she may disagree with" (Herder, 2021).

HBCUs have an opportunity to cultivate more African American women leaders and to promote best practices in this regard. Their student bodies are over 65% women. Not only can HBCUs appoint more African Americans to the leadership ranks of these institutions themselves, but HBCUs—as incubators of talent—produce Black women leaders for corporate America, the larger academy, and state and federal government. They are experts in this regard and can serve as role models for other colleges and universities that endeavor to better support Black women students and future Black women leaders.

Models for Diversity, Equity, and Inclusion

Higher education institutions are often tasked with creating a more inclusive environment to help ensure students feel welcomed, heard, and valued while attending (Campbell-Whatley et al., 2021). At many PWIs there is a lack of commitment to issues of diversity, equity, and inclusion (DEI), which leads to Black students reporting unwelcoming campus climates and feelings of isolation and not being supported. In contrast, students and faculty at HBCUs often describe their institutions as inclusive, diverse, supportive, and reflecting a family-like environment. HBCUs embody inclusion in both their mission and history, and for many Black students who attend HBCUs, the presence of a critical mass has a positive impact on campus climate and leads to feelings of confidence and belonging (S. M. Jones & Phillips, 2020). The core mission of HBCUs is to provide educational access to Black Americans, but these institutions also enroll a disproportionate amount of low-income, first-generation college students compared with PWIs. In many ways, HBCUs have established themselves as institutions that are committed to DEI. Not only have HBCUs been leaders in creating learning environments that are deeply supportive and caring, but these institutions also reflect diversity among the student body as they have had to be responsive to the needs of diverse populations in ways that most PWIs have failed to do. Thus, HBCUs are better positioned to serve as exemplary models of DEI efforts within higher education.

Throughout this book we have shared numerous examples of lessons that can be gleaned from HBCUs, which can also help PWIs address issues related to DEI. For example, those we interviewed noted how HBCUs help foster a healthy sense of self and community. We learned how the culture of HBCUs bolsters Black students' sense of their racial identity. The mentoring and pedagogical practices used at HBCUs also affirm Black students' capacity to succeed, which subsequently leads to a greater likelihood for academic success. We also learned how HBCUs have helped foster academic success in STEM, with students graduating with STEM degrees and entering the workforce. For the foreseeable future, DEI will continue to be a major focus within higher education. PWIs that struggle with integrating DEI into their institutions' core activities should look to HBCUs as models on how to enhance the campus DEI experiences of Black students and faculty.

Final Thoughts

Our goal in writing this book was to examine, in deep and meaningful ways, the power of HBCUs. We used a rigorous research approach that included 50 original oral history interviews and numerous existing oral history collections, as well as myriad and diverse data sources to help tell the unique and remarkable story of HBCUs and to lend credence to the outsize role that HBCUs play in US society and beyond. We provided countless examples of the true power of HBCUs throughout the book, which is reflected in their role in moving generations of Black Americans into the middle class as well as in increasing their socioeconomic mobility. We revealed the power in the ways that HBCUs contribute to the mentoring of their graduates and how these graduates pay it forward by mentoring others. We also showcased the power of HBCUs through the ways they contribute to the economic development of the cities where they reside as well as how they engage with their local and regional communities. We demonstrated that the unique culture of HBCUs has a positive impact on the lives and identities of students, and why philanthropists and alumni alike should invest in that culture. Finally, we showed how the power of HBCUs is present in the way that they shape and propel African American students into leadership and intellectual roles in medicine, literature, law, higher education, art, sports, and business.

As Paul Quinn College president Michael Sorrell stated so passionately, "HBCUs are the great American experiment. There's been nothing in history like them, and I don't think that [fact] gets credit enough. You created a set of schools [for] people who weren't even considered people, right, who were considered chattel, to help them access a life in a land that never wanted them there in this way." HBCUs have earned our respect, deserve our investment, and exemplify the soul of the nation, a soul we desperately need.

APPENDIX A *

The Study

In writing this book, we used a variety of data sources. First, we drew on peer-reviewed articles, books, and reports related to Historically Black Colleges and Universities—including both current and historical sources. Second, we consulted the larger literature related to institutions of higher education and their impact on the lives of students and society. Third, we engaged with national data sets, including those from the National Center for Education Statistics and the Integrated Postsecondary Education Data System, to more fully understand the contributions of HBCUs and their general landscape. To highlight the contributions of HBCUs in the STEM fields, we drew on research by the National Science Foundation. Fourth, we consulted research in the fields of philanthropy, economics, sociology, history, Africana studies, and civic engagement, as well as many other subfields related to topics in the book.

Next, we crafted a list of individuals whom we wanted to interview. These people spanned the HBCU landscape—from graduates to presidents to faculty to administrators, as well as foundation program officers and those in the federal government and in nonprofit organizations who regularly engage HBCUs. Under the auspices of the Institutional Review Board at Rutgers University, we developed a general interview protocol as well as a specific one for each person. We conducted the interviews in the manner of oral histories rather than as qualitative interviews (Gasman, 2010b).

Our interviews lasted 60 minutes. We had them transcribed by Absolute Research, a company we have worked with for decades. None of our interviews are masked in terms of identity as everyone agreed to the use of their real names. On occasion, someone would ask to speak off the record, and we honored that request. Overall, people were incredibly forthright in their discussion of HBCUs. We could tell that everyone cared deeply about HBCUs and wanted the absolute best for these institutions even when they were being critical.

Once we received the transcripts, we shared a copy with each of our interviewees, giving them an opportunity to review and make changes. Individuals made minor grammatical changes but did not change the substance of the interview transcripts. Then, we each read the transcripts multiple times, noting how the interviews fit into our chapters. We then met in person to negotiate the use of the interview data in the various chapters and created two new chapters based on the richness of the interviews and our critical discussion. Although we kept major themes in mind, we did not code the interviews in the manner of a qualitative researcher. Instead, we drew on the interviews to support and complement the book chapters and what we found in our other research. Of note, although we did not use quotes from every individual we interviewed, we did draw on their experiences.

To shape the book, we drew on our previous research knowledge and our personal knowledge: one of us has been conducting historical, qualitative, and quantitative research related to HBCUs since 1994, and the other is a two-time HBCU graduate who has also conducted research related to HBCUs. As part of our writing process, we each wrote sections of the book, shared them with each other, offered extensive critique, and then rewrote each other's sections to reach a common voice. We then worked to smooth out and polish the chapters, as well as our usage of primary and secondary data. Our process also involved reading the chapters aloud to each other to find areas where ideas did not connect and where additional analysis and evidence were needed to make our claims.

We interviewed the following individuals:

Makola Abdullah

Isaac Addae

Antoine Alston

James D. Anderson

Roslyn Artis

Armando Bengochea

Jamila Brathwaite

Brittini Brown

Barbara Cronan

Torrie Cropps

Abdalla Darwish

Joseph Drew

Anthony Driggers

Trina Fletcher

Rick Gallot
Leah Hollis
Thomas Hudson
Kevin James
Amber Johnson
Martha Kanter
Ibram X. Kendi
Walter Kimbrough
Martin Lemelle
Harold Martin
Jeffrey Miller
James Montoya
William Moses
Sierra Nance
Stanley Nelson
Michael Nettles
Robert Palmer

Marquita Qualls
Crystal Sanders
Mary Schmidt Campbell
Ruth Simmons
Michael Sorrell
Louis W. Sullivan
Alton Thompson
Reynold Verret
Danielle Waddell
Kent Wallace
Aaron Walton
Belle Wheelan
Damon Williams
David Wilson
John Wilson
Lynn Wooten

We also used interviews with many other individuals that are publicly available. These interviews are cited in the individual chapters.

Finally, during our interviews, we asked everyone what we should make sure to include in a book about the power of HBCUs. We included every topic they shared in addition to those we originally intended to cover. We worked to make this book as comprehensive as possible, knowing that we surely left things out or could not dig as deep into some of the topics as we would have liked. It was our pleasure to do this research, and we learned from the process both intellectually and professionally.

APPENDIX B

List of HBCUs

Historically Black Colleges and Universities mentioned in the book appear with an asterisk in the list below.

*Alabama A&M University
Normal, AL
1875; Public, 4-year

*Alabama State University
Montgomery, AL
1867; Public, 4-year

Albany State University
Albany, GA
1903; Public, 4-year

*Alcorn State University
Alcorn, MS
1871; Public, 4-year

*Allen University
Columbia, SC
1870; Private, 4-year

American Baptist College
Nashville, TN
1924; Private, 4-year

Arkansas Baptist College
Little Rock, AR
1884; Private, 4-year

Barber Scotia College
Concord, NC
1867; Private, 4-year

*Benedict College
Columbia, SC
1870; Private, 4-year

*Bennett College
Greensboro, NC
1873; Private, 4-year

*Bethune-Cookman University
Daytona, FL
1904; Private, 4-year

*Bishop State Community College
Mobile, AL
1927; Public, 4-year

Bluefield State College
Bluefield, WV
1895; Public, 2-year

*Bowie State University
Bowie, MD
1865; Public, 4-year

Carver College
Atlanta, GA
1943; Private, 4-year

*Central State University
Wilberforce, OH
1887; Public, 4-year

*Cheyney University of
Pennsylvania
Cheyney, PA
1837; Public, 4-year

*Claflin University
Claflin, SC
1869; Private, 4-year

*Clark Atlanta University
Atlanta, GA
1865; Private, 4-year

Clinton College
Rock Hill, SC
1894; Private, 4-year

*Coahoma Community College
Clarksdale, MS
1924; Public, 2-year

Coppin State University
Baltimore, MD
1900; Public, 4-year

*Delaware State University
Dover, DE
1891; Public, 4-year

*Denmark Technical College
Denmark, SC
1947; Public, 2-year

*Dillard University
New Orleans, LA
1869; Private, 4-year

*Edward Waters College
Jacksonville, FL
1866; Private, 4-year

Elizabeth City State University
Elizabeth City, NC
1891; Public, 4-year

Fayetteville State University
Fayetteville, NC
1867; Public, 4-year

*Fisk University
Nashville, TN
1866; Private, 4-year

*Florida Agricultural and Mechanical University
Tallahassee, FL
1887; Public, 4-year

*Florida Memorial University
Miami Gardens, FL
1879; Private, 4-year

Fort Valley State University
Fort Valley, GA
1895; Public, 4-year

*Gadsden State Community College
Gadsden, AL
1925; Public, 2-year

*Grambling State University
Grambling, LA
1901; Public, 4-year

*H. Councill Trenholm State
Community College
Montgomery, AL
1963; Public, 2-year

*Hampton University
Hampton, VA
1868; Private, 4-year

Harris-Stowe State University
Saint Louis, MO
1857; Public, 4-year

*Hinds Community College
Raymond, MS
1903; Public, 2-year

Hood Theological College
Salisbury, NC
1879; Private, 4-year

*Howard University
Washington, DC
1867; Private, 4-year

*Huston-Tillotson University
Austin, TX
1875; Private, 4-year

Interdenominational Theological
Center
Atlanta, GA
1958; Private, 4-year

*Jackson State University
Jackson, MS
1877; Public, 4-year

*Jarvis Christian College
Hawkins, TX
1912; Private, 4-year

*J. F. Drake State Community and
Technical College
Huntsville, AL
1961; Public, 2-year

*Johnson C. Smith University
Charlotte, NC
1867; Public, 4-year

*Kentucky State University
Frankfort, KY
1886; Public, 4-year

Knoxville College
Knoxville, TN
1875; Private, 4-year

*Lane College
Jackson, TN
1882; Private, 4-year

*Langston University
Langston, OK
1897; Public, 4-year

*Lawson State Community
College
Birmingham, AL
1949; Public, 2-year

*Le Moyne-Owen College
Memphis, TN
1862; Private, 4-year

Lincoln University
Jefferson City, MO
1866; Public, 4-year

*Lincoln University
Lincoln, PA
1854; Public, 4-year

*Livingstone College
Salisbury, NC
1879; Private, 4-year

*Meharry Medical College
Nashville, TN
1876; Private, 4-year

*Miles College
Fairfield, AL
1898; Private, 4-year

*Mississippi Valley State University
Itta Bena, MS
1950; Public, 4-year

*Morehouse College
Atlanta, GA
1867; Private, 4-year

*Morehouse College of Medicine
Atlanta, GA
1867; Private, 4-year

*Morgan State University
Baltimore, MD
1867; Public, 4-year

*Morris Brown
Atlanta, GA
1867; Private, 4-year

*Morris College
Sumter, SC
1908; Private, 4-year

*Norfolk State University
Norfolk, VA
1935; Public, 4-year

*North Carolina A&T State
University
Greensboro, NC
1891; Public, 4-year

*North Carolina Central University
Durham, NC
1910; Public, 4-year

*Oakwood University
Huntsville, AL
1896; Private, 4-year

*Paine College
Augusta, GA
1882; Private, 4-year

*Paul Quinn College
Dallas, TX
1872; Private, 4-year

*Philander Smith College
Little Rock, AR
1877; Private, 4-year

*Prairie View A&M University
Prairie, TX
1876; Public, 4-year

*Rust College
Holly Springs, MS
1866; Private, 4-year

*Saint Augustine's University
Raleigh, NC
1867; Private, 4-year

Savannah State University
Savannah, GA
1890; Public, 4-year

*Shaw University
Raleigh, NC
1865; Private, 4-year

*Shelton State Community College
Tuscaloosa, AL
1952; Public, 2-year

Shorter College
North Little Rock, AR
1886; Private, 2-year

Simmons College of Kentucky
Louisville, KY
1869; Private, 4-year

*South Carolina State University
Orangeburg, SC
1896; Public, 4-year

*Southern University and A&M
College
Baton Rouge, LA
1880; Public, 4-year

Southern University at New
Orleans
New Orleans, LA
1959; Public, 4-year

Southern University at
Shreveport
Shreveport, LA
1967; Public, 2-year

Southwestern Christian College
Terrell, TX
1948; Private, 4-year

*Spelman College
Atlanta, GA
1881; Private, 4-year

St. Philip's College
San Antonio, TX
1898; Public, 2-year

*Stillman College
Tuscaloosa, AL
1876; Private, 4-year

*Talladega College
Talladega, AL
1867; Private, 4-year

*Tennessee State University
Nashville, TN
1912; Public, 4-year

*Texas College
Tyler, TX
1894; Private, 4-year

*Texas Southern University
Houston, TX
1927; Public 4-year

*Tougaloo College
Tougaloo, MS
1869; Private, 4-year

*Tuskegee University
Tuskegee, AL
1881; Private, 4-year

*University of Arkansas at Pine Bluff
Pine Bluff, AR
1873; Public, 4-year

University of Maryland Eastern
Shore
Princess Anne, MD
1886; Public, 4-year

*University of the District of
Columbia
Washington, DC
1851; Public, 4-year

University of the Virgin Islands
Charlotte Amalie, VI
1962; Public, 4-year

*Virginia State University
Petersburg, VA
1882; Public, 4-year

*Virginia Union University
Richmond, VA
1865; Private, 4-year

Virginia University of Lynchburg
Lynchburg, VA
1886; Private, 4-year

*Voorhees College
Denmark, SC
1897; Private, 4-year

*West Virginia State University
Institute, WV
1891; Public, 4-year

*Wilberforce University
Wilberforce, OH
1856; Private, 4-year

*Wiley College
Wiley, TX
1873; Private, 4-year

*Winston-Salem State University
Winston Salem, NC
1892; Public, 4-year

*Xavier University of Louisiana
New Orleans, LA
1915; Private, 4-year

NOTES

___

Chapter One: On the Higher Education Landscape

1. Historians disagree over the year 1619, with some arguing that the first Africans were brought to North America in 1526 by Lucas Vazquez de Ayllon. These individuals were in San Miguel de Gualdape, a former Spanish colony that is located in present-day South Carolina (Edgar, 1998; P. Hoffman, 2015).

2. The University of the District of Columbia (UDC) is rooted in the Miner Normal School, which was a school for "colored girls" founded by Myrtilla Miner in 1851. Through a series of mergers with other schools, UDC was formed in 1976. For more information, see https://www.udc.edu/about/history -mission.

3. Of note, Martin Henry Freeman was the first African American president of the all-Black Allegheny Institute (later Avery College), in Pittsburgh, Pennsylvania, between roughly 1851 and 1862 (exact years unknown). The institute offered elementary education and was supported in part by the AME Church.

4. This approach was also a feature at most historically White colleges and universities—starting with Harvard University—during the first decades of their existence.

5. Ida B. Wells, who was a student at three HBCUs—Rust College, Fisk University, and LeMoyne-Owens College—was a leader in promoting antilynching legislation and worked hard to expose lynching activities across the South.

6. The first Morrill Act, which became law in 1862, set aside lands for colleges focused on agriculture and mechanics. Of note, the land for the Morrill Acts did not belong to the United States. It was stolen from various Native American tribes throughout the nation through hostile takeovers and the annihilation of Indigenous people. See Wilder (2013) and Harris (2021).

7. Although there are currently 21 historically Black land-grant universities, only 18 were created as a result of the second Morrill Act. The University of the Virgin Islands was supported in 1962, the University of the District of Columbia in 1994, and Central State University in 2014.

8. Alcorn State University in Alcorn, Mississippi, is also a land-grant institution but was supported by the original land-grant act of 1860. It was the only HBCU created by that act.

9. One of these scandals, the Ludlow Massacre, was a mass killing brought on by an antistrike militia. Members of the Colorado National Guard, along with

private guards supported by the Colorado Fuel and Iron Company, attacked the living space of roughly 1,200 coal miners and their families who were staging a strike in Ludlow, Colorado, on April 20, 1914. John D. Rockefeller Jr., who owned part of the Colorado Fuel and Iron Company, was credited with organizing the massacre. For more information, see McGuire (2004).

10. For a complete list of women presidents of HBCUs, see A. Washington and Gasman (2018).

11. The Harlem Renaissance was an intellectual and cultural movement featuring African American literature, poetry, music, art, fashion, dance, theater, politics, and intellectual contributions centered in the Harlem section of New York City. The Harlem Renaissance spanned the 1920s and 1930s. Although referred to currently as the Harlem Renaissance, at the time it was known as the New Negro Movement, named after *The New Negro*, a 1925 anthology edited by one of the architects of the Harlem Renaissance, Alain Locke.

12. *Plessy v. Ferguson*, 163 U.S. 537 (1896), was a landmark decision of the US Supreme Court in which the Court ruled that laws enforcing racial segregation did not violate the US Constitution as long as the facilities for each race were of equal quality.

13. Black students were admitted in small numbers to historically White institutions before the end of legalized segregation in 1954. For example, Alexander Twilight graduated from Middlebury College in 1823, Edward Jones graduated from Amherst College in 1926, John Russwurm graduated from Bowdoin College in 1826, George Vashon graduated from Oberlin College in 1844, and Anita Hemings graduated from Vassar College in 1897 (Slater, 1994).

14. HNIC is an acronym that means "head Negro in charge."

15. HBCU community colleges include Bishop State Community College (Alabama), Clinton College (South Carolina), Coahoma Community College (Mississippi), University of the District of Columbia Community College (Washington, DC), Demark Technical College (South Carolina), Hinds Community College–Utica Campus (Mississippi), Shorter College (Arkansas), Southern University Shreveport (Louisiana), Southwestern Christian College (Texas), St. Philip's College (Texas), Trenholm State Community College (Alabama), Gadsden State Community College (Alabama), J. F. Drake State Technical College (Alabama), and Shelton State Community College (Alabama).

Chapter Two: Culture and Its Impact on Black Identity

1. The first HBCU marching band was the Tuskegee Normal School Brass Band, which was formed in 1895. Of note, Alabama A&M University and Florida A&M University also formed bands in 1890 and 1892, respectively. See R. Clark (2019).

2. The annual Bayou Classic is a weekend of football and tradition that is enjoyed by fans of Grambling State University and Southern University. It began four decades ago as a football game between two historically Black universities and has grown into one of New Orleans's largest and most anticipated sports competitions.

3. *Tell Them We Are Rising* is a documentary on HBCUs and was directed by Stanley Nelson and Marco Williams for PBS Television, https://www.pbs.org /independentlens/documentaries/tell-them-we-are-rising.
4. Jerry Rice, who was a wide receiver for the San Francisco 49ers of the National Football League (NFL), played college football at Mississippi Valley State University.
5. Walter Payton was a running back for the Chicago Bears of the NFL. Payton played college football at Jackson State University.
6. Doug Williams was a quarterback for the Washington Redskins of the NFL. Williams was the first Black quarterback to both start and win a Super Bowl. Williams played college football at Grambling State University.
7. Althea Gibson was one of the first Black athletes to cross the color line of international tennis. Gibson became the first Black woman to win the French, Wimbledon, and US Open singles championships. Gibson played collegiate tennis at Florida A&M University.
8. Wilma Rudolph became a world-record-holding Olympic champion and international sports icon in track and field. Rudolph was the first American woman to win three gold medals in track and field at the same Olympic Games. Rudolph ran collegiate track at Tennessee State University.
9. Eddie Robinson, born in 1919, was the son of a sharecropper and a domestic worker. He briefly attended Southern University, then earned a bachelor's degree at Leland College in Louisiana. Robinson started his coaching career at Grambling State University in 1941 and is widely known as one of the greatest college football coaches of all time. Robinson retired in 1997 after 56 years of coaching at Grambling. He won 17 Southwestern Athletic Conference championships. The greatness of Robinson and his teams is on display during the Bayou Classic, the annual college football game between Grambling State University and Southern University, which is widely known as the most popular rivalry among all HBCUs. During his tenure, Robinson established himself as the winningest coach in college football history, becoming the first coach to record 400 wins. Robinson retired with a record of 408 wins, 165 losses, and 15 ties. More than 200 of Robinson's players went on to play in the NFL. One of the most notable players coached by Robinson is former Washington Redskins quarterback Doug Williams who was the first Black quarterback to both start and win a Super Bowl Super Bowl. Robinson was also known for his commitment to the academic success of his players, which resulted in an 85% graduation rate among his players.
10. In some years, Howard University, in Washington, DC, sends more African Americans to medical school owing to its size. Xavier, however, continues to produce the most African Americans who pass the medial school graduate exam. See Xavier University website. (2019) https://www.xula.edu/news/2019 /04/xula-still-first-in-african-american-medical-graduates.html.
11. Jack and Jill of America was created in 1938 by African American mothers to foster social and cultural opportunities for interaction among their children.

The first chapter of the organization was established in Philadelphia, the second in New York City, and the third in Washington, DC, where it is now headquartered. The organization typically caters to upper-income African Americans and sponsors cotillions and other cultural and social activities. Annual dues are several hundred dollars, depending on the chapter. Membership is typically by legacy or invitation. All members must be mothers of children between the ages of 2 and 19.

12. For more information, see Camera (2017) and Daniels (2020).
13. The Carlton dance refers to a dance that the character Carlton Banks did on the TV show *The Fresh Prince of Bel-Air*.
14. For more information, see Avery (2003).
15. For more information about increases in Latino and White students at HBCUs, see Bumbardt (2020).
16. See Seymour & Ray (2015).
17. The late Chadwick Boseman played the role of the Black Panther in the Marvel movie by the same name.
18. Blow's books include *The Devil You Know: A Black Power Manifesto* (Harper 2021) and *Fire Shut up in My Bones* (Mariner Books 2015).
19. Although W. E. B. Du Bois attended Harvard College in 1888, he was not allowed to stay in the residence hall with his student contemporaries. In addition, he already had a bachelor's degree, having graduated from Fisk University. Harvard did not honor his degree from a Black college. For a first-person narrative of Du Bois's experience at Harvard, see Du Bois (1960).

Chapter Three: Onward and Upward

1. Research related to HBCUs and socioeconomic mobility uses publicly available aggregate US population-level intergenerational (parent linked to child) income information from the Internal Revenue Service (IRS) and college attendance information from the National Center for Education Statistics' Integrated Postsecondary Education Data System (IPEDS). These data were created in a collaboration between US government employees and researchers affiliated with Harvard's Opportunity Insights. The IRS data link parents' and their children's reported income earnings for children born from 1980 to 1991. Opportunity Insights publicly released aggregated information by postsecondary institutions after merging in key college demographic and institutional characteristics information from IPEDS. Institutions are identified and linked to IPEDS data through their unique Office of Postsecondary Education identifier, assigned by the US Department of Education.
2. Too often comparisons are made between HBCUs and Ivy League universities using performance indicators such as graduation and retention rates. These types of comparisons are neither fair nor accurate in that they compare institutions with a mission of serving low-income students with those that do not embrace this mission but instead one of exclusivity. Moreover, most colleges and universities—Black or White—cannot compete on graduation rates with Ivy Leagues institutions because they are nowhere near as selective,

and even the majority of PWIs have more low-income students than Ivy Leagues institutions. For more on the dangers of false comparisons, see Gasman (2015) and Gasman and Bowman (2011).

3. Ivy Plus refers to the eight institutions that are members of the Ivy League (Harvard, Yale, Princeton, Brown, Penn, Columbia, Dartmouth, and Cornell) and the following institutions: University of Chicago, Stanford, and MIT.

Chapter Four: Inspiring Leaders and Scholars

1. Charles Hamilton Houston was a lawyer who was instrumental in laying the foundation for the *Brown v. Board of Education* decision, outlawing racial segregation in public schools. Houston was a faculty member and dean at Howard University Law School, and he was instrumental in training large numbers of Black law students, including Thurgood Marshall.

2. Percy Julian was a chemistry professor at Howard University and a pioneer in the area of chemical synthesis of medicinal drugs from plants.

3. Ernest Everett Just was a biologist and professor at Howard University. His research focused on the cell surface in the development of organisms.

4. Alpha Kappa Alpha Sorority, Inc. began in 1980 on the campus of Howard University. Nine college women formed the group, which has grown into a global organization of 300,000 women.

5. W. Paul Coates founded Black Classic Press in 1978. The publisher focused on African American authors, including Walter Mosley, Dorothy Porter, and John Henrik Clarke.

6. Charles Drew was a professor at Howard University and a surgeon. He is best known for creating a method for storing blood plasma for transfusion and also organized the first large-scale blood bank in the United States.

7. Poet and author Amiri Baraka, also known as LeRoi Jones, attended Howard University. He was a recipient of the American Book Award.

8. Ossie Davis was a student at Howard University and an actor. He was a recipient of the National Medal of Arts and the Kennedy Center Honors.

9. Doug Wilder was a graduate of Virginia Union University and Howard University law school. He was the first African American to serve as governor of any state since Reconstruction and the first elected African American governor.

10. David Dinkins graduated from Howard University and served as the mayor of New York City from 1989 to 1993.

11. Lucille Clifton was a student at Howard University and a widely respected poet. Her work focused on endurance and strength through adversity in African American communities.

12. Kwame Ture (born Stokely Carmichael) graduated from Howard University and was a prominent leader and organizer in the civil rights movement. He was also a leader in the Pan-African Movement across the world.

13. The term "bald-headed Qs" refers to members of the African American organization Omega Psi Phi, Inc. The fraternity was founded in 1911 on the campus of Howard University by three students and their faculty advisor, scientist Ernest Just.

14. The Ausar Auset Society is a Pan-African spiritual organization that Ra Un Nefer Amen founded in 1973.
15. The author and anthropologist Zora Neale Hurston was a student at Howard University. She is well known for her fiction, including the novel *Their Eyes Were Watching God*, which was published in 1937.
16. Sterling Brown was a professor at Howard University for nearly 40 years. He also held faculty positions at Fisk University and Lincoln University. Brown was a poet and literary critic.
17. Kenneth Bancroft Clark, along with his future wife Mamie Phipps, studied psychology at Howard University. The Clarks performed the famous "doll tests" that were used to demonstrate the impact of segregation on children in the *Brown v. Board of Education* case.
18. Donny Hathaway was a singer, musician, and songwriter who studied music at Howard University.
19. Donald Byrd was a trumpet player who often played at the Blue Note in New York City. He earned a law degree at Howard University. In 1973, he produced the album Black Byrd with his students at Howard.
20. Alain Locke was a professor at Howard University. A graduate of Harvard, he was also the first African American Rhodes Scholar.
21. Although Double Dutch originated in the Netherlands, the jump rope game was made popular by African American girls in the United States.
22. bell hooks was a writer, poet, activist, and social commentator who focused her work on Black women and the Black experience.
23. Sonia Sanchez (born Wilsonia Driver) is a poet and a graduate of Hunter College. She was instrumental in developing Black studies courses at San Francisco State University. She has authored 16 volumes of poetry on Blackness and Black women. She has also written plays and children's books.
24. Frantz Fanon, originally from Martinique, was a political philosopher. His work is deeply influential in the areas of critical theory, postcolonial theory, and Marxism.
25. Of note, the poet and literary critic Sterling Brown was Toni Morrison's professor when she was a student at Howard, and Morrison worked to raise funds to support the creation of the Sterling Brown endowed chair.
26. Kuba art comprises a diverse array of media, which is influenced by the Kuba kings and queens. Kuba refers to a kingdom in Central America. The culture developed in the seventeenth century and peaked in the mid-nineteenth century.
27. Lois Mailou Jones was an artist and teacher.
28. Elizabeth Catlett was a sculptor and graphic artist. She is best known for her interpretations of African Americans in the twentieth century.
29. Jeff Donaldson was an artist who was a major figure in the Black Arts Movement of the 1960s and 1970s.
30. Ernie Barnes was an artist as well as a professional football player.
31. Delta Sigma Theta Sorority, Inc., an African American women's organization that focuses on community and activism, was founded in 1913 by 22 women at Howard University.

32. The Georgia flag did not drop the Confederate symbol until 2003, see Rothberg, 2021.
33. Benjamin E. Mays was the president of Morehouse College from 1940 to 1967. He is credited with laying the intellectual foundation for the civil rights movement, having served as a mentor for Martin Luther King Jr., Julian Bond, and Maynard Jackson while they were students at Morehouse College.
34. The Atlanta University Center, located in Atlanta, is the largest consortia of African American private institutions of higher education. It was created in 1929 and includes its member institutions: Clark Atlanta University, Morehouse College, Morehouse School of Medicine, and Spelman College. Morris Brown College was formerly a member.
35. Of note, Francis was appointed on April 4, 1968, the day Martin Luther King Jr. was assassinated in Memphis, Tennessee (Brack, 2020; Mangan, 2013).
36. Regina Benjamin served as the US surgeon general from 2009 to 2013, under President Barack Obama. She attended Xavier as an undergraduate and earned her MD at the Morehouse School of Medicine.
37. Claude Organ Jr. was a surgeon who did his undergraduate training at Xavier University. He earned his MD from Creighton State University.
38. Keith Amos earned his undergraduate degree at Xavier and his MD at Harvard University Medical School.
39. Herman Hughes received his bachelor's degree at Stillman College and went on to teach high school math. He eventually earned a PhD in computer science at the University of Louisiana, Lafayette. Hughes secured a faculty position at Michigan State University and stayed until retirement. He was a national expert on wireless and high-speed networks.
40. *Knight v. Alabama* was a federal case that lasted nearly 30 years. In 1981, John F. Knight, representative of Alabama's 77th District in Montgomery and the former president of historically Black Alabama A&M University, filed suit against the State of Alabama. He claimed that Alabama's higher education system was racially biased across a variety of areas. He made several attempts to secure justice and various appeals, but the Supreme Court refused to hear the case in 2007 and 2014.
41. Cleveland Sellers was a student at Howard University in the early 1960s. He was also a member of the Nonviolent Action Group, which was an affiliate of the Student Nonviolent Coordinating Committee. He worked diligently in Mississippi to register African American voters. Sellers also served as the president of Voorhees College in Denmark, South Carolina.
42. Langston Hughes started his education in Columbia but left because of the profound racial discrimination. He graduated from Lincoln University. For details on his education, see his autobiography, *The Big Sea*.
43. Reconstruction refers to a period between 1865 and 1977 in the United States. During this time the nation worked to reintegrate the southern states that had left the Union for the Confederacy, as well as integrate into society the 4 million Black people who had suffered the ills of slavery. Congress also introduced the Thirteenth, Fourteenth, and Fifteenth Amendments to the

Constitution, and the Civil Rights Act of 1866 was passed. During this short time, African Americans were allowed to vote and participate in the political process. They were also allowed to purchase land, use public accommodations, and seek employment. However, these minimal freedoms did not last long as those in opposition worked swiftly to curtail any gains that African Americans had made. For more information, see the Library of Congress.

44. Critical race theory (CRT) is a legal framework that signifies that systemic racism is part of American society; it permeates all aspects of society from the legal system to education to health care to employment. CRT sees racism as more than individual bias. For more information, see the NAACP Legal Defense Fund's FAQ, https://www.naacpldf.org/critical-race-theory-faq.

45. Elmer Imes graduated from Fisk University and pursued a PhD in physics at the University of Michigan. He was the second African American to earn a PhD in physics. Of note, Imes was married to Nella Larson, the Harlem Renaissance novelist and author of the famed novels *Quicksand* and *Passing*.

Chapter Five: Legacies of Mentoring

1. Will Packer, a graduate of Florida A&M University, is a film producer and has produced 28 films as well as the 2022 Academy Awards ceremony.

2. Keisha Lance-Bottoms, a Florida A&M University graduate, was the mayor of Atlanta.

Chapter Six: Understanding Philanthropic Support

1. Of note, African Americans have supported educational endeavors through churches, Black Greek letter organizations, Black civic organizations, and Black missionary societies and as individuals. But because of a lack of access to capital on the part of African Americans, as a result of centuries of racial discrimination and systemic racism, they have not been able to contribute at the level they desire (Baradaran, 2017; Gasman & Bowman, 2013).

2. The American Legislative Exchange Council is a conservative organization dedicated to the principles of limited government, free markets, and federalism. See https://alec.org.

3. Vernon Jordan was a civil rights lawyer and powerful political operative. He served as the president of the UNCF and eventually as an advisor to President Bill Clinton. Although he did not attend an HBCU for his undergraduate degree, he attended Howard University for law school.

4. Christopher Edley Sr. was an attorney who graduated from Howard University and then attended Harvard University for law school. Although the UNCF's famed "A Mind Is a Terrible Thing to Waste" campaign began the year before he took on the organization's leadership, he championed the campaign in the years that followed, making the UNCF one of the most widely recognized nonprofits in the nation.

5. Robert F. Smith is one of the wealthiest individuals in the nation, worth $6.7 billion according to *Forbes*. In 2000, he founded the private equity firm Vista

Equity Partners, which focuses on investing in software companies. He did not attend an HBCU; instead, he graduated from Cornell University and earned an MBA from Columbia University. For more on Smith, see https://www.forbes .com/profile/robert-f-smith/?sh=237122702236.

6. White philanthropic donors have been accused of perpetuating privilege by giving enormous donations to PWIs. Dillard University president Walter Kimbrough (2007) has been a vocal critic of White philanthropists, noting the impact that their large-scale PWI donations could have on HBCUs.

7. Harvard University raises roughly $3.8 million per day (Burstein & Caldera, 2020).

8. On March 31, 1960, W. E. B. Du Bois gave a speech to the Association of Social Science Teachers in Negro Colleges in which he warned that roughly 60 HBCUs would cease to exist owing to lack of support from African Americans and others. He also noted the rural locations of some HBCUs and that many African Americans were moving to cities. For more information, see W.E.B. Du Bois Papers, University of Massachusetts, Amherst, Series 2, Speeches, Whither Now and Why, https://credo.library.umass.edu/view/full/mums312-b206-i050.

9. Kimbrough is referring to the 2020 report by the American Institute of Physics: *The Time Is Now: Systemic Changes to Increase African Americans with Bachelor's Degree in Physics and Astronomy*.

10. For more information on the Kresge HBCU Initiative, see Schulze (2005). See also Leak (2018).

11. HBCUs in the MMUF program include Allen University, Benedict College, Bennett College, Bethune-Cookman University, Claflin University, Clark Atlanta University, Dillard University, Edward Waters College, Fisk University, Florida Memorial University, Hampton University, Howard University, Huston-Tillotson University, Interdenominational Theological Center, Jarvis Christian College, Johnson C. Smith University, Lane College, LeMoyne-Owen College, Livingstone College, Miles College, Morehouse College, Morris College, Oakwood College, Paine College, Paul Quinn College, Rust College, Saint Augustine's College, Shaw University, Spelman College, Stillman College, Talladega College, Texas College, Tougaloo College, Tuskegee University, Virginia Union University, Voorhees College, Wilberforce University, Wiley College, and Xavier University of Louisiana.

12. According to a report by the W.K. Kellogg Foundation (2013), African Americans give 25% more of their discretionary income than any other racial and ethnic group. See also Muhammad (2021).

13. Giving Tuesday refers to a movement to encourage contributing to charitable causes. It normally takes place in late November or early December, near the end of the tax year.

14. In 2002, the Southern Association of Colleges and Schools revoked Morris Brown College's accreditation, citing the misuse of federal financial aid by a former president and the financial aid director as well as the college's substantial debt. For more information, see Gasman (2007c).

Chapter Seven: Building Community

1. Morgan State University also benefited from monies from the state that resulted from a decades-long court case accusing the state of failing to desegregate its institutions and failing to support HBCUs. In total, the state allotted $577 million to HBCUs in the state of Maryland. For more information, see Douglas-Gabriel & Wiggins (2021).
2. Thompson is referring to the report *HBCUs make America strong: The positive economic impact of Historically Black Colleges and Universities* by the United Negro College Fund (2017). The report showcases the positive impacts of HBCUs on earnings, employment, and local and regional economies.
3. Ivan Allen Jr. was the mayor of Atlanta for two terms during the midst of the civil rights movement. He is often credited with providing important leadership in the transformation of the South—specifically, moving Atlanta from a segregated and economically depressed city to a more progressive place.
4. The Atlanta Life Insurance Company was founded by Alonzo F. Herndon, a former slave who became Atlanta's wealthiest Black man during his lifetime. The company, which was an outgrowth of the mutual aid societies that served low- and middle-income African Americans, grew to serve Black families throughout the South.
5. For the history of Tougaloo, see Lott (2008).

Chapter Eight: Challenges and Calls to Action

1. *The Hunger Games* is a movie about a televised competition in which teenagers are chosen at random to fight to the death.
2. Tuition discounting is the practice of using a portion of tuition revenue to provide academic merit scholarships and reduce tuition and fees. To do it successfully, a college must enroll a significant portion of upper-middle- and high-income students. According to Owen Daugherty (2021) of the National Association of College and University Business Officers, more private colleges and universities are offering tuition discounts than ever before as a result of the financial pressures arising from the coronavirus outbreak.
3. According to the Brennan Center for Justice (2021), in 2021 alone, at least 19 states passed 34 laws restricting access to voting. More than 440 bills had voter restrictions as their focus in 49 states in the 2021–2022 legislative session. These laws are focused on ensuring that people of color are unable to vote.

Chapter Nine: Opportunities to Sustain the Future

1. Wakanda is a fictional Black utopian society in the film Black Panther.
2. Research 2 refers to the second level of research institution as designated by the Carnegie Classification system.
3. For more information on HBCUs that penalized students for participation in the civil rights movement see Gasman, 2011, and Williamson, 2019.

REFERENCES

Adams, B. (2021, May 17). *United Negro College Fund elects its first Black board chair*. The Grio. https://thegrio.com/2021/03/17/uncf-board-chair-milton-jones

Adams, S., & Tucker, H. (2022, February 1). For HBCUs cheated out of billions, bomb threats are the latest indignity. *Forbes*. https://www.forbes.com/sites /susanadams/2022/02/01/for-hbcus-cheated-out-of-billions-bomb-threats-are -latest-indignity/?sh=73ffe90d640c

African American Registry. (n.d.). *Jewish professors, and HBCUs, a story*. https:// aaregistry.org/story/jewish-profs-and-hbcus

Akintobi, H., T., Sheikhattari, P., Shaffer, E., Evans, C. L., Braun, K. L., Sy, A. U., . . . & Tchounwou, P. B. (2021). Community engagement practices at research centers in US minority institutions: Priority populations and innovative approaches to advancing health disparities research. *International Journal of Environmental Research and Public Health*, 18(12), 6675.

Aladangady, A., & Forde, A. (2021, October 21). *Wealth inequality and the racial wealth gap*. US Federal Reserve. https://www.federalreserve.gov/econres/notes /feds-notes/wealth-inequality-and-the-racial-wealth-gap-20211022.htm

Allen, W. (1992). The color of success: African American college student outcomes at Predominantly White and Historically Black Colleges and Universities. *Harvard Educational Review*, 62, 26.

Allen, W., & Jewell, J. (2002). A backward glance forward: Past, present, and future perspectives on historically Black colleges and universities. *Review of Higher Education*, 25(3), 241-261.

Allen, W., Jewell, J., Griffin, K., & Wolf, D. (2007). Historically Black Colleges and Universities: Honoring the past, engaging the present, touching the future. *The Journal of Negro Education*, 76(3): 263-280.

Allen, W., McLewis, C., Jones, C., & Harris, D. (2018). From Bakke to Fisher: African American students in U.S. higher education over forty years. *The Russell Sage Foundation Journal of the Social Sciences*, 4(6), 41-72.

Allensworth, E. M., & Clark, K. (2020). High school GPAs and ACT scores as predictors of college completion: Examining assumptions about consistency across high schools. *Educational Researcher*, 49(3), 198-211.

Alridge, D. P. (2018). *The educational thought of W. E. B. Du Bois: An intellectual history*. Teachers College Press.

Als, H. (2020, January 27). Toni Morrison's profound and unrelenting vision. *The New Yorker.* https://www.newyorker.com/magazine/2020/02/03/toni -morrisons-profound-and-unrelenting-vision

American Institute of Physics. (2020). *The time is now: Systemic changes to increase African Americans with bachelor's degrees in physics and astronomy.* https://www .aip.org/sites/default/files/aipcorp/files/teamup-full-report.pdf

Anderson, E., & Moss, A. A. (1999). *Dangerous donations: Northern philanthropy and southern Black education, 1902–1930.* University of Missouri Press.

Anderson, J. D. (1988). *The education of Blacks in the South, 1860–1935.* University of North Carolina Press.

Anderson, J. D. (1993). Race, meritocracy, and the American academy during the immediate post-World War II era. *History of Education Quarterly, 33*(2), 15–175.

Anderson, N., & Lumpkin, L. (2020). 'Transformational': MacKenzie Scott's gifts to HBCUs, other colleges surpass $800 million. *The Washington Post.* https://www .washingtonpost.com/local/education/mackenzie-scott-hbcu-donations/2020 /12/17/0ce9ef5a-406f-11eb-8db8-395dedaaa036_story.html

Archibald, P., & Estreet, A. (2017). Utilization of the interprofessional education, practice, and research model in HBCU social work education. *Journal of Human Behavior in the Social Environment, 27*(5), 450–462.

Arroyo, A. T., & Gasman, M. (2014). An HBCU-based educational approach for Black college student success: Toward a framework with implications for all institutions. *American Journal of Education, 121*(1), 57–85.

Arroyo, A. T., Palmer, R. T., Maramba, D. C., & Louis, D. A. (2017). Supporting racially diverse students at HBCUs: A student affairs perspective. *Journal of Student Affairs Research and Practice, 54*(2), 150–162.

Arsenault, R. (2007). *Freedom riders: 1961 and the struggle for racial justice.* Oxford University Press.

Association of Public & Land-Grant Universities. (2020). *How does a college degree improve graduates' employment and earnings potential?* https://www.aplu.org/our -work/college-costs-tuition-and-financial-aid/publicuvalues/employment -earnings.html

Avery, V. (2003). The creation of a center of Black higher education: The Atlanta University Center. *NAAAS Proceedings,* National Association of African American Studies.

Bakari, R. S. (1997). African American racial identity development in Predominantly White Institutions: Challenges for student development professionals. *Different Perspectives on Majority Rules, 19.*

Baker, D. J., Arroyo, A. T., Braxton, J. M., Gasman, M., & Francis, C. H. (2021). Expanding the student persistence puzzle to minority serving institutions: The residential Historically Black College and University context. *Journal of College Student Retention: Research, Theory & Practice, 22*(4), 676–698.

Baradaran, M. (2017). *The color of money: Black banks and the racial wealth gap.* Belknap Press.

Barnett, B. M. (1993). Invisible southern Black women leaders in the civil rights movement. The triple constraints of gender, race, and class. *Gender & Society, 7*(2), 162–182.

Baskerville, L. (2021). *Historical roots: Continued contributions of HBCUs.* https://www.nafeonation.org/wp-content/uploads/2021/11/Historical-Roots-Continues-Contributions-of-HBCUs-w-Technical-Edits.pdf

BBC. (2020, April 22). *George Floyd: Timeline of Black deaths and protests.* https://www.bbc.com/news/world-us-canada-52905408

Beras, E. (2020). *Historically Black Colleges get a $120 million gift. They need it.* https://www.marketplace.org/2020/06/18/historically-black-colleges-get-a-120-million-gift-they-need-it

Betsey, C. L. (2008). *Historically Black Colleges and Universities.* Transaction Publishers.

Bevins, F., Fox, K., Pinder, D., Sarakatsannis, J., & Stewart, S. (2021). *How HBCUs can accelerate Black economic mobility.* McKinsey & Company.

Beyoncé. (2019). *Homecoming: The live album.* Netflix Productions.

Bieze, M. S., & Gasman, M. (Eds.). (2012). *Booker T. Washington rediscovered.* Johns Hopkins University Press.

Blau, P. M., & Duncan, O. D. (1967). *The American occupational structure.* John Wiley and Sons.

Bloomberg. (2016). *Rosalind Brewer: How did I get here?* https://www.bloomberg.com/features/2016-how-did-i-get-here/rosalind-brewer.html

Bly, A. (2008). Pretends he can read: Runaways and literacy in colonial America, 1730–1776. *Early American Studies, 6*(2), 261–294.

Boland, W., & Gasman, M. 2014. *America's public HBCUs: A four state comparison of institutional capacity and state funding priorities.* Penn Center for Minority Serving Institutions.

Booker, K. C., & Campbell-Whatley, G. D. (2018). How faculty create learning environments for diversity and inclusion. *Insight: A Journal of Scholarly Teaching, 13*, 14–27.

Bracey, E. N. (2017). The significance of Historically Black Colleges and Universities (HBCUs) in the 21st century: Will such institutions of higher learning survive? *American Journal of Economics and Sociology, 76*(3), 670–696.

Brack, N. (2020, September). *Norman C. Francis (1931–).* Black Past. https://www.blackpast.org/african-american-history/norman-c-francis-1931/

Brady, K., Eatman, T., & Parker, L. (2000). To have or not to have? A preliminary analysis of higher education funding disparities in the post-Ayers v. Fordice era: Evidence from critical race theory. *Journal of Education Finance, 25*(3), 297–322.

Brazzell, J. C. (1992). Bricks without straw: Missionary-sponsored Black higher education in the post-emancipation era. *The Journal of Higher Education, 63*(1), 26–49.

Brennan Center for Justice. (2021). *Voting laws roundup: December 2021.* https://www.brennancenter.org/our-work/research-reports/voting-laws-roundup-december-2021

Brewer, R. (2018). *Commencement address, Spelman College* [Video]. YouTube. https://www.youtube.com/watch?v=IzBcP8lu5z4

Bridges, B. (2018). *African Americans and college education by the numbers*. United Negro College Fund. https://uncf.org/the-latest/african-americans-and-college-education-by-the-numbers

Brown, M. C., & Davis, J. E. (2001). The Historically Black College as social contract, social capital, and social equalizer. *Peabody Journal of Education, 76*(1), 31–49.

Bumbardt, A. (2020, March 5). *At some HBCUs, enrollment rises from surprising applicants*. American Public Media. https://www.apmreports.org/episode/2020/03/05/hbcu-enrollment-latino-international-students

Burstein, E., & Caldera, C. (2020). Harvard places second among universities in total annual fundraising, per report. *The Harvard Crimson*. https://www.thecrimson.com/article/2020/2/7/harvard-2nd-fundraising

Butrymowicz, S. (2014). Historically Black Colleges are becoming more White. *Time*. https://time.com/2907332/historically-black-colleges-increasingly-serve-white-students

Bynoe, B. (2021, April 19). *HBCUs: The first patrons of African American art*. Black Art in America. https://www.blackartinamerica.com/index.php/2021/04/19/hbcus-the-first-patrons-of-african-american-art/s

Camera, L. (2017, May 19). Black girls are twice as likely to be suspended, in every state. *U.S. News & World Report*. https://www.usnews.com/news/education-news/articles/2017-05-09/black-girls-are-twice-as-likely-to-be-suspended-in-every-state

Campbell-Whatley, G., O'Brien, C., Reddig, K., Sun, T., & Freeman-Green, S. (2021). Non-majority student perceptions of diversity and inclusion at a PWI and an HBCU. Journal for Multicultural Education, 15(3): 253–269.

Carnevale, A., Jayasundera, T., & Gulish, A. (2016). *America's divided recovery: College haves and have nots*. Center on Education and the Workforce. https://cew.georgetown.edu/wp-content/uploads/Americas-Divided-Recovery-web.pdf

Carnevale, A., & Van Der Werf, M. (2017). *The 20% solution: Selective colleges can afford to admit more Pell Grant recipients*. Georgetown University Center on Education and the Workforce. https://1gyhoq479ufd3yna29x7ubjn-wpengine.netdna-ssl.com/wp-content/uploads/The-20-Percent-Solution-web.pdf

Casselman, B. (2015, December 9). *Most Americans aren't middle class anymore*. FiveThirtyEight. https://fivethirtyeight.com/features/most-americans-arent-middle-class-anymore

Castro-Samayoa, A., & Gasman, M. (2018). (Eds). *Contemporary issues in higher education*. Routledge Press.

Clark, L., Heaven, A., & Shah, U. (2016). Mainstreaming and maintaining: Perspectives of social justice from HBCU PETE alumni. *Journal of Teaching in Physical Education, 35*(3), 226–240.

Clark, R. (2019). A narrative history of African American marching band: Toward a historicultural understanding. *Journal of Historical Research in Music Education*, 41(1): 5–32, https://journals.sagepub.com/doi/10.1177/1536600619847933

Clay, P. L. (2012). *Facing the future: A fresh look at challenges and opportunities*. Kresge Foundation, https://kresge.org/sites/default/files/Uploaded%20Docs/Clay -HBCUs-Facing%20the-Future.pdf

CNN. (2018). *Georgia*. https://www.cnn.com/election/2018/results/georgia /governor

CNN. (2020, August 19). Transcript: Kamala Harris's DNC speech. https://www.cnn .com/2020/08/19/politics/kamala-harris-speech-transcript/index.html

Coates, T. (2008, May 1). This is how we lost to the White man. *The Atlantic*. https://www.theatlantic.com/magazine/archive/2008/05/-this-is-how-we-lost -to-the-white-man/306774

Coates, T. (2013). Homecoming at Howard. *The New York Times*. https://www .nytimes.com/2013/10/30/opinion/coates-homecoming-at-howard.html

Coates, T. (2015). *Between the world and me*. The Text Publishing Company.

Cole, D. (2018, October 23). *Stacey Abrams defends presence at 1992 burning of Georgia state flag, which contained the Confederate battle flag design*. CNN. https://www .cnn.com/2018/10/23/politics/stacey-abrams-flag-burning-protest/index.html

Cole, J. B., & Guy-Sheftall, B. (2003). *Gender talk: This struggle for women's equality in African American communities*. One World Press.

Committee on Education and Labor. (2019). *Investing in economic mobility: The important role of HBCUs, TCUs, and MSIs in closing racial and wealth gaps in higher education. Committee Report.*

Commodore, F. (2015). *The tie that binds: Trusteeship, values, and the presidential selection process at AME affiliated HBCUs* [PhD dissertation], University of Pennsylvania.

Connley, C. (January 27, 2021). *Walgreen's new CEO Roz Brewer on bias in the C-suite: 'When you're a Black woman, you get mistaken a lot.'* CNBC. https://www.cnbc.com /2021/01/27/walgreens-new-ceo-roz-brewer-on-dealing-with-bias-in-the-c -suite.html

Conrad, C., & Gasman, M. (2015). *Educating a diverse nation. Lessons from Minority Serving Institutions*. Harvard University Press.

Conrad, C., Gasman, M., Lundberg, T., Nguyen, T., Commodore, F., & Castro Samayoa, A. (2013). *Using educational data to increase learning, retention, and degree attainment at Minority Serving Institutions*. University of Pennsylvania.

Conyers, C. (1990). *A living legend: The history of Cheyney University, 1837–1951*. Cheyney University Press.

Covington, M., & Njoku, N. R. (2021). Answering the call: The role of HBCUs in engaging Black women's identity politics. In Crosby, G., White, K., Chanay, M., & Hilton, A. (Eds). *Reimagining Historically Black Colleges and Universities*. Emerald Publishing Limited, Chapter 11.

Crisp, G. (2010). The impact of mentoring on the success of community college students. *Review of Higher Education, 34*(1), 39–60.

Criss, D. (2019, September 19). *$34 million: How much one man is paying to wipe out a graduating class' college debt*. CNN. https://www.cnn.com/2019/09/20/us /morehouse-student-debt-trnd/index.html

Dance, S. (2012, December 10). Morgan State board votes against renewing president's contract. *The Baltimore Sun.* https://www.baltimoresun.com/maryland/bs-xpm-2012-12-10-bs-md-morgan-president-contract-20121210-story.html

Daniels, N. (2020, October 1). A battle for the soul of Black girls. *The New York Times.* https://www.nytimes.com/2020/10/08/learning/lesson-of-the-day-a-battle-for-the-souls-of-black-girls.html

Daugherty, O. (2021). *Tuition discounting at private institutions hits record high, NACUBO reports.* https://www.nasfaa.org/news-item/21987/Tuition_Discounting_at_Private_Institutions_Hits_Record_High_NACUBO_Reports

Davis, J. (2015). *Intrusive advising and its influence on first- and second-year students: A formative evaluation of a pilot intrusive advising initiative at a HBCU in the south.* [PhD Dissertation], Florida State University.

Deming, D. J., & Noray, K. (2020). Earnings dynamics, changing job skills, and STEM careers. *The Quarterly Journal of Economics, 135*(4), 1965-2005.

DiAngelo, R. (2018). *White fragility: Why it's so hard for White people to talk about racism.* Beacon Press.

Donastorg, M. (2021, October 21). *Despite challenges, HBCUs are drivers of upward mobility.* The Plug. https://www.tpinsights.com/free-articles/despite-challenges-hbcus-are-drivers-of-upward-mobility

Douglas-Gabriel, D., & Wiggins, O. (2021, March 24). Hogan signs off on $577 million for Maryland's historically Black colleges and universities. *The Washington Post.* https://www.washingtonpost.com/education/2021/03/24/maryland-hbcus-lawsuit-settlement

Drewry, H. N., & Doermann, H. (2003). *Stand and prosper: Private Black colleges and their students.* Princeton University Press.

Drezner, N. D. (2008a). *Cultivating a culture of giving. An exploration of institutional strategies to enhance African American young alumni giving* [PhD Dissertation]. University of Pennsylvania.

Drezner, N. D. (2008b). For alma mater and the fund: The United Negro College Fund's National Pre-Alumni Council and the creation of the next generation of donors. In M. Gasman & C. Tudico (Eds.), *Historically Black Colleges and Universities* (pp. 15-26). Palgrave Macmillan.

Du Bois, W. E. B. (1935). *Black reconstruction: An essay toward a history of the part which Black folk played in the attempt to reconstruct democracy in America, 1860-1880.* Harcourt, Brace and Company.

Du Bois, W. E. B. (1940). The future of Wilberforce University. *Journal of Negro Education, 9*(4): 553-570.

Du Bois, W. E. B. (1960). A Negro student at Harvard at the end of the 19th century. *The Massachusetts Review, 1*(3), 439-458.

Du Bois, W. E. B. (2002). *The education of Black people: Ten critiques, 1906-1960.* Monthly Review Press.

Economic diversity among the top 25 national universities. (2021). *U.S. News & World Report.* https://www.usnews.com/best-colleges/rankings/national-universities/economic-diversity-among-top-ranked-schools

Economic diversity and student outcomes at America's colleges and universities: Find Your college. (2017). *The New York Times.* https://www.nytimes.com /interactive/projects/college-mobility

Edelman, M. (2021, February 12). Proud shoutout to my Spelman College sister Rosalind Gates Brewer. *Children's Defense Fund Blog.* https://www.childrens defense.org/child-watch-columns/health/2021/proud-shoutout-to-my-spelman -college-sister-rosalind-gates-brewer

Edgar, W. (1998). *South Carolina: A history.* University of South Carolina Press.

Ehrman, J. (2006*). The eighties: America in the age of Reagan.* Yale University Press.

Elu, J. U., Ireland, J., Jeffries, D., Johnson, I., Jones, E., Long, D., Price, G. N., Sam, O., Simons, T., Slaughter, F., & Trotman, J. (2019). The earnings and income mobility consequences of attending a Historically Black College/University: Matching estimates from 2015 U.S. Department of Education college scorecard data. *The Review of Black Political Economy, 46*(3), 171–192.

Engerman, K., McKayle, C., & Blackmon, A. T. (2021). Presidents' Role in Broadening Participation in STEM. In *Handbook and university leadership* (pp. 186-209). IGI Global.

Esmieu, P. L. (2019). Faculty diversity. In *A Primer on Minority Serving Institutions.* Routledge Press. Espinosa, L. L., Kelchen, R., & Taylor, M. 2018. *Minority serving institutions as engines of upward mobility* (pp. 25-37). American Council on Education.

Ezzell, J. L., & Schexnider, A. J. (2010). Leadership, governance, and sustainability of Black colleges and universities. *Trusteeship, 18*(3), 25–28.

Farmer, E., Kunkle, K., Kincey, S., Willtsher, C., & Hilton, A. (2019). Where do we go from here? Exploring retention and engagement at HBCUs. In Hinton, S. & Woods, A. (Eds). *Examining student retention and engagement strategies at Historically Black Colleges and Universities* (pp. 149–180). IGI Global.

Favors, J. (2020). *Shelter in a time of storm. How Black colleges fostered generations of leadership and activism.* University of North Carolina Press.

Febus, M. (2021). *Realizing potential and achieving possibilities: The value and benefits of mentoring at HSIs and HBCUs.* Rutgers Center for Minority Serving Institutions.

Fenn, P. (2011, February 2). Tea Party funding Koch Brothers emerge from anonymity. *U.S. News & World Report.* https://www.usnews.com/opinion/blogs/peter -fenn/2011/02/02/tea-party-funding-koch-brothers-emerge-from-anonymity

Fester, R., Gasman, M., & Nguyen, T. H. (2012). We know very little: Accreditation and historically black colleges and universities. *Journal of Black Studies, 43*(7), 806-819.

Fleming, J. (1984). *Blacks in college.* Jossey-Bass Publishers.

Florida A&M University. (2022). History of Florida A&M University. https://www .famu.edu/ about-famu/history/index.php

Formisano, R. (2004). *Boston against busing: Race, class, and ethnicity in the 1960s and 1970s.* University of North Carolina.

Fox, M. (April 6, 2019, April 6). Toni Morrison, towering novelist of the Black experience, dies at 88. *The New York Times.* https://www.nytimes.com/2019/08 /06/books/toni-morrison-dead.html

Frankenfield, J. (2021). *What income class are you?* Investopedia. https://www
.investopedia.com/financial-edge/0912/which-income-class-are-you
.aspx#citation-13.

Franklin, J. (2021, November 15). *Howard University students reach an agreement with
officials after a month of protest.* National Public Radio. https://www.npr.org/2021
/11/15/1055929172/howard-university-students-end-protest-housing-agreement

Freeman, K. (1999). HBCs or PWIs? African American high school students'
consideration of higher education institution types. *The Review of Higher
Education, 23*(1), 91–106.

Freeman, K. (2002). Black colleges and college choice: Characteristics of students
who choose HBCUs. *The Review of Higher Education, 25*(3), 349–358.

Freeman, K., & Cohen, R. T. (2001). Bridging the gap between economic development and cultural empowerment: HBCUs' challenges for the future. *Urban
Education, 36*(5), 585–596.

Fresh Air. (August 25, 2015, August 25). *'I regret everything': Toni Morrison looks back
on her personal life.* https://www.npr.org/2015/08/24/434132724/i-regret
-everything-toni-morrison-looks-back-on-her-personal-life

Fry, R., & Kochhar, R. (2018). *America's wealth gap between middle-income and
upper-income families is the widest on record.* Pew Research. https://www
.pewresearch.org/fact-tank/2014/12/17/wealth-gap-upper-middle-income

Fryer, R., & Greenstone, M. (2007). *The causes and consequences of attending
Historically Black Colleges and Universities* (Working Paper 13036). National
Bureau of Economic Research. https://www.nber.org/papers/w13036

Fryer, R. G., Jr., & Greenstone, M. (2010). The changing consequences of attending
Historically Black Colleges and Universities. *American Economic Journal: Applied
Economics, 2*(1), 116–148.

Fulbright-Anderson, K., Auspos, P., & Anderson, A. (2001). *Community involvement
in partnerships with educational institutions, medical centers, and utility companies.*
Annie E. Casey Foundation, Aspen Institute Roundtable on Comprehensive
Community Initiatives.

Funk, C., & Parker, K. (2018). *Women and men in STEM often at odds over workplace
equity.* Pew Research Center.

Gallo, R., & Davis, R. (2009). The impact of town–gown relationships on the
sustainability of African American communities: An examination of the role of
HBCUs. *Journal of African American Studies, 13*(4), 509–523.

Gallup & Strada Education Network. (2018). *Strada-Gallup alumni survey: Mentoring
college students to success.* https://news.gallup.com/reports/244058/2018-strada
-gallup-alumni-survey.aspx

Gallup & USA Funds. (2015). *Gallup-USA funds minority college graduates report.*
file:///C:/Users/lesters/Downloads/USA_Funds_Minority_Report_GALLUP.pdf

Garcia, A. L., Lane, T. B., & Rincón, B. E. (2021). Cultivating graduate STEM
pathways: How alliance-based STEM enrichment programs broker opportunity
for students of color. *Frontiers in Education, 6*: 1–14. https://doi.org/10.3389/feduc
.2021.667976

Gasman, M. (1999). Scylla and Charybdis: Navigating the waters of academic freedom at Fisk University during Charles S. Johnson's administration (1946–1956). American Educational Research Journal, 36(4), 739–758.

Gasman, M. (2002). W.E.B. Du Bois and Charles S. Johnson: Differing views on the role of philanthropy in higher education. History of Education Quarterly, 42(4), 493–516.

Gasman, M. (2004). Rhetoric vs. reality: The fundraising messages of the United Negro College Fund in the immediate aftermath of the Brown decision. History of Education Quarterly, 44(1), 70–94.

Gasman, M. (2006). Salvaging 'Academic Disaster Areas': The Black college response to Christopher Jencks and David Riesman's 1967 Harvard Educational Review article. Journal of Higher Education, 77(2), 317–352.

Gasman, M. (2007a). Envisioning Black colleges: A history of the United Negro College Fund. Johns Hopkins University Press.

Gasman, M. (2007b). Swept under the rug? A historiography of gender and Black colleges. American Educational Research Journal, 44(4), 760–805.

Gasman, M. (2007c). Truth, generalizations, and stigmas: An analysis of the media's coverage of Morris Brown College and Black colleges overall. The Review of Black Political Economy, 34(1–2).

Gasman, M. (2009). The relevance and contributions of Minority Serving Institutions. Report before the Health, Education, Labor and Pensions Committee, Congressional Research Service. https://www.help.senate.gov/imo/media/doc/Gasman.pdf

Gasman, M. (2010a). Comprehensive funding approaches for Historically Black Colleges and Universities. University of Pennsylvania. https://repository.upenn.edu/cgi/viewcontent.cgi?article=1400&context=gse_pubs

Gasman, M. (2010b). The history of U.S. higher education: Methods for uncovering the past. Routledge Press.

Gasman, M. (2011). Perceptions of Black college presidents: Sorting through stereotypes and reality to gain a complex picture. American Education Research Journal, 48(4), 836–870.

Gasman, M. (2012, December 11). Why Morgan State needs David Wilson. The Washington Post. https://www.washingtonpost.com/blogs/therootdc/post/why-morgan-state-needs-david-wilson/2012/12/11/4f4c74ce-43b8-11e2-8061-253bccfc7532_blog.html

Gasman, M. (2013). The changing face of Historically Black Colleges and Universities. Penn Center for Minority Serving Institutions.

Gasman, M. (June 11, 2014a). Give the money back. Inside Higher Education. https://www.insidehighered.com/views/2014/06/12/essay-urges-uncf-reject-major-gift-koch-brothers

Gasman, M. (2014b, September 1). HBCUs' self-imposed leadership struggles. Inside Higher Education. https://www.insidehighered.com/views/2016/09/02/boards-hbcus-should-not-micromanage-their-presidents-essay

Gasman, M. (2015, August 27). Black colleges matter. And we have the data to prove it. Newsweek. https://www.newsweek.com/black-colleges-matter-and-we-have-data-prove-it-366306

Gasman, M. (2016). Exploring issues of diversity within HBCUs. *Journal of College Student Development*, 57(6), 760–762.

Gasman, M. (2020). *21st century college and university presidents: Lessons from Minority Serving Institutions*. Rutgers Center for Minority Serving Institutions. https://cmsi.gse.rutgers.edu/sites/default/files/AspiringLeaders_Report_R6.pdf

Gasman, M. (2021, November 30). Giving spare change and love to Historically Black Colleges and Universities. *Forbes*. https://www.forbes.com/sites/marybethgasman/2021/11/30/giving-spare-change-and-love-to-historically-black-colleges-and-universities/?sh=4f033af0388b

Gasman, M. (2022a). *Doing the right thing: How to undo systemic racism in faculty hiring*. Princeton University Press.

Gasman, M. (2022b, March 1). How HBCUs produce Black business owners. *Forbes*. https://www.forbes.com/sites/marybethgasman/2022/03/01/how-hbcus-produce-black-business-owners/?sh=4799136138ed

Gasman, M., & Anderson-Thompkins, S. (2003). *Fundraising from Black college alumni: Successful strategies for supporting alma mater*. Council for the Advancement and Support of Education.

Gasman, M., & Arroyo, A. (2014). An HBCU-based educational approach for Black college student success: Toward a framework with implications for all institutions. *American Journal of Education*, 121, 57.

Gasman, M. & Bowman, N. (2010). Sending the wrong message about Historically Black Colleges and Universities. *Chronicle of Higher Education*.

Gasman, M., & Bowman, N. (2011). How to paint a better portrait of HBCUs. *Academe*, 97(3), 24–27.

Gasman, M., & Bowman, N. (2012). *A guide to fundraising at Historically Black Colleges and Universities: An all-campus approach*. Routledge Press.

Gasman, M., & Bowman, N. (2013). *Engaging diverse college alumni: The essential guide to fundraising*. Routledge Press.

Gasman, M., & Commodore, F. (2014). The state of research on Historically Black Colleges and Universities. *Journal for Multicultural Education*, 8(2), 89–111.

Gasman, M., & Conrad, C. F. (2013). *Minority-Serving Institutions: Educating all students*. Center for Minority-Serving Institutions. University of Pennsylvania Graduate School of Education.

Gasman, M., Conrad, C., Bowman, N., Nguyen, T., Lundberg, T., & Castro Samayoa, A. (2013). *Telling a better story: Narrating student successes at Minority Serving Institutions*. University of Pennsylvania.

Gasman, M., & Drezner, N. D. (2008). White corporate philanthropy and its support of private Black colleges in the 1960s and 1970s. *International Journal of Educational Advancement*, 8(2), 79–92.

Gasman, M., & Epstein, E. (2002). Modern art in the old south: The role of the arts in Fisk University's campus curriculum. *Educational Researcher*, 31(2), 13–20.

Gasman, M., & Epstein, E. (2004). Creating an image for Black higher education: A visual examination of the United Negro College Fund's publicity, 1944–1960. *Educational Foundations*, 18(2), 41–61.

Gasman, M., Hines, R., & Henderson, A. (2021). *The MacKenzie Scott donations to Historically Black Colleges and Universities: Exploring the data landscape.* Rutgers Center for Minority Serving Institutions. https://cmsi.gse.rutgers.edu/sites /default/files/ScottHBCU_Report%20Final.pdf

Gasman, M., Lundy-Wagner, V., Ransom, T., & Bowman, N., III. (2010). Unearthing promise and potential—Our nation's Historically Black Colleges and Universities. *ASHE Higher Education Report, 35*(5), 1–134.

Gasman, M., & McMickens, T. L. (2010). Liberal or professional education? The missions of public Black colleges and universities and their impact on the future of African Americans. *Souls, 12*(3), 286–305.

Gasman, M., & Nguyen, T. H. (2015). Myths dispelled: A historical account of diversity and inclusion at HBCUs. *New Directions for Higher Education* (170), 5–15.

Gasman, M., & Nguyen, T. (2016). *Historically Black Colleges and Universities as leaders in STEM.* Penn Center for Minority Serving Institutions.

Gasman, M., & Nguyen, T. H. (2019). *Making Black scientists: A call to action.* Harvard University Press.

Gasman, M., Nguyen, T. H., Conrad, C. F., Lundberg, T., & Commodore, F. (2017). Black male success in STEM: A case study of Morehouse College. *Journal of Diversity in Higher Education, 10*(2), 181–200.

Gasman, M., Smith, T., Ye, C., & Nguyen, T. (2017). HBCUs and the production of doctors. *AIMS Journal of Public Health, 4*(6), 579–589.

Gasman, M., Spencer, D., & Orphan, C. (2015). "Building bridges, not fences": A history of civic engagement at private Black colleges and universities, 1944–1965. *History of Education Quarterly, 55*(3), 346–379.

Gasman, M., & Sullivan, L. (2012). *The Morehouse mystique: Becoming a doctor at the nation's newest African American medical school.* Johns Hopkins University Press.

Gasman, M., Toldson, I., & Price, G. (2019). *Covid closures could hit HBCUs particularly hard.* The Conversation. https://theconversation.com/covid-19-closures -could-hit-historically-black-colleges-particularly-hard-134116

Georgia State University Library. (1992). *Stacey Abrams at Spelman College discussing her activism with SAAE in 1992.* Georgia State University Digital Collections. https://digitalcollections.library.gsu.edu/digital/collection/ajc/id/13950

Gibau, G. S. (2015). Considering student voices: Examining the experiences of underrepresented students in intervention programs. *CBE—Life Sciences Education, 14*(3), 28.

Goldberg, B., & Shubinski, B. (2020). *Black education and Rockefeller philanthropy from Jim Crow South to the Civil Rights Era.* Rockefeller Archive Center. ttps:// resource.rockarch.org/story/black-education-and-rockefeller-philanthropy -from-the-jim-crow-south-to-the-civil-rights-era

Golden, A. A., Bogan, Y., Brown, L., Onwukwe, O., & Stewart, S. (2017). Faculty mentoring: Applying ecological theory to practice at historically Black colleges or universities. *Journal of Human Behavior in the Social Environment, 27*(5), 487–497.

Goldrick-Rab, R., Baker-Smith, C., Coca, V., Looker, E., & Williams, T. (2019). *College and university basic needs insecurity: A national #RealCollege survey report.*

The Hope Center. https://hope4college.com/wp-content/uploads/2019/04/HOPE_realcollege_National_report_digital.pdf

Gopalan, M., & Brady, S. T. (2020). College students' sense of belonging: A national perspective. *Educational Researcher, 49*(2), 134–137.

Government Accountability Office. (2018). *Historically Black Colleges and Universities: Action needed to improve participation in education's HBCU Capital Financing Program.* https://www.gao.gov/assets/gao-18-455.pdf

Graham, C. (2021, October 13). *The college athlete experience at HBCUs.* Best Colleges. https://www.bestcolleges.com/resources/hbcu/athletics/#:~:text=What%20Role%20Does%20College%20Athletics,team%20camaraderie%20on%20the%20field

Green, P. E. (2004). A comparative examination of historically disadvantaged institutions in the republic of South Africa and Historically Black Colleges and Universities in the United States. *Race, Gender & Class, 11*(3), 153–176.

Greenfield, D. F., Innouvong, T., Aglugub, R. J., & Yusuf, I. A. (2015). HBCUs as critical context for identity work: Reflections, experiences, and lessons learned. *New Directions for Higher Education, 2015*(170), 37–48.

Greenstone, M., Looney, A., Patashnik, J., & Yu, M. (2013). *Thirteen economic facts about social mobility and the role of education.* Brookings Institute. https://www.brookings.edu/research/thirteen-economic-facts-about-social-mobility-and-the-role-of-education/

Griffin, K., Baker, V., O'Meara, K., Nyunt, G., Robinson, T., & Staples, C. L. (2018). Supporting scientists from underrepresented minority backgrounds: Mapping developmental networks. *Studies in Graduate and Postdoctoral Education.* 9(1): 19–37.

Griffith, J. (1996). *Historically Black Colleges and Universities: 1976–1994.* National Center for Education Statistics. https://nces.ed.gov/pubs/96902.pdf

Guy-Sheftall, B. (2012). Breaking the silence at Spelman College and beyond. *Diversity and Democracy, 15*(1).

Hadley, W. M. (2011). Using the intrusive and nurturing models when advising African American college students with learning disabilities. *Journal of College Orientation, Transition, and Retention, 19*(1).

Haidt, J. (2022, April 11). Why the past 10 years of American life have been uniquely stupid. It's not just a phase. *The Atlantic.* https://www.theatlantic.com/magazine/archive/2022/05/social-media-democracy-trust-babel/629369

Hammond, M., Owens, L., & Gulko, B. (2021). *HBCUs transforming generations: Social mobility outcomes for HBCU alumni.* UNCF.

Hannah-Jones, N. (2015, September 9). A prescription for more Black doctors. *The New York Times Magazine.* https://www.nytimes.com/2015/09/13/magazine/a-prescription-for-more-black-doctors.html

Hannah-Jones, N. (2021). *The 1619 project: A new origin story.* Random House Publishers.

Hanson, M. (2022). *Student debt statistics.* Education Data Initiative. https://educationdata.org/student-loan-debt-statistics

Hardy, P. M., Kaganda, E. J., & Aruguete, M. S. (2019). Below the surface: HBCU performance, social mobility, and college ranking. *Journal of Black Studies, 50*(5), 468–483.

Harris, A. (2017, October 22). Walter Kimbrough's higher calling. *The Chronicle of Higher Education.* https://chronicle.brightspotcdn.com/e4/6e /0a4e71cc6df6c3bc74f922e12923/chronfocus-hbcu-i.pdf

Harris, A. (2021). *The state must provide: Why America's colleges have always been unequal—and how to set them right.* Harper Collins.

Hatter, D. Y., & Ottens, A. J. (1998). Afrocentric world view and Black students' adjustment to a predominantly White university: Does worldview matter? *College Student Journal, 32*, 472–480.

Hauser, R. M., Warren, J. R., Huang, M. H., & Carter, W. Y. (2000). Occupational status, education, and social mobility in the meritocracy. *Meritocracy and Economic Inequality, 5*(13), 179–229.

Hawkins, S. (2021). Reverse integration: Centering HBCUs in the fight for educational equality. *University of Pennsylvania Journal of Law and Social Change, 24*(3), 351–409.

HELP Committee. (2014, May 13). *Strengthening Minority Serving Institutions: Best Practices and Innovations for Student Success.* S.Hrg. 113-835, Hearing of the Committee on Health, Education, Labor, and Pensions, United States Senate. https://www.govinfo.gov/content/pkg/CHRG-113shrg22613/pdf/CHRG -113shrg22613.pdf

Herder, L. (2021, October 21). What women want: Leadership at HBCUs. Diverse Issues in Education, https://www.diverseeducation.com/institutions/hbcus /article/15279799/woman-in-leadership-at-hbcus

Hill, S. (2017, August 23). *The oldest HBCU in America is on the brink of closing.* Black Enterprise. https://www.blackenterprise.com/oldest-hbcu-brink-closing -cheyney

Hillman, N. 2016. Geography of college opportunity: The case of education deserts. *American Education Research Journal, 53*(4), 987–1021.

Hilton, A. A., & McClain, K. S. (2014). HBCU's can maximize minority student achievement and success. *International Journal of Humanities Social Sciences and Education, 1*, 55–69.

Hoffman, J. L., & Lowitzki, K. E. (2005). Predicting college success with high school grades and test scores: Limitations for minority students. *The Review of Higher Education, 28*(4), 455–474.

Hoffman, P. (2015). *A new Andalucia and a way to the Orient. The American Southeast during the sixteenth century.* Louisiana State University Press.

Holsaert, F., & Noonan, M. (2013). *Hands on the freedom plow: Personal accounts by women in SNCC.* University of Illinois.

Howard University. (2019). Ta-Nehisi Coates: A view from the literary top. Howard University Newswire. http://hunewsservice.com/news/ta-nehisi-coates-a -view-from-the-literary-top

Hughes, L. (1940). *The big sea.* Hill and Wang.

International Economic Development Council. (n.d.). *Economic development.* https://www.iedconline.org/clientuploads/Downloads/championing/IEDC _What_is_Economic_Development.pdf

Jackson, E. (2021, June 30). Frederick Humphries was the FAMU president no one saw coming. *Tallahassee Democrat.* https://www.tallahassee.com/story/opinion /2021/06/30/frederick-humphries-famu-florida-a-m-university-president-no -one-saw-coming/7788446002/

Jacobs, P. (2014). *Science and math majors earn the most money after graduation.* The Business Insider. https://www.businessinsider.com/stem-majors-earn-a-lot -more-money-after-graduation-2014-7

James, K. (2021, May 16). *Kamala Harris' road to the White House started at 'The Mecca,' Howard University.* The Undefeated. https://theundefeated.com/features/kamala -harris-road-to-the-white-house-started-at-the-mecca-howard-university

James, W., Scott, L., & Temple, P. (2020). Strategies Used by Historically Black Colleges and Universities to Recruit Minority Teacher Education Candidates. *Teacher Educators' Journal, 13,* 76-104.

Jay, W. (1835). *An inquiry into the character and tendency of the American colonization, and American anti-slavery societies.* Leavitt, Lord & Company.

Jewell, J. O. (2002). To set an example: The tradition of diversity at Historically Black Colleges and Universities. *Urban Education, 37*(1), 7-21.

Johnson, A. (1993). Bid whist, tonk, and *United States v. Fordice*: Why integrationism fails African Americans again. *California Law Review, 81,* 1401.

Johnson, J. M. (2019). Pride or prejudice? Motivations for choosing Black colleges. *Journal of Student Affairs Research and Practice, 56*(4), 409-422.

Jones, B., Lo, P., Wilkerson, A., Xu, A., Hall, L., Cooper, K., Gonzalez, S., & Gasman, M. (2020). *Modeling inclusion: HBCUs and LGBTQ+ support.* Rutgers Center for Minority Serving Institutions.

Jones, L. (2020). *Artist Bisa Butler stitches together the African American experience.* Smithsonian Magazine, https://www.smithsonianmag.com/arts-culture/bisa -butler-stitches-together-quilts-african-american-experience-180975397/

Jones, S. M., & Phillips, G. A. (2020). Re-imagining Campus Climate Assessment at HBCUs. *Research & Practice in Assessment, 15*(2), n2.

Kendi, I. (2016). *Stamped from the beginning. The definitive history of racist ideas in America.* Bold Type Books.

Kendi, I. (2019). *How to be an anti-racist.* Random House.

Kendi, I. (2021, June 9). There is no debate over critical race theory. *The Atlantic.* https://www.theatlantic.com/ideas/archive/2021/07/opponents-critical-race -theory-are-arguing-themselves/619391

Kendricks, K. D., Nedunuri, K. V., & Arment, A. R. (2013). Minority student perceptions of the impact of mentoring to enhance academic performance in STEM disciplines. *Journal of STEM Education: Innovations and Research, 14,* 38-46.

Kim, M., & Conrad, C. (2006). The impact of Historically Black Colleges and Universities on the academic success of African-American students. *Research in Higher Education, 47*(4), 399-427.

Kimbrough, W. (2014, April 2). HBCU presidential crisis: What can be done now. *Diverse Issues in Education.* https://www.diverseeducation.com/institutions /hbcus/article/15094524/hbcu-presidential-crisis-heres-what-can-be-done-now

Kimbrough, W. (2015, June 7). An obscene use of $400 million. *Inside Higher Education.* https://www.insidehighered.com/views/2015/06/08/essay-criticizes -400-million-gift-harvard

Kimbrough, W. (2007, June 11). The perpetuation of privilege. *Inside Higher Education.* https://www.insidehighered.com/views/2007/06/12/perpetuation-privilege

King, M. (2020, November 8). *How Stacey Abrams and her band of believers turned Georgia blue.* Politico. https://www.politico.com/news/2020/11/08/stacey -abrams-believers-georgia-blue-434985

Kochhar, R., Fry, R., & Rohal, M. (2015). *The American middle class is losing ground.* Pew Research. https://www.pewresearch.org/social-trends/wp-content /uploads/sites/3/2015/12/2015-12-09_middle-class_FINAL-report.pdf

Krauskopf, J. (2013). *Samuel Chapman Armstrong: A biographical study.* Forgotten Books.

Leak, H. (2018). *Making bricks without straw. The Kresge HBCU Initiative and fundraising at Historically Black Colleges and Universities* [PhD dissertation], New York University.

Lee, J. (2010). *United States v. Fordice:* Mississippi higher education without public Historically Black Colleges and Universities. *Journal of Negro Education, 79*(2), 166–181.

Lee, J., & Keys, S. (2013). *Land-grant but unequal: State one-to-one match funding for 1890 land-grant universities.* Association for Public-Land Grant Universities. https://www.aplu.org/library/land-grant-but-unequal-state-one-to-one -match-funding-for-1890-land-grant-universities/file

Lee, S., Pfund, C., Branchaw, J., & McGee, R. (2015). Mentoring up: Learning to manage your mentoring relationships. In Glenn Wright (Ed.), *The Mentoring Continuum: From Graduate School Through Tenure* (pp. 133–153). The Graduate School Press of Syracuse University.

Lefrak, M. (2019, August 6). *How Toni Morrison's time at Howard University shaped her career.* National Public Radio WAMU 88.5. https://www.npr.org/2015/08/24 /434132724/i-regret-everything-toni-morrison-looks-back-on-her-personal -life.

Lenning, E. (2017). Unapologetically queer in unapologetically Black spaces: Creating an inclusive HBCU campus. *Humboldt Journal of Social Relations, 1*(39), 283–29.

Levenson, E. (2021, March 30). Former officer knelt on George Floyd for 9 minutes, 29 seconds—not the infamous 8:46. CNN. https://www.cnn.com/2021/03/29/us /george-floyd-timing-929-846/index.html

Li, X., & Carroll, C. D. (2007). *Characteristics of Minority-Serving Institutions and minority undergraduates enrolled in these institutions: Postsecondary education descriptive analysis report.* US Department of Education.

Locke, A. (1925). The new Negro. Atheneum Press.

Logan, L. (2020, July 24). Artist Bisa Butler stitches together the African American experience. *The Smithsonian Magazine.* https://www.smithsonianmag.com/arts -culture/bisa-butler-stitches-together-quilts-african-american-experience -180975397/

Lomax, M. L. (2006). Historically Black colleges and universities: Bringing a tradition of engagement into the twenty-first century. *Journal of Higher Education Outreach and Engagement, 11*(3), 5-14.

Lomax, M. (2021, February 21). How to launch the next great era of Black prosperity. *The Atlantic.* https://www.theatlantic.com/ideas/archive/2021/02/hbcus -black-prosperity/618038

Luedke, C. L. (2017). Person first, student second: Staff and administrators of color supporting students of color authentically in higher education. *Journal of College Student Development, 58*(1), 37–52.

Luedke, C. L., McCoy, D. L., Winkle-Wagner, R., & Lee-Johnson, J. (2019). Students' perspectives on holistic mentoring practices in STEM fields. *JCSCORE, 5*(1), 33–59.

Lumpkin, L. (2022, February 11). Amid the nation-wide enrollment drops, some HBCUs are growing, some see threats, *The Washington Post.* https://www .washingtonpost.com/education/2022/02/11/hbcu-enrollment-growth-bomb -threats

Lundy-Wagner, V. C. (2015). Coming out of the shadows: Rethinking the education policy agenda for diversity and HBCUs. *New Directions for Higher Education, 2015*(170), 91–101.

Lynne, J. (2021, Summer). *School spirit.* Art Forum. https://www.artforum.com /print/202106/jessica-lynne-on-art-and-historically-black-colleges-and -universities-85777

Maddux, H. C., Bradley, B., Fuller, D. S., Darnell, C. Z., & Wright, B. D. (2006). Active learning, action research: A case study in community engagement, service-learning, and technology integration. *Journal of Higher Education Outreach and Engagement, 11*(3), 65-80.

Madyun, N. I., Williams, S. M., McGee, E. O., & Milner, H. R., IV. (2013). On the importance of African American faculty in higher education: Implications and recommendations. *Educational Foundations, 27,* 65–84.

Main, J. B., Tan, L., Cox, M. F., McGee, E. O., & Katz, A. (2020). The correlation between undergraduate student diversity and the representation of women of color faculty in engineering. *Journal of Engineering Education, 109*(4), 843-864.

Malhotra, R., Kantor, C., & Vlahovic, G. (2018). *Geospatial Intelligence Workforce Development in a Changing World–An HBCU Focus. southeastern geographer, 58*(1), 125-135.

Mangan, K. (2013, January 14). America's longest-serving college president has more to do. *The Chronicle of Higher Education.* http://chronicle.com/article/After -More-Than-44-Years/136623/?cid=at

Mangan, K. (2022, January 25). A race to the top in research. *The Chronicle of Higher Education.* https://www.chronicle.com/article/a-race-to-the-top-in-research

Maramba, D. C., Palmer, R. T., Yull, D., & Ozuna, T. (2015). A qualitative investigation of the college choice process for Asian Americans and Latina/os at a public HBCU. *Journal of Diversity in Higher Education, 8*(4), 258–271.

McCaskill, J. (2020, January 6). *What Stacey Abrams means to Spelman College, Georgia and beyond.* Rolling Out. https://rollingout.com/2020/11/11/what-stacey-abrams-means-to-her-alma-mater-georgia-and-beyond

McClay, C. (2021, January 20). *Kamala Harris and a 1986 snapshot of that Howard generation.* BBC News. https://www.bbc.com/news/world-us-canada-55690001

McCoy, D. L., Luedke, C. L., Lee-Johnson, J., & Winkle-Wagner, R. (2020). Transformational mentoring practices: Students' perspectives on practitioner-educators' support during college. *Journal of Student Affairs Research and Practice, 57*(1), 28–41.

McGee, E. O., & Martin, D. B. (2011). "You would not believe what I have to go through to prove my intellectual value!" Stereotype management among academically successful Black mathematics and engineering students. *American Educational Research Journal, 48*(6), 1347–1389.

McGee, M., & Platt, R. (2015). The forgotten slayings: Memory, history, and institutional response to the Jackson State University shootings of 1970. *American Educational History Journal, 42*(½), 15.

McGinnis, F. (1940). *A history of Wilberforce University* [PhD Dissertation]. University of Cincinnati.

McGuire, R. (2004). Colorado coalfield massacre. *Archaeology, 57*(6), 62–70.

McMickens, T. L. (2012). Running the race when race is a factor. *Phi Delta Kappan, 93*(8), 39–43.

Miller-Cotto, D., & Byrnes, J. P. (2016). Ethnic/racial identity and academic achievement: A meta-analytic review. *Developmental Review, 41*, 51–70.

Mobley, S., & Johnson, J. (2015). The role of HBCUs in addressing the unique needs of LGBT students. *New Directions for Higher Education, 170*, 79–89.

Mobley, S., & Johnson, J. (2019). No pumps allowed: The problem with gender expression and the Morehouse College appropriate attire policy. *Journal of Homosexuality, 66*(7), 867–895.

Mobley, S. D., Jr., Johnson, J. M., & Drezner, N. D. (2021). "Why aren't all the White kids sitting together in the cafeteria?" An exploration of White student experiences at a public HBCU. *Journal of Diversity in Higher Education, 15*(3): 300–313.https://doi.org/10.1037/dhe0000298.

Moffitt, E., & Schmidt-Campbell, M. (2021, March 30). *Mary Schmidt Campbell on educating the next generation of Black artists.* Frieze. https://www.frieze.com/article/mary-schmidt-campbell-educating-next-generation-of-black-artists-hbcus

Morgan, I., & Davies, P. (2012). *From sit-ins to SNCC: The student civil rights movement in the 1960s.* University Press of Florida.

Muhammad, H. (2021). *Five facts to know about Black philanthropy.* Tides. https://www.tides.org/accelerating-social-change/philanthropy/five-facts-to-know-about-black-philanthropy

Müller, W., & Pollak, R. (2015). Social mobility. *International Encyclopedia of the Social & Behavioral Sciences*. 10.1016/B978-0-08-097086-8.32092-X.

Murray, A. (1973). The founding of Lincoln University. *Journal of Presbyterian History*, 51(4), 392–410.

Mykerezi, E., & Mills, B. F. (2008). The wage earnings impact of Historically Black Colleges and Universities. *Southern Economic Journal*, 75(1), 173–187.

Nathenson, R., Castro Samayo, A., & Gasman, M. (2019). *Moving upward and onward: Income mobility at Historically Black Colleges and Universities*. Rutgers Center for Minority Serving Institutions.

National Academies of Sciences, Engineering, and Medicine. (2019). *Minority serving institutions: America's underutilized resource for strengthening the STEM workforce*. National Academies Press.

National Association for Equal Opportunity in Higher Education. (n.d.). *About NAFEO*. https://www.nafeonation.org/about

National Research Council. (1995). *Colleges of agriculture at the land grant universities: A profile*. The National Academies Press.

NCES (National Center for Educational Statistics). (2021). *Historically Black Colleges and Universities*. https://nces.ed.gov/fastfacts/display.asp?id=667

NCES (National Center for Educational Statistics). (2018). *Race and ethnicity of college faculty*. https://nces.ed.gov/fastfacts/display.asp?id=61.

Negron, E. (1996. January 6). FAMU gets most talented Black scholars. *South Florida Sun Sentinel*. https://www.sun-sentinel.com/news/fl-xpm-1996-01-12-9601120123-story.html

Nellum, C. J., & Valle, K. (2015). *Government investment in public Hispanic-serving institutions*. American Council on Education.

Nelms, C. (2021, August 6). An open letter to trustees of Historically Black Colleges and Universities. *Diverse Issues in Education*. https://www.diverseeducation.com/leadership-policy/article/15113632/an-open-letter-to-trustees-of-historically-black-colleges-and-universities-hbcus

Nelson, C. A., & Frye, J. R. (2016). Tribal college and university funding: Tribal sovereignty at the intersection of federal, state, and local funding. American Council on Education. Nelson, D. D., & Lang-Lindsey, K. (2020). Rural health-care and telehealth: The importance of social work departments at HBCUs in developing a competent workforce in the rural South. *Journal of Community Engagement and Scholarship*, 12(3), 2.

Nguyen, T., Castro Samayoa, A., Gasman, M., & Mobley, S. (2018). Challenging respectability: Student health directors providing services to lesbian and gay students at Historically Black Colleges and Universities. *Teachers College Record*, 120(2), 144.

Nguyen, T., Gasman, M., Lockett, A., & Pena, V. (2020). Supporting Black women's pursuits in STEM. *Journal of Research in Science Teaching*, 58, 879–905.

Nichols, A. H., & Schak, J. (2014). *Degree attainment for Black adults: National and state trends*. The Education Trust. https://www.brookings.edu/research/closing-the-racial-wealth-gap-requires-heavy-progressive-taxation-of-wealth

Nichols, J. (2011, December 9). The Koch brothers, ALEC, and the savage assault on democracy. *The Nation.* https://www.thenation.com/article/archive/koch-brothers-alec-and-savage-assault-democracy

Nietzel, M. (2021). A new report reveals the false promises of for-profit colleges. *Forbes.* https://www.forbes.com/sites/michaeltnietzel/2021/03/08/a-new-report-reveals-the-false-promises-of-for-profit-colleges/?sh=426843c535fc

Noonan, R. (2017). STEM jobs: 2017 update (ESA Issue Brief# 02-17). US Department of Commerce.

Norwood, A. (2018). Why aren't as many HBCU grads giving back to their college? *MPB News.* https://www.mpbonline.org/blogs/news/why-arent-as-many-hbcu-graduates-giving-back-to-their-college

Ong, M., Wright, C., Espinosa, L., & Orfield, G. (2011). Inside the double bind: A synthesis of empirical research on undergraduate and graduate women of color in science, technology, engineering, and mathematics. *Harvard Educational Review, 81*(2), 172–209.

O'Neal, L. (2017). Ibram Kendi, one of the nation's leading scholars of racism, says education and lover are not the answer. *Andscape,* https://andscape.com/features/ibram-kendi-leading-scholar-of-racism-says-education-and-love-are-not-the-answer/

Opportunity Insights (n.d.). *Social capital and economic mobility.* https://opportunityinsights.org

Organisation for Economic Co-Operation and Development. (2018). *Broken social elevator? How to promote social mobility.* Organisation for Economic Co-Operation and Development.

Owens, L., & Commodore, F. (2018, November 4). Governing HBCUs for the future. *Diverse Issues in Education.* https://www.diverseeducation.com/institutions/hbcus/article/15103563/governing-hbcus-for-the-future

Palmer, R. T., Davis, R. J., & Gasman, M. (2011). A matter of diversity, equity, and necessity: The tension between Maryland's higher education system and its Historically Black Colleges and Universities over the Office of Civil Rights Agreement. *Journal of Negro Education, 80*(2), 121–133.

Palmer, R. T., Davis, R. J., & Maramba, D. C. (2010). Role of an HBCU in supporting academic success for underprepared Black males. *Negro Educational Review, 61*(1-4): 85–106.

Palmer, R., & Gasman, M. (2008). 'It takes a village to raise a child': The role of social capital in promoting academic success for African American men at a Black college. *Journal of College Student Development, 49*(1), 52–70.

Palmer, R. T., & Williams, J. (2021). Peeling back the layers: A deeper look at the diversity among Black students at Historically Black Colleges and Universities, *Journal of Diversity in Higher Education,* https://doi.org/10.1037/dhe0000358

Palmer, R. T., Wood, J. L., & Arroyo, A. (2015). Toward a Model of Retention and Persistence for Black Men at Historically Black Colleges and Universities (HBCUs). *Spectrum: A Journal on Black Men, 4*(1), 5–20.

Parks, D. (2022). Giving to community colleges and HBCUs soared last year. *The Chronicle of Philanthropy*. https://www.philanthropy.com/article/giving-to-community-colleges-and-hbcus-soared-last-year

Parrott-Sheffer, A. (2008). Not a laughing matter: The portrayals of Black colleges on television. In M. Gasman & C. Tudico (Eds.), *Historically Black Colleges and Universities: Triumphs, troubles, and taboos* (pp. 207–222). Palgrave Macmillan.

Pasque, P., Mallory, B., Smerek, R., Dwyer, B., & Bowman, N. (2005). Higher education collaboratives for community engagement and improvement. *National Forum for Higher Education and the Public Good*. https://files.eric.ed.gov/fulltext/ED515231.pdf

Perna, L. W., Gasman, M., Gary, S., Lundy-Wagner, V., & Drezner, N. D. (2010). Identifying strategies for increasing degree attainment in STEM: Lessons from minority-serving institutions. *New Directions for Institutional Research*, 2010(148), 41–51.

Perna, L., Lundy-Wagner, V., Drezner, N. D., Gasman, M., Yoon, S., Bose, E., & Gary, S. (2009). The contribution of HBCUs to the preparation of African American women for STEM careers: A case study. *Research in Higher Education*, 50(1), 1–23.

Pew Research Center. (2014, February 11). *The rising cost of not going to college*. https://www.pewresearch.org/social-trends/2014/02/11/the-rising-cost-of-not-going-to-college

Pew Research (July 12, 2018). *Income inequality in the U.S. is rising most rapidly among Asians*. https://www.pewresearch.org/social-trends/2018/07/12/income-inequality-in-the-u-s-is-rising-most-rapidly-among-asians/

Phillips, R., & Pittman, R. H. (2009). *An introduction to community development*. Routledge Press.

Piety, P. J. (2013). *Assessing the educational data movement*. Teachers College Press.

Pinder, D., Sarakatsannis, J., & Stewart, S. (2021). *How HBCUs can accelerate Black economic mobility*. McKinsey Institute for Black Economic Mobility.

Pittman, R., Pittman, E., Phillips, R., & Cangelosi, J. (2009). The community and economic development chain: Validating the links between processes and outcomes. *Community Development*, 40(1), 80–93.

Plazas, D. (2020, January 2). Civil rights heroes Diane Nash and John Lewis deserve more recognition in Nashville, *Nashville Tennessean*. https://www.tennessean.com/story/opinion/columnists/david-plazas/2020/01/02/diane-nash-john-lewis-nashville-recognition/2777041001

Powell, A. (2022). *The urgency of now: HBCUs at a crossroads*. Association of Governing Boards. https://agb.org/wp-content/uploads/2020/01/Kresge-Report_Urgency_of_Now.pdf

Price, G. N., Spriggs, W., & Swinton, O. H. 2011. The relative returns to graduation from a Historically Black College/University: Propensity score matching estimates from the National Survey of Black Americans. *Review of Black Political Economy*, 38, 103–130.

Public Broadcasting Service. (2000). *From swastika to Jim Crow*. https://www.imdb.com/name/nm0249240/?ref_=tt_ov_wr

Reeves, R., & Joo, N. (2017, January 19). The contribution of Historically Black Colleges and Universities to upward mobility. Brookings Institution. https://www.brookings.edu/blog/social-mobility-memos/2017/01/19/the-contribution-of-historically-black-colleges-and-universities-to-upward-mobility

Riley, J. (2010). Black colleges need a new mission: Once an essential response to racism, they are now academically inferior. *The Wall Street Journal.* http://www.nafeonation.org/hbcu-leaders-respond

Rodríguez, J. E., López, I. A., Campbell, K. M., & Dutton, M. (2017). The role of Historically Black College and University medical schools in academic medicine. *Journal of Health Care for the Poor and Underserved, 28*(1), 266–278.

Rothberg, E. (2021). *Stacey Abrams.* National Women's History Museum. https://www.womenshistory.org/education-resources/biographies/stacey-abrams

Rucker, M. L., & Gendrin, D. M. (2003). The Impact of ethnic identification on student learning in the HBCU classroom. *Journal of Instructional Psychology, 30*(3), 207.

Sanders, C. (2019). Pursuing the unfinished business of democracy: Willa B. Player and liberal arts education in the civil rights era, *North Carolina Historical Review, 96*(1): 1–33.

Saunders, K., Williams, K., & Smith, C. (2016). *Fewer resources, more debt: Loan debt burdens students at Historically Black Colleges and Universities.* UNCF Frederick D. Patterson Research Institute.

Schak, J., & Nichols, A. H. (2014). Degree attainment for Latino adults: National and state trends. *The Education Trust.* https://edtrust.org/wp-content/uploads/2014/09/Latino-Degree-Attainment_FINAL_4-1.pdf

Schexnider, A. (2017, December). *Governance and the future of Black colleges.* Black Past. https://www.blackpast.org/african-american-history/norman-c-francis-1931/

Schrecker, E. (2021). *The lost promise: American universities in the 1960s.* University of Chicago Press.

Schulze, B. (2005). *Changing the odds: Lessons learned from the Kresge HBCU Initiative.* Kresge Foundation. https://kresge.org/sites/default/files/Changing%20the%20odds_lessons%20learned.pdf

Scott, M. (2020a, July 28). 116 organizations driving change. Medium. https://mackenzie-scott.medium.com/116-organizations-driving-change-67354c6d733d

Scott, M. (2020b, December 16). 384 ways to help. *Medium.* https://mackenzie-scott.medium.com/384-ways-to-help-45d0b9ac6ad8?source=user_profile

Scott, M. (2021, June 15). Seeding by ceding. *Medium.* https://mackenzie-scott.medium.com/seeding-by-ceding-ea6de642bf?source=user_profile

Scott, M. (2022, March 23). Helping any of us can help us all. *Medium.* https://mackenzie-scott.medium.com/helping-any-of-us-can-help-us-all-f4c7487818d9.

Seltzer, R. (2017, May 25). Scrutiny of a new Koch grant. *Inside Higher Education.* https://www.insidehighered.com/news/2017/01/13/thurgood-marshall-college-fund-defends-accepting-koch-money

Seymour, S., & Ray, J. (2015, October 27). Grads of Historically Black Colleges have well-being edge. Gallup. https://news.gallup.com/poll/186362/grads -historically-black-colleges-edge.aspx

Shorette, C. R., & Arroyo, A. T. (2015). A closer examination of White student enrollment at HBCUs. *New Directions for Higher Education, 2015*(170), 49–65.

Shorette, C. R., II, & Palmer, R. T. (2015). Historically Black Colleges and Universities (HBCUs): Critical facilitators of non-cognitive skills for Black males. *Western Journal of Black Studies, 39*(1), 18.

Sibulkin, A. E., & Butler, J. S. (2011). Diverse colleges of origin of African American doctoral recipients, 2001–2005: Historically Black Colleges and Universities and beyond. *Research in Higher Education, 52*(8), 830–852.

Siddle-Walker, V. (1996). *Their highest potential: An African American school community in the segregated South.* University of North Carolina Press.

Simen, J. H., & Meyer, T. (2021). Leadership education in professional and graduate schools. *New Directions for Student Leadership, 2021*(171), 113–122.

Sims, A. (2019). *An exploratory case study on the impact of intrusive advising on academic probation students attending an HBCU.* ProQuest Dissertations and Theses. https://www.proquest.com/dissertations-theses/exploratory-case -study-on-impact-intrusive/docview/2247151502/se-2?accountid=13360

Skofstad, C. (2019, March 31). Norman Francis, legendary civil rights and higher education leader, to receive 2019 Laetare Medal. *The Notre Dame News.* https:// news.nd.edu/news/norman-francis-legendary-civil-rights-and-higher -education-leader-to-receive-2019-laetare-medal/

Slater, J. (1994). The Blacks who first entered the world of White higher education. *Journal of Blacks in Higher Education, 4,* 47–56.

Smeeding, T. M. (2016). Multiple barriers to economic opportunity for the "Truly" disadvantaged and vulnerable. *The Russell Sage Foundation Journal of the Social Sciences, 2*(2), 98–122.

Smith, K. C., Boakye, B., Williams, D., & Fleming, L. (2019). The exploration of how identity intersectionality strengthens STEM identity for Black female undergraduates attending a Historically Black College and University (HBCU). *Journal of Negro Education, 88*(3), 407–418.

Smith, K. C., Geddis, D., & Dumas, J. (2021). The role of the HBCU pipeline in diversifying the STEM workforce: Training the next generation of drug delivery researchers. *Advanced Drug Delivery Reviews, 176,* 113866.

Smith, M. P., & Ed, D. (2017). The mis-engagement of higher education: A case for liberation engagement at Historically Black Colleges and Universities. *Penn Center for Minority Serving Institutions.* https://cmsi.gse.rutgers.edu/sites /default/files/The%20Mis-Engagement%20of%20Higher%20Education-%20 A%20Case%20for%20Liberation%20Engagement%20at%20Historically%20 Black%20Colleges%20and%20Universities.pdf

Smith-Barrow, D. (2019, October 21). HBCUs' sink-or-swim moment. *The New York Times.* https://www.nytimes.com/2019/10/21/opinion/hbcu-college.html

Some colleges have more students from the top 1 percent than the bottom 60. Find yours. (2019, January 18). *The New York Times*. https://www.nytimes.com /interactive/2017/01/18/upshot/some-colleges-have-more-students-from-the -top-1-percent-than-the-bottom-60.html

Spofford, T. (1988). *Lynch Street: The May 1970 slayings at Jackson State College*. Kent State University Press.

Stewart, G., Wright, D., Perry, T., & Rankin, C. (2008). Historically Black Colleges and Universities: Caretakers of precious treasure. *Journal of College Admission*, 201, 24–29.

Stewart, P. (2020, July 7). Achieving diversity in STEM faculty requires systemic change, says report. *Diverse Issues in Education*. https://www.diverseeducation .com/stem/article/15107243/achieving-diversity-in-stem-faculty-requires -systemic-change-says-report

Stratford, M. (2017, May 6). *Trump suggests financing for Historically Black Colleges may be unconstitutional*. Politico. https://www.politico.com/story/2017/05/05 /trump-historically-black-colleges-financing-unconstitutional-238061

Strayhorn, T. (2016). Factors that influence the persistence and success of Black men in urban public universities. *Urban Education, 52*(9), 1106–1128.

Strayhorn, T. (2018). *College students' sense of belonging: A key to educational success for all students*. Routledge Press.

Strayhorn, T. (2019). Sense of belonging and student success at Historically Black Colleges and Universities: A key to strategic enrollment management and institutional transformation. In S. Hinton & A. Woods (Eds.), *Examining student retention and engagement strategies at Historically Black Colleges and Universities* (pp. 32–52). IGI Global.

Streitfeld, D. (1995, May 4). Howard's beloved graduate. *The Washington Post*. https://www.washingtonpost.com/archive/lifestyle/1995/03/04/howards -beloved-graduate/8330ae56-5f6f-4aaf-89e0-20735e36b102

Tatum, B. D. (1997). *Why are all the Black kids sitting together in the cafeteria? And other conversations about race*. Basic Books.

Tatum, C. (2019, December 29). Nestled in a poor Dallas neighborhood, Paul Quinn College aims to be a national model for overcoming poverty. *The Dallas Post Tribune*. https://dallasposttrib.com/nestled-in-a-poor-dallas-neighborhood -paul-quinn-college-aims-to-be-a-national-model-for-overcoming-poverty/

Taylor, H. L., & Luter G. (2013). *Anchor institutions: An interpretive review essay*. https://community-wealth.org/sites/clone.community-wealth.org/files /downloads/paper-taylor-luter.pdf

Taylor, I. (2020). *Understanding the role of HBCU boards of trustees in advancing institutional quality and ensuring HBCU survival* [PhD dissertation], University of Pennsylvania.

Taylor, M., & Thompson, T. M. (2019, June 29). The legacy of Dr. Norman C. Francis and Xavier University. Diverse Issues in Higher Education. https://www .diverseeducation.com/students/ article/15096738/the-legacy-of-dr-norman-c -francis-and-xavier-university

The Hundred Seven. (n.d.). *Artists from HBCUs*. http://www.thehundred-seven.org/artists.html

Thelin, J. R. (2011). *A history of American higher education*. Johns Hopkins University Press.

Thurgood Marshall College Fund. (2021). *HBCU infrastructure needs*. https://www.tmcf.org/wp-content/uploads/2021/08/Infrastructure.Needs_.Fact_.Sheet_.Logo_.Final_.8.23.21.pdf

Toldson, I. A. (2019). Cultivating STEM talent at minority serving institutions: Challenges and opportunities to broaden participation in STEM at Historically Black Colleges and Universities. In *Growing Diverse STEM Communities: Methodology, Impact, and Evidence* (pp. 1–8). American Chemical Society.

Tom Joyner Foundation. (n.d.). *Why art at HBCUs*. https://tomjoynerfoundation.org/2021-archives/art-gallery/why-we-believe-in-art/

Trostel, P. (2015). *It's not just the money: The benefits of college education to individuals and to society*. Lumina Foundation. https://www.luminafoundation.org/files/resources/its-not-just-the-money.pdf

Tucker, S. K. (2002). The early years of the United Negro College Fund, 1943–1960. *The Journal of African American History, 87*(4), 416–432.

Uhl, S., & Evans, H. (2021). *The story of the Tallahassee bus boycotts*. Florida State University https://history.fsu.edu/article/black-history-month-story-tallahassee-bus-boycott

UNCF (United Negro College Fund). (2017). *HBCUs make America strong: The positive economic impact of Historically Black Colleges and Universities*. Frederick D. Patterson Research Institute.

UNCF (United Negro College Fund). (2018). *HBCUs punching above their weight: A state level analysis of Historically Black College and University enrollment and graduation*. Frederick D. Patterson Research Institute.

UNCF (United Negro College Fund). (2020). *Gates Millennium Scholars*, https://uncf.org/pages/gates-millennium-scholars-program

Upton, R., & Tanenbaum, C. (2014, September). The role of Historically Black Colleges and Universities as pathway providers: Institutional pathways to the STEM PhD. *American Institutes for Research*. https://www.air.org/sites/default/files/downloads/report/Role%20of%20HBCUs%20in%20STEM%20PhDs%20for%20Black%20Students.pdf

US Census Bureau. (2017). *The nation's older population is still growing*. https://www.census.gov/newsroom/press-releases/2017/cb17-100.html

Valley, P. (2020, September 8). How philanthropy benefits the super-rich. *The Guardian*. https://www.theguardian.com/society/2020/sep/08/how-philanthropy-benefits-the-super-rich

Van Camp, D., Barden, J., & Sloan, L. R. (2010). Predictors of Black students' race-related reasons for choosing an HBCU and intentions to engage in racial identity—relevant behaviors. *Journal of Black Psychology, 36*(2), 226–250.

Van Camp, D., Barden, J., Sloan, L. R., & Clarke, R. P. (2009). Choosing an HBCU: An opportunity to pursue racial self-development. *The Journal of Negro Education, 78*(4): 457–468.

Vanderburgh-Wertz, D. (2013). *An on-campus community grocery store: A social purpose business model for Paul Quinn College.* Duke University, https://dukespace.lib.duke.edu/dspace/bitstream/handle/10161/6669/Darrow%20VW%20-%20Grocery%20Store-Paul%20Quinn%20College%20-%20Body_May%202013.pdf?sequence=1

Vazquez-Martinez, A., & Hansen, M. (2020, May 19). *For-profit colleges drastically outspend competing institutions on advertising.* Brookings Institution. https://www.brookings.edu/blog/brown-center-chalkboard/2020/05/19/for-profit-colleges-advertising

Vedder, R. (2019). Is 'diversity' destroying the HBCUs? *Forbes.* https://www.forbes.com/sites/richardvedder/2019/11/04/is-diversity-destroying-the-hbcus/?sh=34ec38024195

Wagner, V. L., Vultaggio, J., & Gasman, M. (2013). Preparing underrepresented students of color for doctoral success: The roles of undergraduate institutions. *International Journal of Doctoral Studies, 8,* 151–172.

Walker, L. J. (2018). We are family: How othermothering and support systems can improve mental health outcomes among African American males at HBCUs. *Spectrum: A Journal on Black Men, 7*(1), 1–16.

Ward, A. (2000). *Dark midnight when I rise: The story of the Jubilee Singers who introduced the world to the music of Black America.* Farrar Straus Giroux Publishers.

Washington, A., & Gasman, M. (2018). Envisioning equity: Women at the helm of HBCU leadership. In C. Davis, A. Hilton, & D. Outten (Eds.), *Underserved populations at Historically Black Colleges and Universities: The Pathway to Diversity, Equity, & Inclusion.* Emerald Publishing, 201–214.

Washington, B. (1901). *Up from slavery. An autobiography.* Doubleday & Company.

Washington Lockett, A., Gasman, M., & Nguyen, T. H. (2018). Senior level administrators and HBCUs: The role of support for Black women's success in STEM. *Education Sciences, 8*(2), 48.

Watkins, W. H. (2001). *The White architects of Black education: Ideology and power in America, 1865–1954.* Teachers College Press.

Webber, H. S., & Karlström, M. (2009). *Why community investment is good for nonprofit anchor institutions: Understanding costs, benefits, and the range of strategic options.* Chapin Hall at the University of Chicago. https://community-wealth.org/sites/clone.community-wealth.org/files/downloads/report-webber-karlstrom.pdf

Whack, E. (2017, May 26). *Dillard's own 'hidden figures,' one of the smallest HBCUs makes huge marks in physics community.* NOLA.com. https://www.nola.com/news/article_cf566576-3251-53f0-80be-3fcfa86cbafa.html

Whitford, E. (2021, January 31). Back from 2 decades on the brink. *Inside Higher Education.* https://www.insidehighered.com/news/2021/01/12/morris-brown's-accreditation-would-mean-'resurrection'-hbcu-long-brink-closure

Wilcox, C., Wells, J., Haddad, G., & Wilcox, J. (2014). The changing democratic functions of Historically Black Colleges and Universities. *New Political Science, 36*(4), 556–572.

Wilder, S. (2013) *Ebony & ivy: Race, slavery, and the troubled history of America's universities.* Bloomsbury Press.

Williams, D. R., & Williams-Morris, R. (2000). Racism and mental health: The African American experience. *Ethnicity & Health, 5*(3-4), 243-268.

Williams, E. (2013). Women's studies and sexuality studies at HBCUs: The Audre Lorde Project at Spelman College. *Feminist Studies, 39*(2): 520-525.

Williams, H. A. (2005). *Self-taught: African American education in slavery and freedom*. University of North Carolina Press.

Williams, I., Glenn, P., & Wider, F. (2008). Nurtured advising: An essential approach to advising students at Historically Black Colleges and Universities. *Academic Advising Today, 31*(1), 17.

Williams, J., & Palmer, R. (2019). *A response to racism: How HBCU enrollment grew in the face of hatred*. Rutgers Center for Minority Serving Institutions. https://cmsi.gse .rutgers.edu/sites/default/files/A%20Response%20to%20Racism-%20%20How%20 HBCU%20Enrollment%20Grew%20in%20the%20Face%20of%20Hatred_0.pdf

Williams, J. L. (2018). *HBCU by choice: Examining the college choice of Black HBCU undergraduates*. Rutgers Center for Minority Serving Institutions.

Williams, K. L., Burt, B. A., Clay, K. L., & Bridges, B. K. (2019). Stories untold: Counter-narratives to anti-Blackness and deficit-oriented discourse concerning HBCUs. *American Educational Research Journal, 56*(2), 556-599.

Williams, K. L., Mobley, S. D., Campbell, E., & Jowers, R. (2022). Meeting at the margins: Culturally affirming practices at HBCUs for underserved populations. *Higher Education, 84*: 1067-10871.

Williams, L. E. (1980). The United Negro College Fund in retrospect: A search for its true meaning. *The Journal of Negro Education, 49*(4), 363-372.

Williams, M., & Kritsonis, W. (2006). Raising more money at the nation's Historically Black Colleges and Universities. *National Journal for Publishing and Mentoring Doctoral Student Research, 3*(1), https://files.eric.ed.gov/fulltext /ED493566.pdf

Williamson, V. (2021). *Closing the racial wealth gap requires heavy, progressive taxation of wealth*. Brookings Institution. https://www.brookings.edu/research /closing-the-racial-wealth-gap-requires-heavy-progressive-taxation-of-wealth

Williamson-Lott, J. (2008). *Radicalizing the ebony tower: Black colleges and the Black freedom struggled in Mississippi*. Teachers College Press.

Williamson-Lott, J. A. (2018). *Jim Crow campus: Higher education and the struggle for a new southern social order*. Teachers College Press.

Wilson, D. (1987). *Going from Black to Black and White: A case study of the desegregation of Kentucky State University* [PhD Dissertation], Harvard University. https://www.proquest.com/openview/7133dc31b12affo c0cf7e9c2abadb04e/1?pq -origsite=gscholar&cbl=18750&diss=y

Wilson, V. (2007). The effect of attending an HBCU on persistence and graduation Outcomes of African American college students. *The Review of Black Political Economy, 34*(1-2): 11-52.

Winkle-Wagner, R., Forbes, J., Rogers, S., & Reavis, T. (2020). A culture of success: Black alumnae discussions of the assets-based approach at Spelman College. *The Journal of Higher Education, 91*(5), 653-673.

Winkle-Wagner, R., & McCoy, D. L. (2018). Feeling like an "Alien" or "Family"? Comparing students and faculty experiences of diversity in STEM disciplines at a PWI and an HBCU. *Race Ethnicity and Education, 21*(5), 593–606.

W. K. Kellogg Foundation. (2013). *Culture of giving: Energizing and expanding philanthropy by and for communities of color.* https://www.d5coalition.org/wp-content/uploads/2013/07/CultureofGiving.pdf

Wolters, R. (1975). *The new Negro on campus: Black college rebellions of the 1920s.* Princeton University Press.

Wong, A. (2015, October 21). History class and the fictions about race in America. *The Atlantic.* https://www.theatlantic.com/education/archive/2015/10/the-history-class-dilemma/411601

Wood, S. (2021, September 29). How HBCUs are addressing the cost of college. *U.S. News & World Report.* https://www.usnews.com/education/best-colleges/paying-for-college/articles/how-hbcus-are-addressing-the-cost-of-college

Xavier is still nation's top producer of Black doctors. (2012, July 9). *Louisiana Weekly.* http://www.louisianaweekly.com/xavier-is-still-nation%E2%80%99s-top-producer-of-black-doctors/

XULA Still First in African American Medical Graduates. (2019, April 25) Xavier University of Louisiana. https://www.xula.edu/news/2019/04/xula-still-first-in-african-american-medical-graduates.html

Yancy, C. W., & Bauchner, H. (2021). Diversity in medical schools—need for a new bold approach. *JAMA, 325*(1), 31–32.

INDEX

Abdullah, Makola, 068, 181, 200; on culture of HBCUs, 19, 39; on faculty of HBCUs, 239; on graduation rates, 221; on philanthropic support, 153-54, 157, 178-79, 222-23

Abrams, Stacey, 2, 66, 97-102, 128

academic achievement, 67

accreditation, 26, 212, 223, 267n14

Adams, Susan, 229

Addae, Isaac, 127, 137-39, 184-85, 191

admission policies, 17, 60

advising, intrusive, 139

African Institute, 4

African Methodist Episcopal Church, 4

Alabama A&M University, 265n40

Aladangady, A., 54

Alcorn State University, 22, 138, 150, 259n8

Alexander Hamilton (Chernow), 29-30

Ali, Muhammad, 74

Allegheny Institute, 259n3

Allen, Ivan, Jr., 193, 268n3

Allen, Walter, 66-67

Allen University (GA), 6

Alpha Kappa Alpha Sorority, 71, 263n4

Alston, Antoine, 45, 68, 139-41, 196; on alumni giving, 173; on curriculum at HBCUs, 33-34; on faculty of HBCUs, 239-40

American Baptist Home Mission Society, 5

American Council on Education, 55

American Institute of Physics, 162, 267n9

American Legislative Exchange Council, 147, 266n2

American Middle Class Is Losing Ground (Pew Research Center), 53

American Missionary Association, 5

Amos, Keith, 108, 265n38

anchor institutions, HBCUs as, 183-86

Anderson, Anthony, 16

Anderson, James D., 5, 108-13; on alumni giving, 173-74; on belonging, sense of, 48-49; on faculty of PWIs, 69; on mentoring, 127, 129-31; on political activists, 100-101

Armstrong, Samuel Chapman, 8

art, HBCU contributions to, 76-78

Artis, Roslyn, 92-96, 193; on community role of HBCUs, 181, 183, 198-99; on culture of HBCUs, 37-38, 67, 93-94; on institutional stories, 230-31; on philanthropic support, 154-55, 158

Ashmun Institute, 4

Asian American students, 16

Association of 1890 Research Directors, 187

athletics, in HBCU culture, 22, 23-25, 260n2, 261n4, 261n5, 261n6, 261n7, 261n8, 261n9

Atlanta Life Insurance Company, 193, 268n4

Atlanta University, 77

Atlanta University Center, 104, 148, 193-94, 265n34

Auburn University, 89

Ausar Auset Society, 73, 264n14

Avalon Foundation, 168

bachelor's degree, and socioeconomic mobility, 54

"bald-headed Qs," 73, 263n13

Baldwin, William, 7, 142

Baraka, Amiri, 73, 263n7

Barber, William II, 68

Barnes, Ernie, 78, 264n30

Bayou Classic, 22, 260n2

belonging, sense of, 48-51

Clay, Paul, 227
Clayton State University, 56
Clifton, Lucille, 73, 263n11
Coates, Ta-Nehisi, 66, 69, 72–75
Coates, W. Paul, 72, 263n5
Cole, Johnnetta, 86, 146
College Board, 225
college choice decisions, 51. *See also*
    enrollment
Colonial Athletic Association, 24
community colleges, 17, 260n15
community location of HBCUs, 17, 181–202,
    248; in COVID-19 pandemic, 197, 198, 199,
    200; as factor in college choice decision,
    56, 226–27; of land-grant institutions,
    xvi, 186–88; in rural areas, 226–27;
    workforce development in, 188–91, 192;
    of Xavier, 28–29
Congress of Racial Equality, 13
Conrad, C., 55, 157
Conwill, Kinshasha Holman, 77
Cook, Tim, 170
Cooper, Richard, 88
Cornell University, 71, 84
Cosby, Bill, 72, 146
Cosby, Camille, 146
The Cosby Show, 15
COVID-19 pandemic, 1, 149, 216; community
    engagement during, 197, 198, 199, 200;
    customer service during, 207; enrollment
    during, 226
Cresson, Sarah, 4
criminal justice system, 36
critical race theory, 116, 266n44
cultural engagement in community, 191–96
culture of HBCUs, 17, 18–51, 248; and
    academic achievement, 67; Anderson
    on, 110–11; Artis on, 37–38, 67, 93–94;
    belonging sense in, 48–51; and Black
    identity development, 40–51; Brewer
    on, 124; childhood exposure to, 20–22,
    199–200; Coates on, 72–75; Darwish on,
    125–26; diversity of, 25–32, 51; as
    family-like, 37–40, 51, 94, 137–41; Fletcher
    on, 36–37, 121, 124; Harris on, 97; as
    inclusive, 16, 246–47; as inspirational,
    67, 100–102, 125–26; Kendi on, 114–15;
    marching bands in, 19, 20, 21–22, 260n1;
    mentoring in, 127–41; Morrison on, 71,

72; Moses on, 102; music in, 19, 20, 21–22,
    26–28, 260n1; positive impact of, 66–67;
    in resource limitations, 206; Simmons
    on, 79–80; and socioeconomic mobility
    of graduates, 60–61; sports in, 22, 23–25,
    260n2, 261n4, 261n5, 261n6, 261n7, 261n8,
    261n9; Sullivan on, 103, 106; Wallace on,
    25–26, 31, 35–36, 117, 118–19; Wilson on,
    38–39, 88, 90; Wooten on, 85–86
Cummings, Elijah, 90–91
curriculum at HBCUs, 32–35, 227–29; art in,
    77; Black history in, 32–34; in industrial
    education, 8, 9; liberal arts in, 8, 9;
    outside influences on, 6, 8–9; providing
    primary and secondary education, 6.
    See also STEM education
customer service, 203–8
cybersecurity education, 190

Darwish, Abdalla, 125–26
data sources on HBCUs, 247, 249–51
Davis, Ossie, 73, 263n8
Davis, William Boyd Allison, 69
Daytona Educational and Industrial
    Training School for Negro Girls, 9
debt, student, 222
Delaware State University, 7, 150, 166
Delta Sigma Theta Sorority, 85–86, 264n31
Dickey, John, 4
A Different World, x–xi, 15
Dillard University: culture of, 20–21, 50,
    79–80; customer service in, 203–4;
    Darwish at, 125–26; financial aid budget
    in, 224; institutional story of, 162; liberal
    arts curriculum in, 8; philanthropic
    support of, 146, 150, 162, 164; Simmons at,
    79–83, 237; socioeconomic mobility of
    graduates, 57, 58. *See also* Kimbrough,
    Walter
Dinkins, David, 73, 263n10
diversity in HBCUs, 16, 22–23, 31–32, 51, 67;
    community contributions of, 195; of
    faculty, 31, 32, 239; at FAMU, 114; at
    Howard University, 73, 74–75, 97; and
    inclusivity, 16, 246–47; Kendi on, 41, 114,
    115; in sexual orientation, 16, 31, 32; at
    Tuskegee, 87; Wallace on, 117; Walton on,
    126
Dominion Energy, 2, 148

Howard, Otis O., 6
Howard University, 66, 206, 261n10;
  Anderson at, 16; art department in, 77,
  78; Carmichael at, 112; Coates at, 66, 69,
  72–75; culture of, 26, 39–40, 47, 72–75;
  customer service in, 206, 207; diversity
  in, 73, 74–75, 97; Driggers at, 128–29;
  faculty in, 10, 69, 75, 263n1, 263n2, 263n3;
  Flack at, 67; graduation rate in, 220;
  Harris at, 2, 96–97; history of, 6, 10;
  liberal arts in, 8; medical school of, 104;
  Morrison at, 70–72, 73, 74; Palmer at, 22,
  39–40, 144, 206, 225; residence hall
  conditions in, 207; Scott donations
  to, 150; Sellers at, 112–13, 265n41;
  socioeconomic mobility of graduates,
  57, 58; sorority at, 71, 263n4
Hrabowski, Freeman, 110
Hudson, Thomas, 52, 200–201, 227;
  childhood memories of, 20, 61; on
  customer service, 205; on graduation
  rates, 221–22; on leadership of HBCUs,
  212–13; on philanthropic support, 156,
  158–59, 175–76; on research institutions,
  243; role models of, 43–44; on socioeconomic mobility, 61
Hughes, Herman, 109, 265n39
Hughes, Langston, 113, 265n42
humility of presidents, 215, 217
Humphreys, Richard, 4
Humphries, Frederic S., xi–xii, xvii–xviii
Hurston, Zora Neale, 74, 264n15

Imes, Elmer, 120, 266n45
inclusive environment, 16, 246–47
income: of family, 15, 56–57; and
  philanthropy, 267n12; and racial wealth
  gap, 53–54; and socioeconomic mobility,
  17, 52–65; in STEM jobs, 63–65
industrial education, 8, 9
infrastructure of HBCUs, 88, 224, 229–30;
  investments in, 183, 201, 229; president
  leadership role in, 212; residence hall
  conditions in, 207
Institute for Capacity Building of Kresge
  Foundation, 165–66
Institute for Colored Youth, 4
institutional stories, 75, 230–34, 236; and
  color blindness, 226; and philanthropic

support, 157, 159, 161, 162, 231, 233; social
  media posts on, 157, 162, 178, 234
integration: of Boston schools, 104; of
  Kentucky State University, 88
intellectual engagement in community,
  191–96
interviews in HBCU research, 249–51
intrusive advising, 139
Ivy League universities, 57, 79, 220,
  262–63n2

Jack and Jill of America, 28, 261–62n11
Jackson, Jesse, 68
Jackson State University, 20, 61, 200;
  community contributions of, 200–201;
  graduation rate in, 221–22; police killing
  of students in, 13–14; research at, 243;
  sports in, 22. See also Hudson, Thomas
James, Kevin, 26–28, 210; on music programs,
  21–22, 26–28; on social media use, 178,
  234; on socioeconomic mobility, 63
Jewish refugee professors, 10
Jim Crow, 6, 62, 64, 73, 111, 113
Johnson, Amber, 131
Johnson, Charles S., 11
Johnson, James Weldon, 11
Johnson C. Smith University, 164
Jones, Lois Mailou, 78, 264n27
Jordan, Vernon, 147, 266n3
Jubilee Singers, 6
Julian, Percy, 69, 263n2
Just, Ernest Everett, 69, 263n3

Kendi, Ibram X., 41, 66, 114–16, 179, 236
Kennedy, John F., 80
Kent State University, 14
Kentucky State University, 7, 88
Kim, M., 55
Kimbrough, Walter, 50, 66, 68; on board
  effectiveness, 218–19; on community
  engagement, 192; on customer service,
  203–4; on free speech, 244–45; on
  funding constraints, 224; on leadership
  of HBCUs, 209; on philanthropic
  support, 162, 176–77, 180, 267n6; on
  socioeconomic mobility, 62–63
King, Martin Luther, Jr., 15, 68, 112, 265n35
King, Rodney, 98
Knight v. Alabama, 112, 265n40

Koch, Charles and David, 147
Koch Scholars Program, 147
Kresge Foundation, Moses at. *See* Moses, Bill
Kuba art, 77, 264n26

Lance-Bottoms, Keisha, 128, 266n2
land-grant institutions, xv, 6–7, 229;
    community contributions of, xvi,
    186–88; culture of, 26; Morrill Acts on,
    6, 259n6, 259n7
Langston University, x
Latinx population, 16, 31, 46, 53, 54
leaders, 6, 9, 12, 78–96; Artis as, 92–96; in
    business, 123–25; civil rights activism
    of, 12–13, 96–108, 112–13; presidents of
    HBCUs as, 208–17; as role models, 43–44,
    45; Simmons as, 78–84; Wilson as, 87–92;
    women as, 9, 12–13, 123–25, 245–46;
    Wooten as, 84–87
Lee, S. P., 136
Lee, Spike, 63, 68, 128
Lemelle, Martin, 170–71, 175, 184, 204, 207, 214
LeMoyne-Owen College, 5
Lewis, John, 2
Lewis, Sarah Elizabeth, 76
LGBTQ students, 16, 32
liberal arts curriculum, 8, 9
"Lift Every Voice" (song), 11
Lincoln, Abraham, 4
Lincoln University, 4, 58, 150
literacy, in history of slavery, 4, 68, 111–12
literature, contributions of HBCU
    graduates to, 70–75
Locke, Alain, 74, 264n20
Lomax, Michael, 59
Louisiana State University, 57
low-income population, 53; graduation
    rates for, 220–21; and racial wealth gap,
    53–54; socioeconomic mobility of, 52–65.
    See also Pell Grants
Ludlow Massacre, 259–60n9
lynching activities, 6, 259n5

Malcolm, Shirley, 89–90
Mandela, Nelson, 85
marching bands, 19, 20, 21–22, 26–28, 231,
    260n1
Marshall (Thurgood) College Fund, 3, 147,
    149, 170

Marshall, Thurgood, 73, 113, 128
Martin, Harold, 24–25, 186–87, 189, 190, 193
Mason, Beverley, 28
Masters, Christopher, 138
Mays, Benjamin Elijah, 60–61, 103, 106,
    265n33
McDowell, Donald, xix
McKenzie, Fayette, 9
medical education, 64, 65, 103–5, 261n10; of
    Xavier graduates, 28, 107, 108, 233, 261n10
Meharry Medical College, 104, 164
Mellion-Patin, Dawn, xii–xiii
Mellon Foundation, Bengochea at.
    See Bengochea, Armando
Mellon Mays Undergraduate Fellowship,
    168, 267n11
mentoring, xvii–xx, 17, 127–41, 248;
    Anderson on, 127, 129–31; faculty role in,
    34, 128–31, 136, 137–41; HBCU-DAP work
    in, 132–33; of high school students, 132,
    133–34; holistic, 139–41; as intrusive
    advising, 139; by Mays, 106; mentoring
    up and down, 136; by Miller, 37, 136–37;
    paying it forward in, 127, 131–37, 248; by
    Player, 12–13; role models in, 44, 106,
    128–31; of Simmons, 80; in STEM
    education, 132–33, 138, 139; of Wallace,
    118; Wooten on, 85, 134–35
middle class, 53–54; upward mobility to,
    56–57, 58, 63
Miles College, 110
Miller, Jeffrey, 201, 210; on Abrams
    activism, 98–99; on board effectiveness,
    217; on culture of HBCUs, 37, 41–42;
    on economic impact of HBCUs, 186;
    mentoring by, 37, 136–37; on philan-
    thropic support, 171–72
Miner, Myrtilla, 259n2
Minority Serving Institutions, 55, 166, 167
missionary organizations, 5, 6, 7, 26
Mississippi Valley State University, 261n4
Montoya, Jim, 225–26
Morehouse College, x, 8, 166, 194; Glouster
    at, 104–5; graduation rate in, 220; King at,
    68, 112; Lee at, 68; Mays at, 60–61, 103, 106,
    265n33; philanthropic support of, 147–48,
    150; socioeconomic mobility of graduates,
    57, 58; Sullivan at, 47, 60–61, 103, 104;
    Warnock at, 2; Wilson at, 92, 100, 170

Morehouse College of Medicine, 104–5, 161–62. *See also* Sullivan, Louis W.

Morgan State University, 22, 38; Addae at, 137, 138; community contributions of, 185–86, 197; customer service in, 206–7; degree programs in, 228; infrastructure investment in, 229; institutional story of, 232; Palmer at, 22, 44, 144, 206; research in, 241; Scott donations to, 150, 153; state funding of, 268n1; STEM education in, 64. *See also* Hollis, Leah; Wilson, David

Morrill Acts, 6, 259n6, 259n7

Morris Brown College, 194; accreditation of, 26, 37, 223, 267n14; culture of, 26–28, 41–42; financial problems of, 223, 267n14; social media posts on, 178, 234. *See also* James, Kevin; Miller, Jeffrey

Morrison, Toni, 70–72, 73, 74

Moses, Bill, 68–69, 102; on fundraising and philanthropy, 156–57, 164–68, 223; on HBCU leaders, 216–17; on long-term sustainability, 223–24, 226–27

Moses, Napoleon, 138

music programs, 6; marching bands in, 19, 20, 21–22, 26–28, 231, 260n1

Nance, Sierra, 129, 132–33, 199

Nash, Diane, 13

National Association for Equal Opportunity in Higher Education, 15

National Association for the Advancement of Colored People, 113

National Center for Educational Statistics, 226

National Science Foundation HBCU Undergraduate Program, 121–22

National Society of Black Engineers, x, 122, 123, 136

Nelson, Stanley, 23, 45–46, 47, 62

Netflix, 2, 148

Nettles, Michael, 191–92

New Georgia Project, 99

New Negro Movement, 260n11

Nixon, Richard, 14

Norfolk State University, 150

North Carolina A&T State University, xii, xiii, 7; civil rights activism in, xv, xvii, 12; community contributions of, 186–87, 189, 193; culture of, xiv–xv, 24–25, 26, 42,

46; faculty in, 239–40; Jackson at, 68; Martin at, 24–25, 186–87, 189, 190, 193; mentoring in, xix, 85, 134–35, 139–41; Scott donations to, 150; socioeconomic mobility of graduates, 58; Thompson at, 32, 59–60, 189–90; values clarification in, xvi–xvii; Wooten at, 31, 46, 84–87, 102, 134, 174. *See also* Alston, Antoine

North Carolina Central University, 32, 68

North Carolina State University, 59, 60

Obama, Barack, 71, 152, 162–63

Ohio State University, 60

O'Keeffe, Georgia, 11

Old Dominion Foundation, 168

Olorunnipa, Zach, xviii

Omega Psi Phi, 263n13

Onokpise, Oghenekome "Kome," xviii

Opportunity Insights, 55

oral histories on HBCUs, 247, 249–51

Organ, Claude, Jr., 108, 265n37

Ossoff, Jon, 2

Packer, Will, 128, 266n1

Palmer, Robert, 206; on culture of HBCUs, 22–23, 39–40; on financial stability, 225; on leadership of HBCUs, 208–9; on philanthropic support, 144–45; on role models, 44

Pan-African Movement, 263n12

Patterson, Frederick D., 10, 146

Paul Quinn College, 6, 33, 166; community engagement of, 196–97, 201–2; farm program in, 201–2; student focus in, 213–14. *See also* Sorrell, Michael

paying it forward, 127, 131–37, 171–80, 248

Payne, Daniel, 5

Payton, Walter, 23, 261n5

Pell Grants: Artis on, 93; percentage eligible for, 58, 167, 220, 221, 225; and socioeconomic mobility, 58, 62–63

Pew Research Center, 53

philanthropic support, 2–3, 7–10, 17, 142–80, 248; alumni giving in, 171–80, 204, 207, 208, 218; attraction strategies, 157–64, 169–70, 178; Bengochea on, 152, 168–70, 177; *Brown* decision affecting, 11; controversial donations in, 146, 147; customer service affecting, 204, 207, 208;

future of, 170–80; on Giving Tuesday, 177, 267n13; of industrial education, 8, 146; institutional stories affecting, 157, 159, 161, 162, 231, 233; from Kresge Foundation, 164–68; from Mellon Foundation, 164, 168–70; Moses on, 156–57, 164–68, 223; as percentage of income, 267n12; of PWIs, 170, 179, 180, 267n6; reporting requirements in, 151; return on investment in, 151, 152, 158, 163–64; of STEM education, 166; unequal access to wealth for, 143, 266n1. *See also* Scott, MacKenzie, philanthropic donations of

Piety, Philip, 157
plagiarism as teachable moment, 35
Player, Willa, 12–13
Pleas, Danielle, 133–34
Plessy v. Ferguson, 11, 260n12
police actions, 1, 13–14, 48, 143
politics: Abrams in, 97–102; and civic engagement, 191–96; free speech in, 245; Harris in, 96–97; institutional, president understanding of, 209–10, 211
Prairie View A&M University, 26, 58, 166; community contributions of, 187–88; faculty development in, 161, 238; Scott donations to, 150, 160; Simmons at, 79, 83–84, 159–61, 187–88, 215, 218, 237, 238
Predominantly White Institutions (PWIs), ix, 11–12, 15, 16; academic achievement in, 67; belonging sense missing in, 48–49; Black identity development in, xiv; diversity and inclusion in, 246, 247; faculty in, 15, 43, 69–70, 238; graduate education in, 82, 86, 115, 236–37; graduation rate in, 55–56, 262–63n2; historical admission of Black students to, 260n13; philanthropic support of, 170, 179, 180, 267n6; resources of, 205–6; socioeconomic mobility of graduates, 56, 57, 58
Presidential Commission on Campus Unrest, 14
President's Board of Advisors on HBCUs, 14
presidents of HBCUs, 208–17; Black women as, 9, 12–13, 245–46; board selection of, 89, 90, 91, 210, 218–19; personal qualities of, 215–17; student focus of, 213–15; turnover of, 209. *See also specific presidents*

President's Reading Circle, 29–31
Price, G. N., 56
Princeton University, 72, 88
Prophet, Nancy Elizabeth, 77
public relations, institutional story in, 230–34
public service, value of, xvi

Quakers, 4
Qualls, Marquita, 197–98
Quillin, Patty, 148

racial discrimination in federal appropriations, 6–7
racism: critical race theory on, 266n44; Jubilee Singers experiencing, 6; in missionary organizations, 5; in philanthropy, 146, 266n1; in PWIs, 69–70; systemic, 14, 56, 266n1, 266n44
Reagan administration, 93, 96
Reconstruction period, 64, 113, 265–66n43
research, 40; on Black history and culture, 240; corporate partners in, 25; institution focus on, 26, 241–43; philanthropic donations for, 243; on socioeconomic mobility, 55–59
Research 1 institutions, 241–43
Research 2 institutions, 243, 268n2
research methods, 247, 249–51
return on investment in philanthropy, 151, 152, 158, 163–64
Rice, Condoleezza, 110
Rice, Jerry, 23, 261n4
Richardson, Earl, 91
Richie, Lionel, 67–68
Robinson, Eddie, 24, 261n9
Rockefeller, John D., Jr., 7, 11, 147, 259–60n9
Rockefeller, John D., Sr., 7, 142
Rocket Team at Fisk University, 116, 120–21
Rogers, Decatur, 138
role models, 42–51, 106, 128–31
Rosenwald, Julius, 7
Rosenwald Fund, 69, 70
Rudolph, Wilma, 23, 261n8
rural areas, HBCUs in, 226–27
Rutgers Center for Minority Serving Institutions, 55
Rutgers University, 89

Warnock, Raphael, 2, 66
Washington, Booker T., 8, 9, 67
wealth gap, racial, 53–54
Weatherspoon, Dave, xviii
Wellesley College, 81–82
Wells, Ida B., 259n5
"We Over Me" farm program, 201–2
West, Cornell, 245
West Virginia State College, 93–94, 96
Wheelan, Belle, 46, 143–44, 192–93, 194;
on board of trustee members, 218; on
financial issues in accreditation, 223; on
leadership of HBCUs, 209–10, 211; on
long-term sustainability, 228–29
Wije, Michele, 78
Wilberforce University, 4–5
Wilcox, Melanie, 97
Wilder, Doug, 73, 263n9
Wiley College, 129
Williams, Damon, 22, 28–29, 64–65, 172–73
Williams, Doug, 23, 261n6
Williams, Heather, 68
Wilson, David, 87–92; on community
engagement, 197; on culture of HBCUs,
38–39, 88, 90; on economic impact of
HBCUs, 185–86; on infrastructure
investment, 229; on institutional stories,
232; on long-term sustainability, 228; on
Research 1 status, 241; on Scott dona-
tions, 153; as Tuskegee graduate, 87–88,
90, 92
Wilson, John S.: as Morehouse College
president, 92, 100, 170; on philanthropic
support, 152–53, 162–63, 170; in White

House initiative on HBCUs, 18, 78, 100,
152, 162–63
Winfrey, Oprah, 63, 68, 128
Winston-Salem State University, 68, 129,
133, 150, 199
women: as business leaders, 123–25;
enrollment rate at HBCUs, 246; as HBCU
presidents, 9, 12–13, 245–46; historical
education opportunities for, 9; role
models for, 43, 95; as scholar-athletes, 23;
in STEM, 64, 122–23, 125
Woodrow Wilson Foundation, 88–89
Woodruff, Hale A., 77
Wooten, Lynn, 31–32, 42, 84–87, 102; on
alumni giving, 174; on mentoring, 85,
134–35; as North Carolina A&T State
University graduate, 31, 46, 84–87, 102,
134, 174; as Simmons University
president, 31, 46, 84
workforce development, 188–91, 192, 268n2

Xavier University of LA: culture of, 28–29;
drill system in, 107–8; endowment of,
107, 233; Francis at, 106–8, 233, 265n35;
medical education of graduates, 28, 107,
108, 233, 261n10; mentoring in, 141;
peer-led tutoring at, 107, 108; philanthropic support of, 150, 151, 164, 233;
socioeconomic mobility of graduates, 57,
58, 62; STEM education at, 107–8, 233;
Williams at, 22, 28–29, 64–65, 172–73.
See also Verret, Reynold

Yale University, xi, 48, 99, 107